I KNEW A MAN WHO KNEW BRAHMS

A Memoir

NANCY SHEAR

A REGALO PRESS BOOK
ISBN: 979-8-88845-662-0
ISBN (eBook): 979-8-88845-663-7

I Knew a Man Who Knew Brahms
© 2025 by Nancy Shear
All Rights Reserved

Cover Design by Jim Villaflores

Publishing Team:
Founder and Publisher – Gretchen Young
Editor – Adriana Senior
Editorial Assistant – Caitlyn Limbaugh
Managing Editor – Aleigha Koss
Production Manager – Kate Harris
Production Editor – Rachel Paul

As part of the mission of Regalo Press, a donation is being made to Sphinx, as chosen by the author. Find out more about this organization at www.sphinxmusic.org/our-work.

This book, as well as any other Regalo Press publications, may be purchased in bulk quantities at a special discounted rate. Contact orders@regalopress.com for more information.

This is a work of nonfiction. All people, locations, events, and situations are portrayed to the best of the author's memory.

No part of this book may be reproduced, stored in a retrieval system, or transmitted by any means without the written permission of the author and publisher.

Regalo Press
New York • Nashville
regalopress.com

Published in the United States of America
1 2 3 4 5 6 7 8 9 10

To Leopold Stokowski,
and
to the men and women of the Philadelphia Orchestra,
then and now

Author's Note

AFTER SPENDING TIME WITH LEOPOLD Stokowski, Mstislav Rostropovich, and other artists, I wanted to make my experiences permanent—tangible—so I'd jot down notes in a journal or on pieces of scrap paper. Over the years, after moving several times, I lost track of the notes. Long after I started to write this book, I found them. My memory had been startlingly accurate. This ability to vividly remember events—a phenomenon called hypervigilance—enables my mind to function like a movie camera. It's the result of dealing with the emotional instability of one parent and the volatility of the other; I constantly had to be aware of what was happening so that I could prevent or cope with threatening situations. I'm able to recall many conversations verbatim and recollect details about performances I heard as a teenager—small things, as well as the major events of that time.

Contents

Prelude 11

Chapter One 17
Chapter Two 21
Chapter Three 34
Chapter Four 54
Chapter Five 67
Chapter Six 88
Chapter Seven 105
Chapter Eight 111
Chapter Nine 120
Chapter Ten 132
Chapter Eleven 145
Chapter Twelve 151
Chapter Thirteen 167
Chapter Fourteen 178
Chapter Fifteen 194
Chapter Sixteen 212
Chapter Seventeen 219
Chapter Eighteen 230
Chapter Nineteen 242
Chapter Twenty 268
Chapter Twenty-One 295
Chapter Twenty-Two 313

Coda 315
Acknowledgments 316

Prelude

ON JULY 21, 1960, LEOPOLD Stokowski was to conduct members of the Philadelphia Orchestra at the Robin Hood Dell, an outdoor amphitheater where they performed for eight weeks after the regular Academy of Music season. Stokowski, who brought the Philadelphia Orchestra to global prominence years earlier, had been away from the city for almost two decades. This would be his first appearance at the Dell in twenty-seven years, and although I was only fourteen, I was desperate to hear him conduct.

That concert became a landmark in my memory. Five summers later, backstage in his dressing room at the Dell, Stokowski would ask me to work with him as his personal orchestra librarian and musical assistant. It would be the beginning of a close, complex relationship that would bring me not only into his home but into his musical mind.

I was too young to travel alone in 1960. My mother probably wasn't well, because my older neighbor, Eileen, went with me. Luckily, the tickets were free, available by clipping coupons from local papers.

Eileen and I arrived early—more than an hour before concert time—but long lines had already formed at the entrance. Inside, green wooden seats lined the vast bowl-shaped venue. The extensive concrete paving was softened by a grove of trees to the left of the seats and an expansive grassy embankment to their right. A huge angular shell leaned protectively over the stage.

That July evening, more than thirty thousand music lovers filled the seats and covered the immense sloping lawn. Some people even climbed into the trees. Two thousand more stood outside the facility, listening through loudspeakers. Eileen and I were lucky to have gotten in.

As we waited for the concert to begin, I observed what is still one of my best-loved rituals—something most concertgoers don't even notice: an orchestra tuning up. The musicians wander onstage, talking and laughing. They settle into their seats and begin fussing with their instruments. Wind players assemble and reassemble the various components of their instruments like pieces of puzzles to get just the right alignment, and the brass players press and pull valves and slides and squirt streams of valve oil from little plastic squeeze bottles. Oboists, clarinetists, and bassoonists suck on reeds, pulling them in and out of their mouths to keep them moist. String players twist the black pegs above their instruments' fingerboards to adjust pitch, and rub the horsehair of their bows against cakes of rosin. Percussionists arrange bass drums and snares, timpani and triangles, ratchets, bells, chimes, gongs, and cymbals so that they can move swiftly from one instrument to another without colliding.

The orchestra begins to warm up. The winds play through runs—rapid ascending and descending scales—and the brass play long sustained tones, octaves and arpeggios—the individual notes of a chord, upward or downward. String players produce soaring, virtuosic phrases, or work through intricate, tricky passages. It's always a game for me to identify the threads of melodies and scraps of phrases that will soon become part of the full tapestry of sound.

At a signal from the stage manager, the concertmaster—the principal violinist—walks onstage to the area near the podium, faces her colleagues, and pointedly looks at them, a demand for silence. I watch as she nods at the principal oboist to sound the note "A," which orchestras tune to.[1] After tuning her violin, the concertmaster turns in all directions to engage the full orchestra, listening intently to decide if the instruments are properly tuned or if the process should be repeated. She will also decide how the orchestra will tune: all sections at once, or separately.[2] An orchestra member once told me that the concertmaster's role is largely ceremonial; while the musicians could tune directly to the oboe, it's in recognition of the concertmaster's authority—and a nod to tradition—that he or she plays this important role. When she is satisfied that the instruments are correctly tuned, she takes her seat, the lights dim, and the conductor walks onstage to ascend the podium.

For me, the best part of orchestral tuning is the wild improvisation of notes that fly around the "A," leaving it and returning to it, like a flock of birds taking flight then landing. After the tuning, when the orchestra—and the audience—become silent, there is always a moment of intense anticipation.

At the Dell, even though we were sitting almost a block away from the stage, I caught sight of Stokowski just before the concert began. He was dressed in white tie and tails as he stood at the open backstage doorway. More than half a century later, I can still feel the thrill of seeing him in person for the first time.

Seconds later, to wild cheers and applause, the Maestro made his way onstage. Mounting the podium, he bowed several times in different directions, then—in one quick motion—pivoted to face the orchestra and launched a vibrant performance of Berlioz's

---

[1] Because of the way it's constructed, the oboe doesn't have as much flexibility of intonation—the ability to alter a given pitch—as most other instruments possess, so everyone tunes to the oboe. Also, its stable, penetrating tone can easily cut through the sound of the full orchestra. The oboist's tuning "A" will always be the most beautifully-shaped, focused note he or she is capable of playing. It is, in a way, the first note of the concert.

[2] In the 1960s, when the Philadelphia Orchestra concertmaster gave the "A," all the players tuned simultaneously; today, many orchestras have the winds, then the brass, then the strings, then the entire ensemble tune. Anshel Brusilow, the former concertmaster of the orchestra, told me that it was rarely necessary for him to tune individual sections. Many European orchestras tune backstage; the players walk onstage together, ready to perform. I always feel cheated at those concerts!

Roman Carnival Overture. Ravel's *Alborada del Gracioso* followed, castanets clicking away, all color and seduction. Then came Debussy's "Nuages" and "Fêtes" ("Clouds" and "Festivals"), two of the three sections of the *Nocturnes*.

Atmospheric and mysterious—mostly soft winds and muted strings—"Nuages" gave way to the brisk and spirited "Fêtes," with its swirling winds and scurrying strings. A few moments after "Fêtes" began, a train, chugging far off in the distance, tooted a rude counterpoint to the music and the performance abruptly stopped. People looked at each other questioningly, then at the stage. Facing the orchestra, Stokowski stood motionless, his hands at his sides. He held the pose for four interminable minutes. Then, once silence was restored, his hands moved, the music resumed, and the audience visibly relaxed. The peace, however, was short-lived. A loud diesel horn blew, the crowd laughed, and Stokowski flew offstage. Another four minutes elapsed before he returned. But back on the podium, before he resumed conducting, he turned to face the audience. "We must be patient with modern civilization," he commented, and the crowd cheered.

During the second half of the concert, which included a powerful performance of Shostakovich's Symphony No. 1, he stopped the music two more times for train noise but didn't leave the podium. The shouting, foot-stamping crowd brought him back for ten curtain calls.

"I hear you asking for an encore," he teased the audience. "We would be delighted to do it, but do not wish to disturb the Pennsylvania Railroad!" Everyone laughed but no one left. "If you will protect me," he said into the microphone, "and you are sure we will not offend the Pennsylvania Railroad, we will play a little something."[3] He repeated the last movement of Amirov's "Azerbaijan: Symphonic Suite," which had already been performed in its entirety.

---

3   Back at the Dell a year later, he apologized to the Pennsylvania Railroad; it had been the Reading Company railroad.

On the way home I didn't want to talk to Eileen. I only wanted to replay the music in my head and to picture Stokowski on the podium. He had been elegant and imposing, even when he was joking with the audience. He fascinated me, and I longed to know him.

Chapter One

I CANNOT PICTURE THE LIVING room of my childhood home without thinking of the music that was constantly playing there. As a toddler, I often stood on tiptoe looking into the groove of a record as it spun on the turntable, watching the blurry disc rotate faster than I could follow. Some sort of magic had to be embedded in its shallow, winding ridge because, at the touch of the phonograph needle, the sound of a symphony orchestra would emerge from the flat black vinyl.

Mom and I listened together, eating lunch on tray tables as we sat on the sofa in our row house in suburban Philadelphia. Because I was an only child, it was always just the two of us. Mom would make doll salads—hardboiled egg faces with raisin eyes, a pimento mouth, and grated-carrot hair—or elephant-shaped pancakes. Early in the evening, I'd wait for the smell of dinner cooking—a signal that Mom would soon shower and change her clothes and we'd be able to listen to another record. I knew we might not get through an entire piece. When my father's car pulled into the driveway, we'd have to switch off the music, and by the time his keys jangled in the door lock, the house would be hushed and filled with tension as though it had been pumped in.

We chose the records from a small collection stored in the bottom of our floor-model Farnsworth radio–record player. Mom had started saving for the player as soon as she learned she was pregnant and bought it when I was a few weeks old. It was a rare luxury for our family, purchased because Mom felt that great music was essential to a child's life.

A formidable piece of furniture that dominated our living room, the Farnsworth had a reddish-brown mahogany cabinet that Mom kept polished and dusted. But it wasn't the Farnsworth's appearance that Mom and I treasured, it was its sound—rich and resonant. I imagined that an orchestra would sound just like that if I heard it in person.

We owned two or three dozen LPs—new technology in the early 1950s—and a dozen or so of their predecessors: shellac 78s, which played a few minutes of scratchy music that abruptly stopped just before the next disc dropped heavily onto the turntable. Even now, in live performances of works like the César Franck Symphony in D minor, which I first heard on 78s, I anticipate interruptions in the music and the slight hiss of a needle finding its way into the groove.

"What images do you see?" Mom would ask, as Beethoven or Tchaikovsky or Rachmaninoff flowed from the speakers. I imagined clouds—billowing white masses moving across a brilliant blue sky during lyrical pieces, roiling gray-black swirls during turbulent works—or the angels and ogres that inhabit a child's dreams and nightmares. Mom usually described landscapes—fields and forests and farmland—and told me about things that had happened when she was a little girl: knowing she was loved by her father but not by her cold, distant mother; being left on her grandparents' farm when her parents were too busy to take care of her; looking after her baby brother, Stan, whom she adored. These moments were precious to me. From the time I was six months old, my mother had suffered from a severe form of obsessive-compulsive disorder, perhaps even paranoia. We spoke of it only as "emotional illness," but I never knew if she'd be able to spend time with me, or if she'd be possessed by panic or be deep in depression.

My father didn't like "long-hair" music, as he called it, so he turned on the TV as soon as he got home. My mother and I never objected because we were both frightened of him. It's still difficult for me to refer to him as my father, and impossible for me to call him "Dad." I prefer calling him Leonard, as my mother and I did when he wasn't around, or Len, as he was known to family and friends.

At five-eleven, Len was almost a foot taller than Mom and he loomed over me like a giant. It's hard for me to picture him without a sarcastic smile stretched across his lips and his head shaking with disapproval over something I'd said or done. We'd be together no more than twenty minutes before he'd start to tease and criticize me, so I tried to stay out of his sight when he was home. He was gone most of the day, working as a salesman, first for General Foods—their products included Jell-O and Maxwell House coffee—then for a company that manufactured locks and keys. I don't remember ever having a conversation with Len. It was Mom who told me about his mother's sadistic treatment of him and his two brothers. I was too young then to know that abused children often become abusive adults. As I matured, I would often draw on this information to understand my father's behavior, but it never made his treatment of Mom and me easier to tolerate.

※

After my first evening at the Dell, I thought constantly about Stokowski. He seemed more like a god than a man—long white hair swept back behind his ears; a large, finely shaped nose; intense blue eyes; and full lips that may or may not have been smiling. He always tilted his head slightly upward, as if he were contemplating something important.

I had seen Stokowski in the movie *Fantasia* when I was four. He stood high above the orchestra and moved his hands as the music filled the theater. He looked a little scary, but when Mickey Mouse climbed up on the podium and tugged at his coat tails, Stokowski bent down and shook his hand. I didn't think anyone willing to do that could be very dangerous.

My parents pronounced Stokowski's name with a "V" sound, not a "W," which seemed exotic, and they spoke about him with the same awe and respect they showed when talking about President Roosevelt, who had died the year before I was born. I overheard them say that "Stoki"—which was his widely-used nickname—had conducted orchestras all over the world and had been married to someone famous. I wasn't sure what a conductor did, but I noticed that whenever a recording was especially intense or emotional, Stokowski was conducting. Something happened inside me when I listened to his music. My chest filled with a kind of warmth when melodies soared, and my stomach tightened when he ratcheted up the tension. I felt slightly dizzy when he made the music seethe with passion, although I couldn't yet put a name to that feeling.

At night, it wasn't the sound of the Farnsworth or the TV that rose through the heating vent into my bedroom, but my parents' fighting—strangled sounds of suppressed fury that crescendoed into my father's screams and my mother's anguished cries. I didn't dare block out the sounds of their battles with blankets over my head or my hands over my ears; I had to be alert in case my mother needed my help. The fighting often continued for hours until there was sudden silence, shattered only by the sound of my father slamming doors throughout the house.

My childhood memories are like photos that have never faded. In one, Mom is sitting on the kitchen floor, sobbing. Her back is against the cabinet doors, her legs are stretched out in front of her, and I'm walking toward her, about to cover her with a blanket from either my crib or my bed. I'm only three or four, but this was probably not the first time I had taken care of her. Terrified of being separated from her, I sobbed my way into kindergarten, not knowing that Mom had sneaked around to the back of the building to watch me through the windows. She, too, had been frightened. Throughout my childhood, I was terrified that Mom would die, particularly when I wasn't there to protect her. That wasn't just because I loved her; if she died, there'd be no one to take care of me.

Chapter Two

I LONGED TO PLAY A musical instrument, but had access only to the old upright piano my parents had bought—a scratched, battered object that hardly qualified as a real instrument. Not all the keys worked, and a few, mostly in the upper register, produced only a dull clunking sound. I never felt at one with the piano; its chipped, yellowed keys seemed like a wide mouth grinning menacingly up at me.

I wanted to play the flute—to produce the shimmering, fluid tones that blended into the orchestra, and the high-pitched notes that pierced or soared above it, as I had heard on our records. When I got to middle school, however, where students could have free lessons and borrow instruments, there weren't any flutes available. Mom greeted me at the door one day, startled to see a cello case almost as tall as I was.

But at my first lesson, when the teacher handed me the cello, it seemed to fit. My knees anchored the lower part of its body; the fingers of my left hand pressed the strings; my right hand grasped the bow; and the top of the instrument's back rested on my chest, near my heart. I learned to keep the horsehair of the bow flat against the strings, drawing it evenly from the frog of the bow, where it's held, to the point, at the far tip. The initial screechy, strident sounds began to smooth into full-throated tones that, with the application of a bit of vibrato in the left hand, started to sing. My fingers found their correct place on the strings, cautiously navigating up the fingerboard toward the wooden bridge for higher-pitched notes. Tedious exercises paved the way for simple songs and my repertoire grew to include melodies like "Welcome, Sweet Springtime," one of Mom's favorites. She'd listen nearby, her smile turning into a grimace as I ventured up the fingerboard. It would take many months of hard work to sweeten the shrill and screechy sounds I first produced.

At dinner one evening, my uncle told my mother about an unusual new recording he had just obtained. "It's a rehearsal, not a performance—Bruno Walter conducting the Columbia Symphony in Beethoven's Ninth. Wait until you hear this!"

Why would anyone want to hear a rehearsal? I wondered. Now almost fifteen, I'd recently joined the school orchestra and didn't consider rehearsals very interesting. They were basically about playing the right notes at the right time. Curious, I followed Mom and my uncle Stan into the living room.

Holding the edges of the LP between his palms, Stan carefully lowered the disk onto the turntable and placed the needle in the groove. The sound remains vivid in my memory: The opening crackles and hisses, then the string players tap their bows against their stands as a tribute to Walter. "Good morning, gentlemen, good morning," he says in his pleasant, German-accented voice, and asks them to start with the second movement, the scherzo. He informs the double basses that he wants a "little accent" on the first note, and the orchestra begins. A pattern of three short, powerful notes, played twice by the strings, demands your attention. It's then played by the timpani, then by the strings, winds, and brass. The orchestra sounds fine to me, but not to Walter. The rhythm, he says, is slightly off. To illustrate what he wants, he sings to them. The musicians understand, and they begin again. Now the emphasis is different: The accents are more pronounced; the theme is more assertive. A few moments later, Walter tells the musicians that a crescendo must be extended—the speed and volume should increase at a slower pace—"gradually, gradually, gradually," he tells them—and you can feel him almost physically holding back the music.

A bit farther along, he tells the players again that the rhythm is not quite right. This error, he says, is "an old crime in orchestras all over the world!" They heed his instructions and alter their approach. It takes five tries, each from the beginning of the movement, for the musicians to deliver the accents and pacing Walter wants. "You got it!" he finally tells his players.

There was more to music than I had realized—small but critical details that musicians must consider: a slight shift in the way a note or phrase is shaped, or a subtle change in spirit or mood. Even a modest alteration in tone, rhythm, or phrasing can have a powerful effect on the listener.

My uncle gave me the LP. I shared it with my friends—we were all learning to listen as well as play—as four or five of us sat on a living room floor or sprawled on a bed. It was a time of discoveries—the soaring melodies of Schumann, Mendelssohn, and Dvořák; the slippery chromaticism of Berlioz; the lush and harsh harmonies of Richard Strauss; the primitive rhythms of Stravinsky; the anguish of Mahler.

"Did you hear the way that theme repeated?" we'd ask each other about a work new to us, trying to figure out how the piece was organized. "Now it's in the flutes, but only the first few notes of it.... Now there's just the theme's rhythm, not the melody!"

"Listen how slowly and gently he's taking that section," we'd comment about a new interpretation of a familiar work. We'd try to compare recordings of the same piece by different conductors: Stokowski and Toscanini, Walter and Mitropoulos, Bernstein and Koussevitzky. We'd beat out the rhythms of symphonies on tabletops and discuss the love lives of composers like Brahms, Schumann, and Wagner as if they were current hot gossip.

We talked about Stokowski and Toscanini more than any other conductors.[1] In the 1950s and '60s, everyone knew their names. Toscanini (who had died in 1957, when I was eleven) had been the autocratic leader of the NBC Symphony; he seemed to adhere to performance rules and traditions. Stokowski, the glamorous iconoclast, broke them. The more I listened to Stokowski's recordings, the more my fascination with him grew. And from what I read about him at the library, his life seemed as colorful as his music.

"Stoki" championed radical works that some people didn't consider music at all. He talked to audiences from the stage—which conductors rarely did—often scolding them for coughing or talking or booing a work he considered a masterpiece. He had front-page marriages and love affairs and played himself in the movies. In addition to *Fantasia*, he had appeared in *The Big Broadcast of 1937* (1936), *One Hundred Men and a Girl* (1937), and *Carnegie Hall* (1947), always portraying himself. His movie career during Hollywood's Golden Age—before television—expanded not only his fame but also classical music's popularity. I thought that was impressive, but many music professionals did not. "How dare he take serious art to lowbrow Hollywood!" they were quoted as saying. It would take decades for them to forgive him. (Many still have not.)

I read that he didn't want to be photographed, but the photos I saw of him—several in profile—were dramatic: his head tilted back arrogantly, his nose (which writers described as "heroic") extending beneath an illuminated mane of white hair. But most celebrated were his hands; unlike most conductors, he didn't use a baton. Large and expressive, as if reaching into the air to sculpt sound, his hands became his trademark. They enhanced the aura of mystery that seemed to surround him.

Stokowski became the model for the generic image of The Conductor. He was parodied in cartoons like *Baton Bunny* (1959), in which a coughing member of the audience incurs the wrath of

---

1   Leonard Bernstein, who had started televising his *Young People's Concerts* a few years earlier, didn't capture our imaginations as much as they did.

the rabbit on the podium, and *Long-Haired Hare* (1949), a Warner Bros. Looney Tunes cartoon in which Bugs Bunny appears in white tie and tails, with long white hair and a haughty attitude. Orchestra players gasp, "It's Leopold! It's Leopold!" as the bunny mounts the podium, takes the baton, and snaps it in half.

There were movies like *Unfaithfully Yours*, starring Rex Harrison (the film was said to have been based on Sir Thomas Beecham but carried obvious Stokowski influence) and *Once More, with Feeling!* starring Yul Brynner as the egocentric, glamorous, amorous maestro.[2]

I wasn't advanced enough to play in the All-Philadelphia Senior High School Orchestra, a group comprised of the city's best young musicians. I was better suited to listening to music than to performing it. I hated practicing—the long, solitary hours, the constant repetition, and the almost imperceptible progress. So, my friends had the thrill of playing under Stokowski in January 1962 when he rehearsed the ensemble at Girls' High. I was there as a guest.

Because I arrived late, I had to sit several rows back from the orchestra pit where the players were seated. The regular conductor began by taking them through their paces in Stokowski's transcription of Bach's Passacaglia and Fugue in C minor, not easy music. He wanted the young musicians to play as well as possible. Then he turned to address members of the audience, who were mostly friends and parents of the players. He warned us not to make a sound when Stokowski arrived or while he was conducting.

Through a side door of the auditorium, Stokowski entered, taller up close than anyone I'd ever seen. He wore a dark pinstriped suit, a black shirt and a white tie, and with an expression of great seriousness, he took his place on the audience level, above the pit, separated from the musicians by a low metal railing. The fact that

---

[2] Pianist, composer, and actor Oscar Levant, in his memoir *The Unimportance of Being Oscar,* G. P. Putnam's Sons, 1968, took credit for the concept of the original play and the film. "There's a play in that man," he'd told their writer, Harry Kurnitz, referring to Stokowski. Kurnitz had lived in Philadelphia during Stokowski's heyday with the orchestra and was, Levant said, "well-acquainted with the maestro's idiosyncrasies."

he walked with a cane—the result of having broken his hip a year earlier—didn't lessen his dignity, nor did it make him seem frail.

The Maestro, as everyone called him, raised his hands toward the young musicians and the rich sonorities of the Bach swelled throughout the hall. My skin broke into goose bumps, but the sound wasn't full enough for him.

"Violins!" he shouted, banging his hand on the railing. "There is more music inside your instruments than that! Make the room vibrate!" The kids dug in and I saw him smile down at them. The cellos hadn't had any such problem and he told them they were champions. "Your attacks are splendid!" he declared, and they grinned up at him. He worked through the entire piece, and when the session ended, he and the young musicians applauded each other.

My friends began to pack up their instruments, but I told them to leave without me. At a discreet distance, I followed Stokowski through the auditorium exit and down the long hallway. Suddenly, he stopped and turned around to face me. "Hello," he said quietly.

"Hello," I answered, and continued to follow him until he reached the exit.

Someone at the rehearsal had mentioned that the Maestro was staying at the Barclay Hotel on Rittenhouse Square. The next day I stood for hours in the park, hoping in vain to catch a glimpse of him. That was the fantasy, nothing more. He was a god; I was a kid. In my sacred world of music, Stokowski had become a religious figure. It's not a stretch to imagine a religious teenager's reverence for the Pope.

Every week, the member of the school orchestra who had "made the most progress" was rewarded with a ticket to a Philadelphia Orchestra matinee. I think everyone eventually won, even if they hadn't made great progress, but I was thrilled when my name was announced.

The following Friday, I entered the red velvet, crystal and gold leaf auditorium of the Academy of Music. From a front-row center seat in the first balcony, I watched and listened as the one hundred-plus musicians warmed up. Then the concertmaster walked from the wings to his spot just left of the podium, the musicians tuned, and the lights dimmed. After a few seconds, as the audience applauded, the conductor crossed the stage and mounted the podium. Then I heard the Philadelphia Orchestra.

This was not the amplified, slightly distorted sound of the Robin Hood Dell, which competed with birds and leaves and trains and planes. This was the acoustically renowned Academy. The sound filled the vastness of the hall and reverberated in my chest and stomach. More powerful than anything I had ever experienced, this music expressed joy, sadness, and longing.[3]

In class the following week, I tried to concentrate on schoolwork but could think only of my escape plan for Friday. I wouldn't have an excuse from school or a ticket to the concert, but I had no choice; I had to hear the orchestra again. When that afternoon came, I looked around to make sure no one was watching, then furtively exited the school building and hid inside the doorway of the dry cleaners across the street near the bus stop. The bus took me to the "El"—the subway line that started at the rooftops then made a screeching, grinding, metal-against-metal descent into the subterranean part of its route. Arriving in Center City, I walked a few blocks to the Academy at Broad and Locust Streets, ending the hour-long journey.

At the box office, I asked the cost of the cheapest ticket and was stunned by the answer—$1.25—nearly all of my weekly allowance.

---

[3] The orchestra had long been one of "The Big Five," as the top ensembles in the industry are known, the others being the Boston Symphony, Chicago Symphony, Cleveland Orchestra, and the New York Philharmonic. Cleveland was known for its precision, Chicago for its burnished brass, New York and Boston for general excellence. Philadelphia was, and is, famous for its rich sound—opulent, flowing, and seamless, adaptable to all styles and periods but best suited to works of the Romantic era: Wagner, Brahms, Mahler, and Rachmaninoff. This distinctive sound was cultivated and perfected by Stokowski.

I must have been a sad little figure because when I froze at hearing the price, the woman in the box office quickly—and gruffly—scribbled a seat number and her signature on a small white form.

"All right," she barked, as if I had protested the cost, "here's a pass for the concert. It's for the Amphitheater." That's where the cheapest seats were located, but I didn't care.

In the Academy's European splendor,[4] the Amphitheatre (known affectionately as "the peanut gallery") was the only area that was unadorned, the bare wood of its seats rising above the gilt-encrusted, red plush of the two lower balconies. Sitting there, I was level with the crystal chandelier and the top of the grand proscenium arch that framed the stage. From this height, I could see the tops of the musicians' heads, not their faces.

Friday became my orchestra day. For several weeks after my first visit to the box office, "Mom Haley"—a nickname, I learned, that the orchestra and Academy staff used (her real name was Catherine)—handed me the coveted piece of paper that provided entry into the perfect world of the concert hall. But one day, her demeanor having softened, she kindly explained that she couldn't continue to give me passes because she might get into trouble.

"Go over there," she instructed, pointing to a mirrored, white marble lobby down the hall from the box office where an older, mostly female, crowd was gathering. "These women usually buy two season subscriptions and the husbands don't come. Some of them might like to have your company."

My everyday outfit in those days, before girls wore pants to school, consisted of a dark skirt, white blouse, black cardigan, and thick white socks and sneakers—not the dressy suits and substantial jewelry worn by the ladies who lunched then went to the orchestra. But the strategy worked. I stood in the lobby, a five-foot-two, fair-skinned, eager teenager, dark-blonde hair pulled into a ponytail, looking genuinely dejected. After ten or fifteen minutes, someone would ask if I needed a ticket and I was ushered into the Parquet,

---

4 The Academy's design was based on Milan's magnificent opera house, La Scala.

the most expensive location in the Academy, able to hear what I now thought of as "my" orchestra. But after a few weeks, I either ran out of luck or exhausted the novelty of being the only kid in a grown-up setting. Standing alone, after dimming lights signaled the start of the concert, I could hear only muffled applause, not music, emanating from the hall.

I needed a new strategy. The Amphitheatre could be accessed through its own doorway around the corner, on Locust Street. Concertgoers always jammed that narrow space, presenting their tickets to an usher before hiking up the steps. My heart pounding, I mixed in with the mob then sneaked past the ticket-taker when his attention was diverted. Once upstairs, I saw only a single empty seat, in the back row. Afraid that someone would claim it, I waited until the lights lowered to sit down. But after all that effort, I couldn't concentrate on the music; I kept thinking about the usher I had evaded. *What if he had chased me or called the police?* I'd have to find a less risky route into the concert hall.

I thought about the stage door, just up Locust Street from the Amphitheatre entrance, where I paused every Friday to watch the musicians arrive. Carrying all kinds of instrument cases, they were always laughing and talking. Everyone going through that doorway seemed happy. Someone there might have an extra ticket.

The following week, I arrived more than an hour before concert time but no one seemed to mind my standing, or occasionally sitting, on one of the shallow stage door steps. After two or three weeks, several orchestra members recognized me and smiled, and some even paused to say hello. Then one day, the short, limping figure of Eugene Ormandy, the music director and conductor of the orchestra, stopped in front of me. He had conducted several of the concerts I'd attended and usually passed me on the steps without a word.

Ormandy, who had a Hungarian accent, sounded annoyed. "I always see you. Every week. What are you doing here?"

"I love the orchestra."

"Do you have a ticket?"

"No," I replied, not telling him I couldn't afford one. He hesitated, then nodded toward the doorway.

"Come with me," he ordered, and I followed him past the Green Room guard, through the cluttered, cavernous backstage area where musicians were warming up for the concert, and into his office. He picked up the receiver of the black rotary phone on his desk. "I'm sending a friend of mine. Please give her a ticket," he stated matter-of-factly. He then directed me to the opposite side of the backstage area and told me to go through a doorway marked "NO EXIT."

Mom Haley had the pass ready. Her eyes widened when she saw whom Eugene Ormandy had sent. "You!" she exclaimed. "A few weeks ago you couldn't afford a ticket, and now you're Eugene Ormandy's friend!"

The pass to that concert was a treasure, but more importantly, I had learned the backstage layout. If I could get through the stage door unchallenged, I'd have access to the corridor that led directly into the concert hall, bypassing the ticket-takers.

Coming in through the stage door was now easy. My entrance with Eugene Ormandy had given me credibility, so no one stopped me. The guard even smiled and waved when I walked in.

The stage door led directly into the Green Room, where I'd chat with the musicians before the concert began. I regarded them as celebrities but they didn't act that way. They always seemed happy to see me, and eagerly shared stories about conductors and soloists and their own predecessors in the orchestra. When it was time for them to go onstage through a door on the right, I'd slip through one on the left, into the concert hall. Ticketless.

I knew my chances of finding a seat were best in the Amphitheatre, where the atmosphere was relaxed and informal. Up there, I wouldn't be too conspicuous. An almost-sure bet was a second-row seat on the extreme right of the hall's horseshoe curve, a few seats in from the aisle. Concertgoers bought tickets for this location only if no other seat was available, so it was rarely occupied. Classified as "partial view," it was really "partial comfort," sharing its space with a white column that rose in front of it, where one's left leg should have gone. I didn't feel the hardness of the chair's wood or the narrowness of its width. To be able to see the stage far below, I had to sit forward on the edge of the seat, my left arm wrapped around the pillar, both legs jammed into half the normal floor space. But rather than being uncomfortable, there was something comforting about embracing part of the building. It was a way of making physical contact with the sounds that emanated from the stage. To this day, listening to certain works of music, I can sense the curves in the column and the rough texture of the flat white paint against my skin.

I felt no guilt about sneaking into concerts. I wasn't able to pay and the seats I sat in would have been empty anyway. I thought everyone benefitted: I got to hear the concert, and the audience was larger than it otherwise would have been. Even after I became a legitimate ticket holder, it took decades for me not to feel like a gatecrasher.[5]

Stokowski was back at the Academy on March 17, 1962. I didn't sneak into that concert; I must have saved for the ticket or got it at school. My proof is a ticket stub—*Amphitheatre Sec. A, Row B, Seat 3*—stapled to the cover of the program booklet.[6]

Walking down the Amphitheatre's steep wooden steps that evening, I became aware of the uniqueness of a Stokowski audience. There was palpable anticipation—loud, excited chatter, not the usual subdued pre-concert conversation. Instead of looking at each

---

[5] In 1965, the assistant conductor of the orchestra, William Smith, calculated that I had "crashed" $5,000 worth of concerts. In 2025, that would amount to nearly $50,000.

[6] Programs for almost every concert I have attended—numbering several thousand—are safely stored in boxes, ticket stubs fastened to the covers, newspaper reviews tucked inside. In marginal notes, my youthful handwriting details my impressions of the music and the musicians. Many programs contain signatures of the performers and composers.

other, audience members constantly glanced at the door at the back of the stage. They stopped talking only when the orchestra completed the ritual of tuning and the house lights dimmed. Then, as a unit, everyone turned to focus on the doorway, the sudden hush of the hall heightening the suspense. Finally, the door swung open and the imposing figure of Stokowski emerged. The audience was on its feet—rare in those days—before a note was played.

I watched him stride onstage—his head raised, his back straight—with dignity that bordered on arrogance. His gait was stiff and stately—he no longer used a cane—but his long legs carried him quickly through the violins and toward the podium, the tails of his cutaway waving slightly behind him. He acknowledged the audience by raising his right hand into the air as he walked.

The ovation peaked as Stokowski reached the front of the stage. He bowed to the audience directly in front of him, then to the immediate right and left. His right hand grasped the thick brass railing and he mounted the two steps to the top of the podium, turning to bow again, now to the far right and left of the hall, then up to the Amphitheatre. In one swift dramatic gesture, he turned to face the musicians, raised his hands, and the soft pizzicato pulses of the Webern Passacaglia began to throb.

All the works on that program were new to me: the Webern, the Sibelius Symphony No. 4, Debussy's *La Soirée dans Grenade*, and Mussorgsky's *Pictures at an Exhibition*. The last two pieces were orchestrated by Stokowski.

Russian composer Modest Mussorgsky had composed *Pictures*, originally for solo piano, to honor his late friend, artist/architect Viktor Hartmann. A number of Hartmann's paintings, on exhibit in St. Petersburg in 1874, had fired Mussorgsky's imagination. He used the paintings as points of departure, conveying his impressions through music. Stokowski's version, expanding the set of piano pieces to the full forces of the symphony orchestra, seemed to portray the visual scenes even more vividly than the original, which I'd heard in recordings. This orchestration was, in the truest sense, theatrical. Elements of the orchestration came close to, but never actually employed, sound effects; these were produced strictly by conventional instruments.

One of the ten movements found in *Pictures*, "The Gnome" is pure evil: shrieking brass; thunderous timpani; suspenseful strings; stealthy woodwinds and brass. In "The Ballet of Unhatched Chicks in Their Shells," chirping flutes, biting strings, and fluttering trumpets depict the frenetic scurrying of the little creatures. *Pictures* builds in intensity to the grand finale: "The Great Gate of Kiev," with fanfare-like brass so triumphant that my body seemed to levitate.[7]

The music, I thought, described not only how the paintings looked but how seeing them might make you *feel*: terrified by the gnome; frantic at the plight of the unhatched chicks; scared at the idea of the catacombs; awed by the grandeur of the Great Gate.

Emboldened by the power of the *Pictures* performance, I rushed to the Green Room after the concert, hoping to see Stokowski leave the building. About two dozen others also waited, and a larger group stood outside on Locust Street. After almost an hour, he came quickly through the crowd, waving regally.

---

[7] Maurice Ravel's orchestration of *Pictures*, dating from 1922, is far better-known than Stokowski's, from 1939. Stokowski's is more Russian in feeling; Ravel's is more French.

Chapter Three

IN THE SUMMER OF 1962, when I turned sixteen, my friend Jean and I applied for work as ushers at the Dell. We were a year too young but, by displaying my passion for the job, I was able to talk the officials into hiring us.

The affluent Friends of the Dell, who sat in seats close to the stage and dressed in summer finery, funded the free admission for the general public by paying for season subscriptions. But even the Friends' seats were not under cover—not protected from rain, dust and birds.

From reading program notes and the backs of record albums, I'd learned a lot about the composers and their music. And, from speaking with orchestra members in the Green Room, I also knew something about the workings of an orchestra. As I walked with ticket holders from the gate to their seats, I delivered mini-lectures on the works to be played, the composers' lives and the functioning of the orchestra, and ended by vigorously dusting the slatted wooden chairs. I was tipped well.

One of the perks of the job was being allowed to sit in a reserved section of benches that bordered a grove of mimosa trees. I was often the only person there, and free to stand and move to the music. I will forever associate the perfume of the mimosa with the music I heard as an usher, much of it for the first time. During one concert, the orchestra played Dvořák's Symphony No. 8 in G Major (known then as the Fourth), which I'd never heard. I adored its soaring cello lines like mountain ranges, French horn flourishes like hunting horns, and flute warbles like bird songs—a celebration of nature to which the real birds and rustling leaves of the Dell added their own soundtrack.

After every concert, I'd run backstage to talk with the soloists, conductors, and orchestra players, often asking for autographs. I got signatures from pianist/conductor José Iturbi; cellist/conductor Pablo Casals; conductors Charles Munch, Georg Solti, and the young Zubin Mehta; violinists Michael Rabin, Henryk Szeryng, and Zino Francescatti; and pianists Byron Janis and Van Cliburn.[1] Then, alone or with a friend (Jean had lost interest in ushering at this point), I'd wait in the dark for the bus—the first leg of a journey that would take more than an hour.

If Mom was well, she'd come into my room while I got ready for bed. Whispering while my father slept down the hall, I'd share stories about the works I'd just heard and what I'd learned about the orchestra. But I never knew what I'd find at home—Mom in a panic or my father in a rage.

*

For Stokowski's return to the Dell that summer, in 1962, the *Philadelphia Bulletin* reported that the city had gone to "elaborate lengths to cut down outside noises since Stokowski's 1960 flights of temperament. Airline pilots and airports have been notified to steer clear of the Dell."

The edicts didn't work. During Tchaikovsky's *Capriccio italien*, at the first overhead hum, Stokowski froze in place, his head bowed; the players sat motionless. But he didn't leave the podium. In the *Bulletin* the next day, noting that Stokowski had stopped conducting but had stayed onstage, a reporter wrote: "It had some old time concert-goers wondering if the maestro is getting mellow."

---

[1] Some of these legendary musicians became my friends; others became clients when I began consulting and doing press representation. I interviewed many of them when I became a broadcaster and journalist.

Between pieces, Stokowski bantered with audience members as if they were old friends. His unconventional behavior continued during the encores; before the hornpipe from Handel's *Water Music*, he asked if any sailors were present, and he dedicated his rousing, almost rowdy version of Sousa's "The Stars and Stripes Forever" to Philadelphian Betsy Ross, signaling four piccolo players, then the entire brass section, to stand up and play. Watching this outrageous, outsized personality violate concert etiquette, I began to realize that his musical interpretations reflected the same willfulness and lack of inhibition. His behavior was the perfect complement to the emotional extroversion and unpredictability of his conducting.

The following December 1962, I saved for and bought a ticket to Stokowski's Pension Foundation benefit at the Academy that featured works by Wagner, Beethoven, Debussy, Ravel, Revueltas, and Stravinsky.

At the end of the concert, the Maestro cleverly devised a way of getting his worshipful audience to leave. (It was also a way of providing humor and drama.) He programmed the final movement of Haydn's Symphony No. 45, "Farewell," as the last of four encores. Haydn had written the work to have the musicians, one by one, finish playing and leave the stage.[2] Stokowski asked each musician to add his or her own touch: wipe down the instrument, take it apart, or place it in its case before exiting. The score calls for two musicians to remain onstage at the end of the piece, but Stokowski had all of them leave. Concertmaster Anshel Brusilow, the last to go, played the final bars of his violin solo en route to the door. Midway, he turned and waved goodbye to Stokowski, who returned the gesture. The audience laughed as the Maestro, alone

---

[2] In 1772, Haydn's patron, Prince Nikolaus Esterházy, had kept the court orchestra at the summer palace longer than expected. To respectfully convey a complaint to the prince, Haydn wrote the last movement of the symphony to have one musician after another stop playing, blow out the candle on his stand, then leave the stage. The not-so-subtle hint worked: the day after the performance, the prince dismissed the musicians. Audiences have enjoyed the symphony and the story for almost two-and-a-half centuries.

onstage, acknowledged the ovation for himself before extending his arms toward the empty chairs as if the players were still present.

Just before each concert, when I leaned forward in my Amphitheatre seat, I'd be able to catch a glimpse of backstage life. On the left side of the stage, waiting to make their entrance, the conductor and soloist stood at the doorway, talking and looking out at the audience. After the orchestra tuned and the lights lowered, I'd see the conductor gallantly gesture for the soloist to precede him through the violin section to the front of the stage. A few other people often stood with them: the librarian, who put the music folders on the stands before concerts; the assistant conductor, who sometimes led performances I attended; and one or two stagehands. I longed to be backstage with them, but one person stood in my way.

Ruddy-faced and sandy-haired, stage manager Edward Barnes walked with great authority among the chairs and music stands onstage and throughout the city block–long area backstage. If the Green Room guard wasn't watching, I'd slip through the doorway leading backstage rather than going into the hall to find a seat. I'd rarely get halfway to the other side before I encountered Edward Barnes. I can't picture Mr. Barnes—I never called him anything else—without a kind smile on his face, even when he was throwing me out of the building.

Standing with his arms folded across his muscular chest, towering over me, he'd begin by shaking his head, then, quietly and with a note of regret, say, "I can't let you stay. I have to ask you to leave. We can't have people walking around back here because it's not safe with all that's going on." I always replied that I understood then made my way into the hall. After a few weeks of prowling around, I discovered an unlocked entrance off Shubert Alley, on the south side of the building. When Mr. Barnes—always gently—asked me to leave, I'd come back in through the Shubert doorway. He'd turn around and there I'd be. He'd never express anger or annoyance but would repeatedly, kindly, ask me to leave as if it was the first time, always with an expression of regret on his face. A decade later, when I returned to the Academy as a grown woman, "Eddie," as I now called him, sweetly apologized: "I'm so sorry, so sorry," he kept repeating.

※

Visually, backstage was intriguing: expansive raw brick walls; massive rope pulleys holding opera scenery, props and lighting fixtures; handcarts and dollies to move equipment. Enormous wooden double bass cases lay strewn about the floor like coffins, and cello cases, standing upright, looked like human silhouettes in the dim lighting mounted high above the dark-red velvet curtains. Battered black trunks served as moveable closets, their doors ajar to reveal concert dresses, dark suits, and sets of tails draped on wooden hangers. Larger trunks fitted with shelving stood ready to receive and transport the music folders for one hundred-plus players.

The entire backstage area smelled of music: the scent of bow rosin, the perfume of valve oil, and the aroma of freshly-pressed concert clothing mingled with the mustiness of decades of dust. That smell was like a drug. As it filled my lungs, I was infused with a sense of well-being.

After successfully evading Mr. Barnes, I'd go exploring. In a room jammed with vintage opera props and costumes, a wooden spinning wheel sat atop a jumble of scenery. In another, a Civil War–era mural depicting a group of minstrels, contemporary with the building, was plastered to the wall. Inside the concert hall itself, I came to know the terrain so intimately that—in almost-total darkness—I could negotiate its shallow steps and small ramps, and the quirky dips and rises in the old flooring, without missing a step.

I loved to walk across the abandoned, darkened stage after rehearsals, peering first through the crack of the door to be certain no one was there. Empty chairs and music stands fanned out from the podium, and the ghost light—a single bare bulb screwed into the top of a wrought-iron stand at the edge of the stage—threw elongated shadows high against the walls. The silence had a tone of its own, a kind of prelude to the music that would soon replace it.

In 1963, when I was almost seventeen, Mr. Barnes finally gave up the battle. I was allowed to go where I wished backstage. Just off stage right, a few concrete steps led to a utilitarian-looking metal door and on one of my explorations, I opened it. Two men sat at a long, worn, pale-green linoleum table. A fluorescent lamp with a piece of paper taped to its side illuminated the end of the table nearest the door, where the assistant conductor of the orchestra, William Smith, sat puffing on his pipe. Jesse Taynton, the orchestra's good-natured, white-haired librarian, sat to Mr. Smith's left, a cigarette burning itself out in the ashtray in front of him. He was penciling strange-looking marks, like hieroglyphics, onto sheets of music. I always said hello to these two backstage, but they were obviously hard at work now. Wordlessly, I began to close the door. "You may come in," Mr. Taynton said, and I pushed the door back open.

"This is the library, where we prepare the music," he explained. I was confused. Composers wrote the notes. I knew that from playing the cello in the school orchestra. Why would anything have to be added to what the composers had written? I was also shocked. The music was sacred, like the Bible, and not to be tampered with.

"Pull up a chair," he invited, "and I'll show you what I'm doing." Bill Smith smiled at me, his pipe clenched between his teeth.

Mr. Taynton explained that the printed music couldn't convey everything needed for a performance. It instructed the musicians on what notes to play and basically how loud or soft, long or short, fast or slow, to play them. But the conductor, through gestures and sometimes verbal directions at rehearsals (as I'd heard years ago in the Bruno Walter recording), would communicate specific tempos, volume (called "dynamics"), phrasing, and the subtleties of expression that make each conductor's interpretation uniquely his own. To further convey his wishes, a conductor would give the librarian directives to mark into the parts.

The most heavily marked parts, Mr. Taynton explained, were those for the string players. They had to deal with bowings—markings that indicated the directions in which the bows should move, up or down, which varies the quality of sound. The conductor, the concertmaster,[3] or the principal player of each string section determined the bowings. (Ormandy, a former violinist, did the bowings for many of his concerts.) The librarian then had to transfer those directions—hundreds or thousands of them—into every string part. There were also indications of how phrases should be shaped; if certain notes should be played aggressively or subtly, given relatively more or less emphasis; and a myriad of other interpretive details. A conductor might also decide if certain notes should be omitted.

The markings, Mr. Taynton continued, must reflect the style of playing that a conductor will ask for through gesture. The markings for a conductor who wants a lean, classical approach differ substantially from those of someone who wants an emotional, romantic interpretation. Markings, therefore, would have to be changed from conductor to conductor.

Fascinated, I listened as Mr. Taynton talked. Pipe smoke curled in the air and the sound of the Philadelphia Orchestra flooded the room from a wall speaker mounted above a metal cabinet. I returned to the library the next afternoon, and started going there a few days a week, not just on Fridays. My mother knew I was spending time at the Academy, but not during school hours. I never lied to her; she assumed I'd go there after classes ended.

In June 1963, that same year, Stokowski's sense of humor and fiery temperament were again in evidence onstage at the Dell, but this time I got to see him backstage, up close.

---

3   The concertmaster is, in effect, the principal violinist. He or she sits at the head of the first violin section, just to the left of the podium, on the side nearest the audience. The concertmaster's many duties include serving as "ambassador"—relaying questions and comments—between conductors and players. Conductors and concertmasters often have close relationships.

After an eventful first half (colorful, exotic music plus train whistles), Dell President Fredric R. Mann presented Stokowski with a plaque commemorating the fiftieth anniversary of his appointment as conductor of the Philadelphia Orchestra. "To praise Stokowski," Mann said, "would be gilding the lily."

"I have been called many things during my long life," the eighty-one-year-old Stokowski replied, "but I think this is the first time I have been called a lily!"

When the program, which included a driven, intense performance of Tchaikovsky's Fifth Symphony, came to an end, he turned to the audience. "May we on the stage, we lilies, thank you for your reception of this great music." He then asked, "Would you like to go home now?" A chorus of thousands yelled "No!" He asked the same question before each of six encores. After the final work, hearing the audience roar "No!" he suggested, "Let's ask the orchestra."

"Yes!" the musicians yelled, and the concert ended.

From the paved area in front of the stage, a friend of mine had taken photos of Stokowski accepting the plaque. We ventured backstage. In the bare painted-cinderblock dressing room, the Maestro was reclining in an armchair, his body almost straight. My friend, his camera hanging from his neck, slowly approached Stokowski. Politely, cautiously, he asked if he could take his picture. One of the Maestro's long legs shot out, missing the camera only by inches. "I am not an animal in the zoo to be photographed!" he bellowed. Then, just as abruptly, he conversed with us as if nothing had happened. His behavior, however, didn't scare me. Something inexorably drew me to him.

A crack in the sidewalk ran beneath the chain link fence that marked the boundary of Northeast High's property. I'd stare at the line beneath my feet and think, *Cross it, go to school, and your day will be wasted,* so a few times a week I'd head into town. My grades remained acceptable and no one at school seemed to notice my absence; the music department probably thought I was in class, and my teachers probably thought I was practicing.

When I arrived at the Academy, I'd choose between going to the library to watch what Mr. Taynton and Mr. Smith were doing, or sitting in the hall to listen to the orchestra rehearse, often with conductors and soloists whose recordings I'd heard at home—Igor Stravinsky, Byron Janis, Van Cliburn, Nathan Milstein, Rudolf Serkin, and David Oistrakh (the latter, I believe, spoke Yiddish in rehearsals).

I always sat a few rows back from the stage, on the left side of the hall. There, I'd be able to hear the conductor's comments and see his gestures and expressions. As the rehearsals began, I'd look at the empty seats around me then high up to the Amphitheatre, picturing what I looked like from there, alone in the hall, with the Philadelphia Orchestra onstage.

"What are you doing here?" Mr. Taynton asked when I showed up on a weekday. "It's not a holiday."

"I have off from school," I'd answer as convincingly as possible, but also with a laugh that let him know I wasn't completely trying to lie. He'd stare at me with good-natured doubt, shake his head, and invite me to watch what he was doing. Lengthy orchestral works, he explained one afternoon, were often subjected to cuts decided by the conductor, despite the fact that there was often controversy about conductors "second-guessing" a composer. I watched as he drew two marks that resembled the capital letter "I," one at the beginning of a section to be cut, and one at the end. He then connected the two with a sweeping, curving line. In the heat of a performance, there would be no ambiguity; the musicians' eyes could move swiftly and easily along the line, passing notes that were not to be played, before reaching the point where they were to resume playing. Every cut, whether it involved a single beat or a substantial section (referred to in the business as a "bleedin' chunk"), had to be marked in the parts of all orchestra members.

I arrived one day to see Mr. Taynton, thick-nib fountain pen in hand, writing musical notes for the second violins across a blank sheet of staff paper. When the first line, six measures long, was complete, he wrote out the same notes on the staff below, continuing the process until he had eight identical sets, one for each stand. (All of this had to be done by hand; it would be a year or two before photocopy machines became widely available, and the orchestra didn't yet own one.) He said he was doing something that the composer, long dead, might not approve of since the work originally stated that those notes be played only by the violas. But the orchestra's wind, brass, and percussion instruments were now better constructed, and therefore louder, than their counterparts in the late eighteenth and early nineteenth centuries, when many of the works in the orchestra's repertoire had been written. (Even string instruments could play at greater volume, due to better quality strings.) Because of this, some inner voices—secondary but still essential—might be drowned out. Having additional instruments play those notes would change the texture of the sound but allow the line to be heard clearly. There were also orchestrations that were especially dense, where some instrumental lines could be overpowered; the buried notes could be supplemented by other instruments of a similar range and tonal quality. I understood this better a few weeks later when Mr. Taynton showed me bassoon notes that were being drowned out when the orchestra played at full volume. Because the range and timbre of the cello was close to those of the bassoon, he was writing out those notes for members of the cello section—twelve musicians, two each at six music stands; again, he had to write out the six identical sets of notes by hand. With a pair of scissors, he meticulously cut out each line so it would fit perfectly over the notation it would replace. Now the cellists in the orchestra would supplement the bassoon line so that those notes would be heard. Mr. Taynton said that these cutouts were called "inserts," but joked about "cutting out paper dolls." I was thrilled to learn some of the lingo of the music business. I was inside the creation of a concert.

I asked him where he had learned all this. He had studied harmony, theory, and counterpoint in college and had been a professional bass player, but there wasn't any school that taught orchestra library skills. They had to be learned on the job. My education continued in rehearsals, where the markings he had made translated into sound: I could hear the augmented viola part, and the bassoon line played by the cellos. Because of the accuracy of Mr. Taynton's work, the orchestra was able to concentrate on making music—not correcting errors.

Sitting in on rehearsals, I was able to build on what I had heard in the Bruno Walter recording. Conductors must coordinate the interpretive and expressive details of pieces they perform—the way the notes flow and fit together, the way the pacing and phrasing and articulation match or develop within a movement and from one movement to another—and this process goes beyond what's written in the parts.

I heard one conductor stop the violin section midway through a beautifully played phrase in the first movement of Dvořák's "New World" Symphony, commenting that one of the notes had been shorter and more separate when stated by the solo flute a bit earlier. They had to match, or at least be similar, to unify the interpretative concept.

No musical decision, I learned, is ever arbitrary; there are technical, historical, and traditional reasons behind every choice a knowledgeable professional will make. Most performers base their decisions on what they think will best serve the composers' intensions. Orchestra members, of course, have studied their instruments with great pedagogues and know the historical contexts and traditional interpretive approaches to the works they are playing. They also have their own feelings and viewpoints to express, but their responsibility is to give the conductor exactly what he wants, even if it means suppressing their own preferences.

Hearing the players comment about the men (I don't recall a woman on the podium in those days) who conducted them, I began to see that a conductor who doesn't know the scores well, who steps onto the podium with undue arrogance or who talks too much—a trait musicians loathe—will lose players like an inept tour guide being abandoned by his group. The musical equivalent, however, can be more subtle: The players won't leave, but will go through the motions. The expressive intensity and sense of "ensemble"—an indefinable state in which the musicians almost read each other's minds, breathe as one organism, and "catch fire" in the heat of the performance—will not develop, nor will the players be able to fully communicate the "message" of the music.

I often heard the players refer to conductors as their "natural enemies"; they seemed to harbor resentment toward many of their leaders. But the great majority of the time, the musicians followed the conductor's every directive, verbal or physical. (They wanted to serve the music but were also fearful of being reprimanded.) The complex dynamics of the conductor–player relationship are still pure mystery. Almost any musician can be taught the basic techniques of conducting; few, however, are able to unite and ignite one hundred individuals of diverse backgrounds and personalities and, mostly through gesture, bend them to their own will. The essential qualities cannot be fully explained. In interviews, Stokowski said that what makes a great conductor is indefinable—a quality he called "X." There might be a parallel to different chefs using identical recipes, ingredients and equipment, and producing totally different results. Conductors, however, must influence *others* to create the end result.

Most conductors didn't care who attended their rehearsals, as long as they weren't music critics. (Guests could be distracting, but no one wants to be judged by a performance that isn't fully prepared.) Stokowski was different; except for the orchestra staff, he rarely allowed *anyone* at his rehearsals. Even family members of the musicians were rarely permitted to attend.

I didn't know that the rehearsal on the morning of February 3, 1964—for a benefit concert the following night—was more restricted than usual. Stokowski had ordered the session closed: *no* guests, including the orchestra's administrative and office staff. Mr. Taynton said I wouldn't be able to get in, but I decided to try.

Arriving at the stage door more than an hour early, I kept pacing back and forth from the brick wall of the Academy to the curb, trying to evade the icy wind, breathing the mix of cold, sweet air and exhaust fumes from the traffic moving down Locust Street.

A black sedan finally stopped at the curb and the commanding figure of Stokowski emerged, his face and shock of white hair dramatically set off by a white silk scarf and a long dark overcoat. He gripped a stack of scores in one large, chamois-gloved hand, and strode toward the stage door. I ran after him, my heart pounding. Startled, he paused, first turning his head, then his upper torso. I walked toward him as he turned to face me.

"Maestro, would it be all right if I attended your rehearsal? May I come in?"

He hesitated, then, almost ceremoniously, with the upturned palm of his right hand, motioned for me to walk ahead of him into the Green Room.

He took me off to the side and bent down toward me. "Why do you wish to hear the rehearsal?" he asked, his pronunciation shaped by a richly exotic, unidentifiable accent. I can't remember my response, but I recall that he threw his head back and laughed out loud—not, I'd come to learn, a characteristic Stokowski response. He again became intensely serious.

"What instrument do you play?" he asked.

"The cello," I told him, and he nodded approvingly.

"You may attend the rehearsal on one condition," he said as I looked up at him. "You must come backstage when it is finished and tell me your impressions." I considered this a serious responsibility.

"I will, Maestro," I assured him. He put his hand on the top of my back.

"Now, go!" he commanded, and with a shove, propelled me toward the concert hall.

The stage blazed with light; the house itself had been dimmed into semi-darkness. I sat in the first row on the left side of the hall, where I could hear as well as see Stokowski.

I was amazed to find all of the musicians already in their seats, warming up—no latecomers for this rehearsal! Themes from Shostakovich's Fifth Symphony and Rachmaninoff's "Vocalise" broke through the din like fish jumping out of the sea, while the musicians' "noodling"—playing rapid runs and flurries of notes—tested the instruments' ability to respond without hesitation and showed if they were properly tuned, focused, and colored.[4]

The orchestra tuned, and the personnel manager, standing beside the empty podium, made announcements about scheduling. Then, facing the orchestra, he clapped loudly three times—the universal signal for an orchestra to be silent. From the stage right doorway, Stokowski emerged, moving swiftly through the first violin section toward the front of the stage. The players broke into cheers, knocking the wood of their bows against the metal of the music stands and shuffling their feet in tribute. As he walked, Stokowski waved at the players and nodded in acknowledgement. Then, mounting the podium, he turned to face the orchestra, raised his arms, and cut through the air with both hands. The two-

---

[4] Different instruments, playing at the same pitch and degree of loudness, have different tonal characteristics and colors (also called timbres). The sounds of the flute and bassoon, for example, will not be easily confused because they are so dissimilar. Combining them—having them play together—will produce a different type of color, not unlike the process of mixing two shades of paint. Orchestrating well is a specialized talent not every orchestral composer possesses. Deciding which instruments to assign to which parts—alone and in combination—is the basis of orchestrating. An accomplished player has the ability to produce an endless variety of tonal colors on a single instrument. He will imbue every note with specific coloration—some nuanced and subtle, others strong, even coarse; even a single extended note can have many colorations. This is yet another element of performance, along with pitch, duration of notes, shaping of phrasing, and emotional expressiveness. Stokowski considered this a crucial element of interpretation and often asked for highly specific colorations from his players.

note motif that opens the Shostakovich Fifth, stated first by the cellos and basses, then echoed by the violins, resounded throughout the hall. He knew how to play that orchestra; he had created it. In the years following this rehearsal, in live performances and in recordings, I would hear Stokowski convey a huge range of emotions through these opening notes: anger, defiance, introspection, sadness, tragedy. I'd come to learn that his interpretations, more than those of other conductors, were spontaneously shaped by his moods. (I'd also come to learn that he could begin a rehearsal without a smile or a greeting. He could be charming then intimidating, without warning.)

As I watched and listened, it became clear that there were sounds in his imagination he was striving to replicate. Tension built as he had the musicians repeat the same phrase over and over, wordlessly adjusting the contour or tempo or sonority with only a turn of his wrist or the slight lift of a finger. Then he heard what he wanted.

"That's it, that's it. Do it that way in the concert," he said matter-of-factly as the players shot relieved glances at each other.

He knew when to ratchet up tension, pushing the players to an almost intolerable level of pressure. Then he'd sense when they needed a collective deep breath. Sitting back on the high stool, he began to tell stories. Setting the scene of his travels in Bali years earlier, he moved his hands evocatively in front of him, palms up, and described sailing slowly down a river in total darkness, without even moonlight to illuminate clusters of natives chanting on the river banks. The orchestra members were mesmerized. Then he told amusing stories of working with other orchestras, joining lightly in the laughter of the players.

That morning, I realized that his stories were not merely entertainment. They gave the musicians a break while putting them into the proper frame of mind for the works they were rehearsing. The tales of his travels to the Far East primed the players for works like Eichheim's "Japanese Nocturne" from *Oriental Impressions*, an atmospheric, mystical converging of Eastern and Western musical styles that he'd conduct as an encore. A more dramatic story set the mood for the intense, extroverted final movement of the Shostakovich Fifth. He even used rehearsal letters, which serve as points of reference in the parts for musicians to know where to resume playing, to communicate the mood of the music. "Letter H! Hor-ri-ble!" he yelled, in tones of distress, when the music expressed ferocity or anguish. "Letter C, please, calm," he intoned so quietly that the players could barely hear him before he led them into a section of Shostakovich's solemn slow movement.

Even during Stokowski's lighthearted comments, when the orchestra wasn't playing, the musicians sat with their instruments poised, ready to start. String players kept the fingers of their left hands in place on the fingerboards, their right hands gripping the bows in playing position; woodwind and brass players held instruments with their fingers hovering just above the keys; and percussionists stood close to their mallets, beaters, and sticks. The musicians' eyes never strayed from Stokowski, who often shouted out a rehearsal number or letter and, in a flash of motion, resumed conducting. There was no clapping to get attention, no second or two of conversation among the players or a repeat announcement of the rehearsal number or letter. There wasn't even a final pause before the full attention of the orchestra had to focus on his downbeat.

I suspected that Stokowski's practice of resuming the playing with no more than a split-second's notice was a way of keeping his musicians off balance. Focusing fully on him, totally under his control, they were able to give him the flexibility and spontaneity he demanded.

For two and a half hours, I absorbed every word he uttered and studied every gesture, amazed at the subtle and powerful effects they had on the evolution of the performance.

When the rehearsal ended, I rushed backstage to Eugene Ormandy's suite, which Stokowski was using. I knocked on the door and he answered. He motioned toward a swivel chair in front of a desk and I sat down. Wordlessly, holding up his index finger, he signaled that he'd be back, and in a moment, through the open bathroom door, I heard water running in the sink. I was shocked that the great Stokowski, like a mortal being, would need to wash. Waiting for him to return, I spun around a few times in the chair, watching the room revolve around me.

The Maestro reappeared. I sat still in the swivel chair as he walked toward me.

"What did you think of the rehearsal?" he asked, looking at me intently.

"It was remarkable!" I answered. "Thank you for allowing me to be there. But I didn't understand something you did in the Shostakovich."

Near the end of the first movement, he had suddenly pushed the tempo forward and then pulled back, slowing the speed like a rider pulling the reins of a horse. His hands had moved high above his head, his index fingers pointing upward like beacons, his eyes making contact with virtually every player so that he could control the orchestra's winding down, done in a matter of seconds, as one cohesive unit. It was like watching a movie scene suddenly shift into slow motion, and I had found it difficult to breathe. Then he'd pushed ahead again, moving the tempo urgently, impulsively. I had heard the symphony in recordings and its speed had never fluctuated as dramatically as it had in this rehearsal.

"Why did you slow the orchestra, then speed up?" I asked. Stokowski opened his score and pointed to the section in question, then explained briefly what he had done and why. His playing with tempo—a slight hesitation, then a surging ahead, or the reverse—was, I would learn, a characteristic of his conducting. This elasticity is called *tempo rubato*, translated from the Italian as "stolen time"—time taken from the regular, measured pulse of the tempo. He was a master of this push-and-pull expressiveness. Then, in what I would come to know as a characteristic Stokowski move, he dismissed me.

I returned for the second rehearsal later that day, not bothering to ask Stokowski's permission. He smiled and waved when he saw me.

At the end of that rehearsal, I walked onstage to thank him. Standing a few yards from the podium, I watched and listened as orchestra members, music in hand, approached him to clarify stylistic details—if a note should have slight emphasis or none at all; whether another note should be extremely short or somewhat sustained; if he wanted a slight delay and, if so, would he provide a cue for them to play. He suggested to a few players that they turn their instruments in unconventional directions to achieve unusual colors or effects. The musicians seemed to revere him, but even those who shared a smile or laugh with him seemed to be in awe.

As he stepped off the podium, Stokowski began to chat with me. He continued the conversation as we walked toward Ormandy's dressing room. I hesitated at the doorway and he gestured for me to enter. He put his pinstriped vest, which had been draped on the railing of the podium, over his navy blue silk shirt, then his suit jacket over that. Mr. Taynton walked in with the scores he had retrieved from the stage and handed them to Stokowski, who handed them to me. "Would you put these in my bag?" he asked. Then he gestured for me to precede him out the door. We walked the length of the backstage to the Green Room. I carried the briefcase as he walked beside me, his left hand resting gently on my right shoulder.

I went to the following evening's performance with a violin student my age named Pat. She attended all of Stokowski's concerts and always came backstage to see him. We sat in the front row just below the stage. (I snuck in; she probably bought a ticket.) Like the unsold obstructed-view locations in the Amphitheatre, these seats weren't desirable; we had to crane our necks to see what was happening. But they were easy to "crash," and we had proximity to the performers, including the Maestro.

The excited scribble in my diary details what took place:

> Once, Stokowski winked at me, and three times he smiled at Pat and me. After the concert, on his way for a curtain call, he stopped where we were and

bent down slightly, and laughed when we yelled "Bravo!" He began to have fun with the audience. "Well, what's the next question?" he said slyly when the program ended. A man in the balcony shouted, "What are we going to play next?" Politely, and a little facetiously, Stokowski replied, "Would you like to come up here and play for us?" Then he conducted five encores. After the last, he looked directly at Pat and me and said, "Isn't it time you were home?" We yelled, "Oh, no! Please play more!" He laughed heartily and shook his head. Everyone in the hall joined in the laughter. There were two more encores, then he dismissed the audience by wishing them "pleasant dreams." When Pat and I went backstage, he excused himself from his guests and walked over to us, starting to laugh again. "Here are the noisy girls from the first row!"

Adding to the excitement of the concert, I was harboring a thrilling secret: That was the last concert I'd have to crash.

The day before, when I arrived for the second rehearsal, Mr. Taynton was placing music folders on the stands and I asked how he was. "Not so good," he replied, looking troubled. "My assistant quit unexpectedly."

"Here I am!" I yelled, throwing my arms out to my sides for emphasis. He threw his head back and laughed, then reached out to muss my hair.

"We'll call you if we need you," he joked.

Later that afternoon, after I had returned home, my mother knocked on my bedroom door. "Mr. Taynton is on the phone," she said.

I could hear the orchestra playing in the background. "If you want a job," he said, "get back here tomorrow." At seventeen, I was on the payroll of the Philadelphia Orchestra.

Four months remained until my liberation from Northeast High. Classes ended at about three in the afternoon, so I was able to work a few hours each day. I set my combination lock to the last number so that I could tug on the lock, get my belongings, and run to the bus.

Mr. Taynton—Jesse—and Bill made room for me at the green linoleum table. I needed a chair, and Bill pointed to a tall wooden stool with a cane seat lying on top of a cabinet. I recognized that stool. I had looked down on it from the Amphitheatre sixteen months earlier, when the great German conductor Otto Klemperer led a series of Beethoven symphonies. At age seventy-seven, Klemperer had survived a stroke and been burned in a fire, and during the concerts the stool had supported his large, fragile frame. Sitting with one leg extended, Klemperer gave the beat with his right hand, balled into a fist, and signaled the players' entrances with his palsied left hand. I still remember the slow, grand gait of the second movement of the Seventh.

I occupied one of the long sides of the table, opposite Jesse; Bill was at the short end to my left. Pens, pencils, erasers, rulers, scissors, glue, and small square bottles of black ink littered the space not occupied by scores and parts, and a drinking glass and an ashtray sat in front of each man. I put a framed postcard of the exterior of the Academy of Music on my part of the desk. The piece of paper taped to the fluorescent lamp, I learned, had nothing to do with music; it listed winning poker hands.

A few days after I started the job, Hugh Walsh Sr., one of the managers of the Academy, stopped me near the entrance to the library. He held something out to me.

"Here's a passkey to the stage door," he explained. "You might have to get in here in the middle of the night if there's an emergency." The key glinted like gold in the palm of my hand.

Chapter Four

A YEAR OR TWO BEFORE I started working with the orchestra, my parents and I had driven to see a new tourist attraction—the Cherry Hill Mall in New Jersey, one of the first indoor megamalls on the East Coast. There I discovered a large paperbound book with an intriguing cover: dark gray musical notes against a light gray background, the title in bold red script running across its center: *The Nine Symphonies of Beethoven in Score*. This book wasn't about the symphonies; it contained the works themselves—the complete orchestral scores, reduced in size so that four original pages now fit onto a single one.

The "Beethoven book" became my talisman, representing the foundation of Western classical music; those nine symphonies, Bill Smith often commented, were "the rocks on which the orchestral repertoire was built." The book also became my teacher, inadvertently preparing me for my job. Because I knew the basics of musical notation from playing the cello, and because the names of the instruments were written in the left-hand margins next to their lines of music, I was able to follow the scores while playing recordings of the symphonies; I looked for the notes I was hearing. I memorized the order in which the instruments appeared on the page: woodwinds at the top, then brass and percussion, with strings last, each instrumental group listed in order of pitch, higher to lower. A few weeks after I began working in the library, Jesse asked me to collect the folders from the stands after a performance. "Would you like them in score order?" I asked, to his and Bill's surprise.

Although orchestral music is highly complex, the basic terminology, I quickly learned, is simple: Conductors conduct from scores; players play from parts. Scores show every note played by every musician; each instrument has its own line. The score is what composers actually create. Copyists or music publishers then "extract" the parts from the score by writing out the individual lines for each instrument. The resulting part is what each musician has on his or her music stand. The complete collection of parts for every member of the orchestra is called a set.

Just before a concert, I'd step up on the podium and put the scores on the conductor's stand, opening the first piece to the first page of music. Then I'd place the baton (always referred to in the business as a stick) beside the score. There was something ritualistic about this procedure, and I did it slowly, reverently. When the concert ended, the score usually remained open to the final page, the stick lying across it.

After a concert, I'd make two or three trips from the stage to the library, carrying the folders from the stands, all loaded with parts from each of the pieces. At first, feeling at home onstage, I had kicked off my shoes, not realizing that there were little puddles of condensation and spit throughout the wind and brass sections, released from the innards of the instruments. I never did that again.

If the program was going to be repeated, I'd stack the folders in the library; if it was not, I'd break them down, separating the parts for each piece into its own pile. If a set was complete, I'd use a specially made folder that had flaps and ties to secure the music, then put it back into its horizontal space in one of the green metal cabinets. If a part was missing, I'd hunt down the musician who had played it or go through sets of other works on the program to see if I had misfiled it.

Jesse soon had me marking parts—bowings, rehearsal numbers, phrase markings, cuts and dynamics—putting into practice what he had taught me during my after-school visits. There could be no ambiguities, no conflicting directions, or we'd hear our mistakes.

None of us did our work automatically. Both Bill, who was the orchestra's keyboard player as well as assistant conductor, and Jesse, a former bass player, were hearing the notes as they entered the markings. "Look at this!" Jesse would say to Bill. "How does the conductor expect the violinists to have enough bow to last the length of this phrase without changing directions?" I too began to hear what I was marking.

At one point, Jesse asked me to mark a small cut, just a few measures, into each of the parts—a job that would take hours. Why couldn't such a simple change be announced at the rehearsals? I asked. It would take only a minute or two for the musicians to mark it into their parts. It was our job, he explained, to protect every minute of rehearsal time for rehearsing—the precious, limited, and expensive time orchestra members and conductors have together.[1]

From playing in the school orchestra and from spending time with Jesse, I knew that all the musicians within each string section—first violins, second violins, violas, cellos, and double basses—play basically the same notes, with two players sharing a stand.[2] Most members of the wind and brass sections—flutes, oboes, clarinets, and bassoons; horns, trumpets, trombones, and tuba; as well as some of the percussion and miscellaneous instruments—require individual parts; each musician plays different notes and must have his or her own part and stand. On average, there are about seventy parts for every piece an orchestra plays. (There's little doubt

---

[1] It's still not unusual for a two-hour concert to require one hundred hours of library work. In 2016, it took the library staff of the Philadelphia Orchestra a total of twenty-four hours to mark only the first and second violin parts for Mahler's arrangement of a Beethoven string quartet.

[2] The number of players in each section can vary from orchestra to orchestra and from concert to concert, depending on the repertoire. In string sections, two musicians sit at each music stand, reading from a single part. Most often, in the Philadelphia Orchestra, we had nine copies of the first violin part, eight of the seconds, six of the violas, six of the cellos, and five of the basses, plus an extra or two as spares.

that someday soon orchestra musicians will all play from electronic devices instead of paper. They use them now mainly for practicing at home. Occasionally a soloist will read from a device during a performance.)

One of the most dreaded problems, I soon learned, is that parts can vanish; one minute they're on the stand then they're nowhere to be found. Thankfully, it doesn't happen often. Losing the music for a string instrument can be a nuisance, but because there are duplicates, it's not a disaster. Missing a wind, brass, piano, harp, or other part can be calamitous because there's only one copy of each. A set that's missing a single part or even a section of a part (unless it's a string part, for which there are duplicates) is no longer usable; the work can't be played without every instrument it's scored for.[3]

When a part went missing, our only immediate option was to photocopy one from another set in our collection, if it existed. Often, it did not; although the Philadelphia Orchestra library housed almost 1,100 individual pieces, we had duplicates only for works in the standard repertoire. And, during my first year or two on the job, we didn't own a photocopy machine. If we didn't have a duplicate (or couldn't get one from the Curtis Institute up the street), there was little we could do on short notice. Copying out the part from the conductor's score, while technically possible, wasn't usually feasible. Unless it involved a short piece, the process would take too long, and the chance of mistakes was high.

I didn't always mind these emergencies because I'd get to make spur-of-the-moment train trips to New York to obtain replacement parts from publishers, Juilliard, or the New York Philharmonic. Even though the replacement parts didn't contain the markings we had entered before rehearsals, or the additional markings the musicians had made during those sessions, the Philadelphia musi-

---

[3] How I wish we'd had today's technology in the 1960s! Librarians now often scan one each of the string parts to use in emergencies. These scans can be printed but they won't be ideal, lacking the markings from rehearsals. Librarians can also now find replacement parts for standard works online, or they can try to find a music publisher who can scan and send suitable material.

cians were able to compensate. Whenever rehearsals ended, I'd see players carefully tuck their music into their instrument cases or their briefcases. It was their responsibility not just to care for their precious instruments, but for the parts they took home to practice. And it was my responsibility, at age seventeen—while my friends were earning money after school as babysitters—to help keep track of the music for one of the world's great orchestras.

We'd often have to do extra work when "modern" repertoire (Stravinsky, Prokofiev, Shostakovich, Bartók, Ravel, and others) was programmed. Most of this music was still under copyright and legally couldn't be purchased; copyrighted parts could only be rented. Entire sets of rented materials, therefore—after we had marked them to the conductor's specifications—had to be returned to the publishers after the concert. (Parts are usually returned with markings intact; it's up to the next orchestra's librarians to replace whatever markings aren't relevant with their own. We removed only inserts—evidence that the conductor had changed the composer's notes, which is always controversial.) When our orchestra played any one of these pieces again, we'd have to redo all our work. There were a few rental pieces, however, like Bartók's Concerto for Orchestra and Ravel's *Daphnis et Chloé*, Suite No. 2, that we performed every few seasons. With the permission of the rental company, we'd hold that music in the library so that we wouldn't have to make the huge investment of time to re-mark the parts. If, however, the publisher had requests from more orchestras than it had sets of parts, we'd have to return the material.

When I opened packages of rented music, I knew I'd soon be erasing markings from performances by other orchestras, conducted by the likes of George Szell, Fritz Reiner, Leonard Bernstein, William Steinberg, and Erich Leinsdorf. Jesse and I could have used an electric eraser to facilitate the job; spinning furiously, its rubber tip would easily have devoured the existing markings. However, its abrasiveness would have shortened the life of the paper. Using a soft white rectangular eraser, I'd scrub the parts clean, feeling my arm go numb after an hour or two. When the time came for us to return a set to the publisher, I'd double-wrap it in heavy brown paper, write the name and address of the company in thick black letters on the package, and carry it in my arms to the post office. I made certain that every package was heavily insured.[4]

Most of the top conductors maintained their own libraries of scores and parts containing their markings, so all we had to do was make certain that the sets were complete before putting the music on the stands. Conductors who didn't have their own libraries sent us their marked scores several months in advance of the first rehearsal, and we'd begin the arduous process of transferring every marking in the scores into each of the parts. I was fascinated when Jesse told me that there was practically nothing for him to do when Stokowski conducted the orchestra. He brought his own sets of parts and, in any case, he required fewer markings than most other conductors.

I sat in on as many rehearsals as I could, which was a bigger bonus than being able to attend concerts. I'd hear the music being shaped and polished, and I'd listen for the changes Jesse and I had marked in the parts. Some conductors let the music unfold for whole sections before they heard something they wanted to change, while others constantly started and stopped. I understood then why Jesse and I spent so much time marking rehearsal numbers and letters into the parts: The players had to have frequent, coordinated points where they could resume playing as a group after being stopped by the conductor. Although publishing companies print rehearsal numbers and/or letters in the music to note these locations, there are often too few of them,[5] so Jesse and I

---

4 Today, there's a shortcut. When preparing works that are under copyright (and therefore rented), librarians can scan one each of the marked string parts (called "masters"). When the piece is next performed, the librarians will be able to transfer the markings into the players' parts. That work, however, still must be done by hand.

5 Having to stop mid-piece during a concert is rare—a nightmare come to life—but it happens. Zubin Mehta, while rehearsing the superb orchestra of the Curtis Institute of Music in *The Rite of Spring* in the 1970s, had difficulty keeping the orchestra together at one point in the score. "If this happens during the concert," he told the young musicians, "meet me at letter O!"

would mark additional ones into the scores and parts. (Bill marked parts only when there was a rush job.) With Jesse's permission, I transferred the rehearsal numbers and letters from the orchestra's parts into my Beethoven book. Then, when the orchestra was rehearsing one of the symphonies, I could follow along.

As Jesse had mentioned when I first showed up in the library, the most intense part of our job involved bowings. Virtually every conductor in history has wanted all the string players within each section to "bow in sync"—to have all the bows move up and down at the same time—a kind of choreographed look where they all change direction simultaneously. Just above the notes, we'd indicate symbols for upbows, where the bow travels away from the player, and downbows, where it moves toward the player. The directions in which the bows move help determine subtle, variable qualities of tonal color. Bowings also help the string player shape phrases as the conductor wishes. They convey how the conductor wants notes to be articulated—very short, sustained, emphasized, connected to each other, detached, and so on (phrase markings serve the same purpose for winds and brass players; we'd jokingly call them "blowings"). Some conductors determined the bowings they wanted, but most asked the concertmaster or the first-chair players of each string section to make those decisions. Jesse told me that there was only one conductor who didn't want bows to move in unison: Stokowski. I began to gain insight into how he created his unique, signature sounds.

As librarians, we even had to be concerned with page turns. If the bottoms of righthand pages involved rapid or sustained notes, musicians wouldn't be able to play and turn the page at the same time. String players, sitting two to a stand, could share the responsibility: One person could quickly turn the page while the other continued to play. But the winds, brass, harp, percussion, and others, having a single person reading from each part, were on their own; we'd have to copy the measures at the top of the following page, locating a point where there was a rest or a sustained note that could be played with one hand. We'd then tape those measures to the bottom of the preceding page.

At fast tempos—even with good page turns—string players often had to turn pages quickly, then slap them flat with their bows. And some of the sets, decades old, had the brittle consistency of dead leaves; we always had parts to repair, even for non-string instruments. We dreaded finding a small piece that had flaked off, bearing only a few notes of music. We'd have to begin the detective work of identifying the piece, then the part, and repairing it before its next performance.

I began to learn about the form and structure of music and the distinctive characteristics of composers' styles—how composers influenced each other, and why they made the choices they did. I gained insight into the works themselves and what made them great; what they expressed emotionally, even philosophically; and I began to know where they fit into music history.

My best teacher sat only a few feet away from me at the green linoleum table. Bill had an expansive and deep knowledge of many subjects, from Civil War history to Sherlock Holmes. He was able to connect disparate facts about world history and music history, and consider those connections from various perspectives.

He also had a sense of humor. When things got tense, Bill would pick up the phone and "call" Beethoven, asking him a lot of questions. Of course I only heard Bill's side of the conversation—long monologues that contained appropriate gaps for the Master's responses. These hilarious discussions became serious revelations for me about the interpretive options musicians had to consider.

People who passed through the library were often links to music history. Many of the players had studied with former members of the orchestra, so I heard about these distinguished musicians from people who had known them well. And a few piano soloists I met traced their teachers back to Beethoven. They'd recite the lineage, calling themselves "grand pupils of the Master." But one of the most thrilling moments occurred one afternoon when a diminutive, elderly, pale-complexioned man with round glasses and a thin, dark moustache appeared.

"Raoul!" Bill shouted with delight. Pointing to our guest, Bill ordered, "Shake this man's hand!" and I reached across the table toward him. Bill let a dramatic second pass.

"You are now shaking the hand that shook the hand of Brahms!" he declared. It took a moment for me to comprehend what Bill had said.

"Where did you meet Brahms?" I asked.

"In Hanslick's apartment," he answered. At age eighteen, I'd met someone who had not only known the great composer, but had met him in the home of the legendary music critic, Eduard Hanslick.[6] Our visitor, Raoul Hellmer, told me that his father had been a pharmacist in Vienna at the end of the nineteenth century and when Brahms requested that his prescriptions be delivered, the pharmacist called on his music-loving son to serve as messenger. On one occasion, Brahms was visiting Hanslick, so Hellmer delivered the medication to Brahms at the critic's home. Hellmer had even taken walks through the Stadtpark with Mahler. He'd also known the mayor of Vienna, who had given him a facsimile of the Mahler Tenth score that Bill and I had compared to the completed version, done by Deryck Cooke, that the orchestra had recently performed; Hellmer had passed that treasure on to Bill.

In contrast to the chaos at home—my father's tirades, my mother's descents into depression—the warmth and stability of the library was comforting. Most of the musicians surfaced there during rehearsal breaks to get their music for upcoming performances, discuss markings in the parts, or to share stories, jokes, gossip, and complaints about conductors. The intercom brought sounds from

---

[6] Wagner had used the pro-Brahms, anti-Wagner Hanslick as the model for the unprogressive, fastidious character of Beckmesser in *Die Meistersinger*.

the stage right into the library; whenever the music stopped, everyone went silent and stared at the speaker, anticipating Ormandy's anger-edged voice.

The orchestra members basically lived together. They went home to their families but spent the bulk of their time rehearsing, playing concerts, recording, and touring. They had to be acutely sensitive to each other, coloring and shaping their sounds to blend as a unit. While there were occasional disagreements among the players, for the most part they seemed to love being together. I was always amused to hear them moan about the hard work and impossible schedule (complaining is a universal orchestra trait), say they couldn't wait to have a break from one another, then make plans to vacation together (one year, a sizeable group went to the Bahamas). Before extended breaks, Jesse, Bill, and I would say goodbye—but a day or two later, one by one, we'd all show up at the library. "What are you doing here?" we'd ask each other, laughing. There was nowhere else we'd rather be.

Despite their complaining, the musicians obviously loved what they were doing. Unlike other orchestras I knew about, the Philadelphians always delivered the finest possible performances, even for conductors they didn't like or respect. On many occasions, I'd see the attention of the musicians subtly shift from a weak conductor to the concertmaster, taking the beat from the slightly exaggerated movement of his head or bow. These performances were always adequate; the audience had no reason to suspect that there was a problem. But without a strong conductor, it wasn't possible for the musicians to realize the full potential of the music.

It was also unusual for a mostly masculine group to protect a young woman constantly in their midst. I had problems only with Ormandy—every woman in the orchestra and on the staff had to fend off his advances—and one staff member. The players protected me as if I were their child or younger sibling. I remember one such incident, in the fall of 1964. I was alone in the library during one of Arthur Fiedler's rehearsals for a pops concert. During a break, I noticed that several of the players were staying longer than usual, chatting and looking through the music folders. When the bell rang to summon them back on stage, I saw one of them, at the top of the stairwell, glance at the others. "What's going on?" I had to ask twice to get a response. Sheepishly, they confessed that they had arranged among themselves for me not to be left alone, in case Fiedler, well-known for his womanizing, came to visit.

Although we had fun, no one ever laughed at me or teased me about my youthful devotion to music and to Stokowski. The musicians, and Jesse and Bill, encouraged that admiration, but they also told me to be careful.

"Watch out!" several of them warned. "You can't trust him! He tries to seduce every woman he meets, and he usually succeeds! Don't *ever* be alone with him!"

They knew a lot more about Stokowski than I did. I was aware that the iconic image of the conductor—dictatorial and seductive—was based largely on him. The tyrannical part of the profile was shared by many conductors: Toscanini, Reiner, and Szell among them. The amorous part seemed to come with podium territory; everyone in the business knew about "conductor tricks" which, at that time—a very different era— were accepted if not admired. But the musicians were aware that Stokowski had taken that behavior to extremes. (One Philadelphia Orchestra old-timer said no one could figure out how he'd had time to study his scores.) His three marriages had ended in divorce, and his serial infidelities had caused the first two breakups. His affairs were an open secret during his first marriage, and heavily publicized during his second. The media attention generated by all his marriages—which he probably coveted—was unavoidable: His first wife, Olga Samaroff,[7] was a concert pianist (more famous than him at the time of their marriage);

---

7   Samaroff was married to Stokowski from 1911 to 1923.

his second, Evangeline Love Brewster Johnson,[8] was an heiress (a member of the pharmaceutical family); and his third wife was the young Gloria Vanderbilt,[9] already famous because of the custody battle waged by her mother and her aunt. Madam Samaroff, as she was known, tolerated her husband's infidelity for years, and the indiscretions during his second marriage (played out with global press coverage) involved, among others, the most celebrated, glamorous woman in the world: Greta Garbo. Retired members of the Philadelphia Orchestra told me they knew when Stokowski had begun a new love affair by the presence of *Tristan und Isolde* on concert programs. (They played it often.) While I was working with the orchestra, a story still circulated about two Philadelphia matrons arriving at the Academy for Stokowski's return in 1960. "You will have the musical experience of a lifetime," one told the other. "Just try to forget about his deplorable morals!"

Jesse also had stories, even though he had started working for the orchestra years after Stokowski's departure as music director. The route to the Maestro's dressing room, Jesse said, cut through the library, and there had been a buzzer hidden under a desk for the librarian to warn Stokowski when his second wife, Evangeline, was en route—in spite of the fact that they had agreed to an "open" marriage.

Even now, I continue to discover evidence of Stokowski's romantic adventures. Browsing through books at the library, I find a biography of writer–aviatrix Beryl Markham. Markham was involved with Stokowski, possibly during his marriage to Gloria Vanderbilt. A biography of Blanche Knopf—*The Lady with the Borzoi: Blanche Knopf, Literary Tastemaker Extraordinaire* by Laura Claridge[10]—reveals her affair with him as well as that of journalist Virgilia Peterson. (Peterson is quoted as having told a mutual friend: "At least I didn't have a nervous breakdown after my affair

---

8 Evangeline Johnson and Stokowski were married from 1926 to 1937.
9 Stokowski and Gloria Vanderbilt were married from 1945 to 1955.
10 Laura Claridge, *The Lady with the Borzoi: Blanche Knopf, Literary Tastemaker Extraordinaire*, Farrar, Straus & Giroux, 2016.

with Stokowski the way Blanche did.") In the book *The Pink Lady: The Many Lives of Helen Gahagan Douglas*,[11] author Sally Denton writes about the actress–stateswoman's thwarted relationship with Stokowski in the 1920s, when she was a budding actress:

> She exuberantly accepted a part in *Fashions for Men*, written by the Hungarian playwright Ferenc Molnár. That play's opening in Philadelphia brought her to the attention of the famous Philharmonic Hall [sic] conductor Leopold Stokowski, who attempted to take the starlet as his mistress. Then at the height of his career, Stokowski had a harem of European and American stage and opera stars.

These stories reinforced the Stokowski legend. But I didn't have to be concerned; I wasn't in his league.

---

[11] Sally Denton, *The Pink Lady: The Many Lives of Helen Gahagan Douglas*, Bloomsbury Press, 2009.

Chapter Five

AT HOME, I WAS CONSTANTLY dealing with my father's explosions of anger and my mother's bouts of anxiety and fear. I'd spend hours trying to calm her, sitting close beside her or holding her in my arms as she sobbed. If I had to leave the house, I'd write reassuring statements on pieces of paper that she'd obsessively read. Her panic could be so powerful that her glasses would steam up from the inside—flat white discs that obscured her eyes. When the situation became unbearable, I'd think about Stokowski's next visit to Philadelphia to guest conduct the orchestra, but the time until then seemed interminable. To make the waiting manageable, I constructed a countdown calendar that showed the dates between his departure, his return, and the number of days that remained. Every morning when I awakened, I'd cross a number off the calendar. A week or two before he arrived I'd lose at least five pounds from excitement, a lot of weight for a slender teenager. (Years later, I told Stokowski about the weight loss. "That's the worst thing about music I've ever heard!" he said.)

I had to cross 132 days off the calendar between February 4, 1964, the day of Stokowski's concert at the Academy—when I got my job—and June 17, when he was back at the Dell. Unlike other conductors, he preferred not to rehearse on the day of a concert; his dress rehearsal almost always took place the day before. Although I was now working for the orchestra, and although Stokowski had allowed me into his other rehearsals, Jesse felt that he should ask permission for me to attend. Like everyone I had seen interact with the Maestro, Jesse seemed fearful of angering him.

The Maestro arrived early that morning. Jesse and I found him sitting onstage in the concertmaster's chair, pencil in hand, leaning over to write something in one of the parts on the stand. Jesse told him that I was now his assistant and asked permission for me to attend the rehearsal. "Of course," he said to Jesse, nodding toward me. "Now it is even part of her work."

After helping Jesse put the music on the stands, I went out front to sit in one of the sun-warmed wooden seats. The program included Handel's Overture in D Major; Beethoven's Symphony No. 8; Stravinsky's *Petrushka* Suite; and Rachmaninoff's *Rhapsody on a Theme of Paganini*, with pianist Jerome Lowenthal as soloist.

As I'd heard in February, Stokowski's rehearsals weren't like those of other conductors. He hardly spoke; the orchestra understood what he wanted solely through his gestures, all without a baton.[1] He didn't conduct the works straight through, choosing to skip sections he knew the orchestra would play well. Whenever he stopped the orchestra there was absolute silence—no laughing, no chatting; like Jesse, the musicians seemed to fear him. And at no point did the playing become routine; the music always had the intensity—the "edge"—of a performance.

When the rehearsal ended I went to the podium to thank Stokowski for allowing me to attend. "Tomorrow night, before the concert, would you come to my dressing room and work with me?" he asked. "There are so many little things that must be done." Thrilled at the thought of spending time with him, I said I would. I was not concerned about his intentions. When I had been with him in his dressing room the day I got my job, there was nothing remotely flirtatious in his manner, and I sensed that I could trust him.

---

[1] In 1929, Stokowski developed bursitis and temporarily had to stop using a baton. He loved the freedom he felt using only his hands and never went back to a stick. "Why should I use one," he would say, "when I can have ten?" Although occasionally there are conductors who don't use a baton (and others who use only their hands in specific works or in sections of works), most conductors feel that their gestures are clearer and easier to follow when they use a baton.

The following morning, Jesse and I were working in the Academy library when the phone rang. Jesse answered. "Believe it or not," my diary notes, "it was Stokowski asking if 'Nancy could please come up to my hotel room in the Barclay to help me write some music.' I was ecstatic until Jesse found out that I wasn't allowed to do this because of musicians' union regulations." (Jesse was considered a member of the orchestra and had to belong to the union.) It didn't occur to me then—and would not until decades had passed—that Jesse might have been lying to prevent my being alone with Stokowski. (My suspicion was confirmed fifty-two years later, in February 2016, when I called the president of the local Philadelphia musicians' union. As a former copyist who knew union rules from the 1960s, he said he'd never heard of such a restriction.) When Bill returned to the library shortly after Stokowski's call, Jesse looked at him.

"The Maestro called, looking for Nancy," he said with a little smile.

"Uh oh," Bill said, not looking at me.

Jesse went to the Barclay himself, returning about an hour later with a souvenir for me: a few bars of the Handel Overture handwritten by Stokowski on hotel stationery. He also brought a message: "You tell Nancy that I send my love," Stokowski had told Jesse, adding, "Ah, you are a lucky man, Jesse."

That evening, June 18, I went to the Dell two hours early. Hoping to see the Maestro arrive, I trekked through the staff parking lot at the rear of the facility, down the steeply sloping driveway leading to the East River Drive on a bank of the Schuylkill River. I was halfway up the hill on my way back when his black limousine drove into view. Stokowski, sitting in the front with the chauffeur, began to wave vigorously. The car pulled up beside me and the window lowered. "Would you like a ride?" Stokowski asked, smiling. I suddenly grew shy and shook my head no. I walked beside the car as it moved up the hill and maneuvered into the parking space beside the stage door.

Once we were inside, the door marked "CONDUCTOR" swung open every few minutes. "Nancy, would you come here, please?" the Maestro asked firmly, and sent me on "wild missions for pencils and people," according to my diary. I watched as he gave the concertmaster and a few first-chair players specific directives about stylistic details and ways of adjusting orchestral balances. Even with the concert only minutes away, he was replaying the dress rehearsal in his memory, continuing the process of perfecting the performance. That was the reason he had asked for help at the Barclay—to make changes in the Handel parts after the final rehearsal.

The day before, the only other people attending the rehearsal were two middle-aged women who had sat in front of me. I only wanted to listen to the music and to Stokowski's comments, but they insisted on making conversation, telling me that they had driven from New York where they lived. I didn't want to alienate people he knew, so I didn't ask them to be quiet. When Stokowski had walked onstage at the beginning of the rehearsal, I saw him nod to them; they waved. This was my first encounter with Faye and Natalie, whom Stokowski, during the break, addressed as "Feodora" and "Natasha." I identified them in my diary as:

> Stokowski's two friends who follow him all over…
> They were constantly babbling in my ear, telling
> me all of Stokowski's personal business from his
> morning exercises to the Stokowski-Vanderbilt feud
> last summer over a summer camp for their two boys.

In the years that followed, I would come to know Faye and Natalie extremely well.

I crossed 181 days off my calendar before the Maestro returned to Philadelphia for concerts in December 1964. During that visit, I began to see the constant shift between the harsh and gentle sides of his personality.

His program included the world premiere of Henry Cowell's Concerto for Koto and Orchestra—a piece that embodied the mix of East–West cultures that Stokowski loved, written for western orchestral forces but with Asian colors and effects. Kimio Eto, a blind virtuoso, walked through the Academy's backstage area holding my arm. He wasn't able to find his dressing room without help, but during performances he would instantaneously locate and move the bridges under the thirteen strings of his koto, a long wooden instrument, lying horizontally on the floor in front of him.

One section of the concerto, marked *grave*,[2] two beats to the measure, wasn't coming together. Stokowski clapped his hands, stopping the players.

"*Grave*," he intoned slowly and quietly, foreshadowing the sobriety of the section, asking them to repeat it. It still wasn't right. "*Grave*," he said again, his eyes narrowed, his mouth set, his right hand giving the downbeat. For the third time, it didn't work. "*Grave*," he stated yet again, no louder than before. Tension was building, and I was afraid he'd explode. He offered no explanation, no instructions, nor did I see any change in his gestures. But he must have altered his breathing or his eye contact (which, from the back, I couldn't see), because the players then gave him what he wanted. As they continued playing past the end of the *grave* section, I saw the musicians shooting relieved glances at each other.

After the rehearsal, I knocked on the door of Stokowski's dressing room. I had found a copy of his book *Music For All of Us* at a used bookstore and wanted him to sign it. He was wearing a black overcoat, ready to leave for his hotel but, as I wrote in my journal, I "bravely" asked if he'd autograph the book. He took it from me, sat down, and asked me to do the same. Then he began to question me about my job, "chattering on," as I detailed in my diary, while inscribing the title page opposite his photograph. "Be careful, it's wet," he warned as he handed me the open book. He continued to talk.

---

[2] It's pronounced "GRAH-vay," and means slow, serious, solemn, or heavy.

"To work as a librarian, one must be a very good musician, as I am sure you are. Not many people realize that."

"It's too bad that the public doesn't know how a great orchestra functions," I told him. "I certainly never did, before I began working here." A smile spread across his face.

He started to say something when Mary Krouse, Ormandy's secretary, walked in.[3] Stokowski's car had arrived.

"Already?" he said. He seemed disappointed. I was, too. Mrs. Krouse took Stokowski's black leather briefcase from the desk, and I walked over and took it from her.

As we walked through the vast darkness of the backstage area, he turned to me. "Why don't you write an article about your job and the orchestra? Call it 'Behind the Scenes.' I'd like to see that!"

I told him I was interested in journalism. "Then you know how to write such an article. But make it frank and open. Don't hide anything!"

"Maestro, that's the only way to write about anything," I answered.

"That's how all of life should be," he said.

It was a noble statement, but when I began to do research on him at the library, I discovered many autobiographical falsehoods he had invented and perpetuated.

At the first rehearsal that week, I had worn a white wool blazer that had an embroidered patch bearing the red, white, and green insignia of the Philadelphia Musical Academy—the school I was now attending part-time—on the breast pocket. Before the session

---

3 Mary Krouse, Ormandy's longtime secretary, was a gruff, gray-haired woman who had worked for Arthur Judson, the legendary impresario–manager of prominent musicians like Ormandy and Stokowski, and of orchestras including the Philadelphia and the New York Philharmonic. Jesse, Bill, and Mrs. Krouse, as I always called her, were co-conspirators in the ongoing effort to deal with Ormandy's often unreasonable demands. They constantly traded stories of The Boss's quirks. Mrs. Krouse was in on the secret of my growing closeness to Stokowski but I don't think she cared.

began, I went to Stokowski's dressing room to mark the rehearsal numbers from the orchestra's parts into his personal score of Bedřich Smetana's "Šárka" (from the cycle of six symphonic poems, *Má Vlast*). When I arrived, he was seated in a swivel chair talking to the orchestra's manager and assistant manager.

"Come in, Nancy, sit down," he said. A few moments later, he interrupted the business talk to tell me I looked pretty. I marked his score, then left to listen to the rehearsal ("the only person," I wrote in my diary, "in a hall able to seat 3,000!").

Early the next morning, before anyone else arrived for the first of two rehearsals that day, I knelt on the floor at the front of the stage, examining two round openings in the low stand that supported the koto. Suddenly Stokowski appeared. His hand jutted out.

"Good morning, Nancy."

"Maestro, I was wondering if you could explain something to me."

He looked at me thoughtfully. "I don't know too much," he said, a statement that surprised me. "I don't know if I can tell you, but ask me."

"Are these holes for acoustical purposes or for carrying the instrument?"

"I really don't know. I would imagine for both."

As I got up from the floor, he moved close to me, pointing to the emblem on the blazer. "Nancy, this is your pretty jacket. This is my favorite. Always wear it for me, please." Thrilled to have a bond with him, I told him I would.

During the break between rehearsals, the backstage area was deserted. I was standing near the door of the library when I saw him walk toward the stage. He hadn't seen me, and a subdued quality in his posture stopped me from greeting him. I secretly watched as he cautiously made his way across the darkened stage, through chairs and stands, to the high stool on the podium. There, he sat still and silent. Neither he nor I moved for at least five minutes. I wondered if he was reliving his great triumphs in that hall, dating back more than half a century. Then I saw him stir, and I walked onstage.

Jesse and Bill had returned from their lunch with a tin of expensive Abdulla Turkish cigarettes they'd bought for me to give to Stokowski as a gift. I approached him with the tin.

"Here's a Christmas present for you," I said, handing him the package. He playfully tossed the can high into the air and caught it, but it was too dark to read the label.

"What is it?" he asked, and I said it contained cigarettes. "What kind of cigarettes?"

"Turkish."

"Oh, I like those!"

"I know you do," I told him. He shook my hand, smiling. I watched him set the tin on the small table next to the podium that held his scores, jacket, and tie.

"Do you want me to put them in your room?" I asked.

"Yes. Know where you can put them? In my black briefcase on… Oh, you know, the one you carry for me!"

I was halfway across the stage when he called me back.

"Do you know how to roll cigarettes?" he asked.

"Well, Maestro, I saw it done in cowboy movies when I was little."

He chuckled. Then, with imaginary paper and tobacco, on the top of his music stand, he mimed the entire process: smoothing out the paper, sprinkling the loose tobacco, rolling the cigarette, and sealing the finished product with an imaginary lick. "I used to roll cigarettes," he quietly confessed.[4]

---

[4] In my research about Stokowski shortly after meeting him in 1962, I was impressed to read that he never smoked or drank. But not long after, following one of his concerts, my friends and I were ushered into a room where Stokowski sat at the center, studying a bottle of wine, a cigarette poised between the thumb of his right hand (underneath) and the index and middle fingers (on top), bringing it straight to his puckered lips and drawing on it. I would later see him hold a cigarette between the ring and middle fingers of his right hand. Never did I see him hold a cigarette conventionally. (And even though he didn't smoke often, whenever he did, I never saw him smoke his own cigarettes. He always asked someone to give him one.) He rarely did anything conventionally. He often held cups or glasses not on the sides but from underneath, close to the bottom, the vessel sprouting from his fingertips. The belts of his pants were often buckled on the side, not in front.

I waited for him inside the stage entrance before the Saturday evening performance. As I wrote in my diary, I had never seen him look handsomer. He glanced in my direction, nodded, then turned away. I was deeply hurt. Seconds later, I heard the famous accent—"Is that Nancy?"—and I walked toward him.

"Where is my jacket?" he asked.

"I thought I'd get a bit more dressed up tonight, Maestro."

He eyed my sleeveless red knit dress top to bottom. "Why can't you wear it over this dress?" he asked. "It would look *so* good."

"Next time, Maestro."

"Do you have it here?"

"No, Maestro. If I did, you know I'd wear it for you. Next time. When I come to your concert with the orchestra in New York. I promise."

"All right," he said, "but New York is not tonight!" Off he walked.

My parents were going to pick me up after the concert, so I phoned them to bring the jacket. My father, never eager to do favors, was impressed by Stokowski and complied.

After the performance, which included "Sárka," the Sibelius Symphony No. 2, the world premiere of the Koto Concerto, and excerpts from Wagner's *Die Meistersinger*, a crowd of more than a hundred jammed the hall in front of Stokowski's dressing room. Suddenly the door opened and everyone gasped. There stood Stokowski. The crowd surged forward, but he raised his hand to hold them back: "Not yet, please." He craned his neck, peering down the hallway, searching, until his eyes met mine, then he motioned for me to come to him. As everyone stared, I made my way through the crowd. "Maybe we'll do some talking tonight," he said quietly as I walked ahead of him into the room. Then he noticed the jacket. "Good girl!"

He closed the door behind us, motioning for me to sit in a chair opposite Henry Cowell, the composer. The two of them talked about the concerto. I didn't utter a word, nor did they speak to me; I was the fly on the chair. It was, for me, a historic event. (Cowell, one of America's most prominent and original composers, would die the following year.) I never learned why Stokowski wanted me there—if for some reason he didn't want to be alone with Cowell; if he wanted Cowell to see that he had a young woman friend; or if he wanted me to experience a bit of music history.

Kimio Eto entered the room. Adrian Siegel, the orchestra's official photographer, who had been in the room with Cowell and Stokowski when I arrived, arranged and took a few pictures of Stokowski standing between Cowell and Eto.

"Good. That's all," Stokowski said, but Siegel had other plans.

"Only two more, Maestro."

The observant Stokowski challenged him. "You already have four."

"Then I'll have six," Siegel answered.

"You are a greedy man," the Maestro coolly replied.

Cowell left. Stokowski, leaning back against a desk, sipped a large cup of soda through two straws. A diminutive Japanese woman who had accompanied Eto timidly approached him.

"You are a great conductor," she quietly told him.

Noisily drinking his soda, without lifting his head, he responded, "Of course I am great!"

She didn't know quite what to do, so she continued: "You look well."

"Of course I look well!" he replied between sips. "I lead a very virtuous life. Why shouldn't I look well?" His shoulders shook with laughter.

Everyone except Adrian Siegel left, so I started out of the room.

"No, Nancy," Stokowski ordered. "You stay. Adrian, Nancy and I are going to have our picture taken together." Side by side—me in my white jacket, him in his tails and white tie—we smiled into the camera. "Adrian," Stokowski instructed, "no publicity, please. If Nancy wants a copy, she may have one, and I definitely want one for myself." He hugged me as I started to leave.

"I'll see you in New York, Maestro," I told him.

"Baltimore," he said (pronouncing it BAHL-tee-more), naming one of the three cities—Baltimore, Washington, and New York—where he'd conduct the orchestra in addition to Philadelphia.

"No, Maestro, in New York."

"In Washington!"

"No, Maestro, only in New York."

The crowd of admirers was finally admitted, my parents among them, and I introduced them to the Maestro. As everyone listened, Stokowski said, "Nancy is a wonderful girl. She is extremely intelligent. We are fortunate to have such a capable assistant. You know, she never does her music in any way mechanically. It is all understood." Miming the act of writing on his palm, he said, "And she is a wonderful copyist. I depended on her very much this week."

Half an hour later, Jesse, my parents, and I were chatting backstage when Stokowski, heading toward the exit, made a detour to where we stood.

"Jesse," Stokowski implored, "why can't Nancy come to Washington and Baltimore with us? I want her to come."

"Maestro, she's coming to New York."

Stokowski thought for a moment. "What if there is copying to be done? We couldn't let Jesse do it all by himself!" Everyone laughed, and winking at me, he was gone.

Two weeks later, after Christmas and New Year's, he was back in Philadelphia to conduct the final concert of the series. He called me at home the morning of the performance. Would I do him a favor and find bone studs for his dress shirt? They could not be plastic or metal or stone; they had to be bone. I frantically called every clothing store I knew, then went into Center City to check additional shops. I finally went to the Barclay Hotel, where he was staying, to admit defeat.

He answered the door in a white terrycloth robe and, with a little laugh, said that he "just had a bath with Epsom salts." I had never seen him dressed informally nor heard him speak about anything personal; he also sounded more British than I'd ever heard him sound. I was both thrilled and uncomfortable to see him in such human guise. I apologized profusely for not being able to get what he wanted, but he dismissed it as something no longer important. I started to leave when he motioned toward a chair, and we sat and talked for some time. When I finally rose to go, he suddenly stepped forward and enveloped me in his arms, holding me tightly, tenderly, quietly, then, wordlessly, he released me. I remember the feel of his back through the terrycloth. That evening, I didn't tell anyone about my quest for the studs or my trip to the Barclay, and certainly not about the embrace from Stokowski. He had established a new closeness between us, and I didn't want to violate his need for privacy. I had sensed, from his usual regal bearing, that he didn't freely bestow expressions of pure affection; there was no hint of anything sexual in the embrace or in the sweetness of his smile when he had released me, and I treasured this shift in our relationship.

In 1962, around the time we first met, Stokowski had founded the American Symphony Orchestra, which was based at Carnegie Hall—a place I'd heard about all my life but hadn't visited. In early 1965, I asked Stokowski for tickets to one of his concerts there. I told Jesse about my plans to attend with one of my school friends, Judy Kornfeld. "If you're going to New York," he said, smiling, "why don't you take the Maestro's music to him at his apartment?" Knowing how much this visit would mean to me, Jesse was willing to trust me with Stokowski's scores and marked parts from his performances three weeks earlier. He told the Maestro that I'd deliver the materials.

On a bitterly cold afternoon, I lugged Stokowski's tan suitcase, decorated with colorful hotel stickers from all over the world and loaded with music, from 30th Street Station in Philadelphia to Pennsylvania Station in New York. I called the Maestro from a pay phone when we arrived. First there was a busy signal, but on the second try the line clicked.

"Allo?"

"Hello, Maestro, this is Nancy Shear. How are you?"

"All right." Then, in an agitated voice, "Where are you?"

"Pennsylvania Station. I have your music."

"Are you coming to my concert tonight? Do you have tickets?"

"You wrote to me last week and said that you'd put two tickets at the Box Office."

"Yes, but that was last week! Listen, if you have any trouble, I want you to come to the stage door and ask for me and we'll straighten it out."

"All right, Maestro. When may I bring you your music?"

"When is convenient for you?"

"How about right now?"

"Yes," he said. "Do you have the address?"

"I do."

"Ten-sixty-seven Fifth," he told me, "between Eighty-Seventh and Eighty-Eighth Streets."

"All right, Maestro."

"That's between Eighty-Seventh and Eighty-Eighth," he repeated. I could detect concern in his voice. "Now, listen. You get into a taxi and come right here."

"I will, Maestro."

"See you!"

I wonder now why he didn't tell me to bring the suitcase to Carnegie Hall instead of coming to his apartment, especially on the afternoon of a concert.

After a fifteen-minute taxi ride, Judy and I stopped in front of an elegant Fifth Avenue apartment building. A dark-green awning stretched from above the curb to the door, and inside, upholstered sofas; crystal chandeliers, and fresh flowers were reflected in the lobby's mirrors. The doorman announced our arrival. Excited and nervous, we took the elevator to the fourteenth-floor penthouse, getting off in a small, dark, private vestibule that had a table with a vase, and several framed drawings on the wall. (All the art, I'd later learn, was the work of Stokowski.) Glass wind chimes hung from the ceiling. I wondered if they were always silent in this breezeless room.

As the elevator doors closed, the room became totally dark. I could hear Stokowski's deep laugh—he seemed to be on the phone—before I rang the bell. In a few moments the door opened and there he stood, in dress pants but shoeless, shirt unbuttoned, white bowtie draped around his neck.

Towering over us, he greeted us with powerful handshakes and gestured for us to enter. We crossed a large room where a long, narrow desk jutted out at a right angle from windows overlooking the reservoir in Central Park. A famous Monet—I think it was "The Artist's Garden at Giverny"—hung low on one wall. I put the suitcase in the nearest corner of the living room.

"Please sit down," he ordered more than offered. "I will be with you in a minute." He disappeared into another room.

We lowered ourselves into wingback chairs—one covered in a green and orange Asian fabric, the other in a green and pink rose pattern—our backs to a barren fireplace. We looked around. I wanted to remember every detail of the Maestro's home.

A tall, open-door armoire held little statues (including a white bust of Bach and, in clear blue glass, one of Stokowski); photos (a young woman with long blonde hair who resembled him); and what appeared to be a curved-top treasure chest. There were also photos on the walls: Stokowski walking through a cathedral with a man who appeared to be Pope John XXIII, and black-and-white shots of two happy little boys on ice skates. A black lacquer Oriental cart held bottles of liquor and drinking glasses, and a huge oil portrait of a young Stokowski in profile hung frameless above the fireplace. Most intriguing, a hand-sketched circle about six feet in diameter, drawn right onto the wall, filled the area between two bookcases. A metal wand, extending from the circle's center to its perimeter, moved slowly past lines that intersected the circle's circumference. I wondered if it was some sort of clock. Consulting my watch, I realized that the wand indicated the time like the single hand used to set an alarm clock. Near the center of the room, a patch of paint peeled from the ceiling.

After about fifteen minutes, the Maestro returned, now dressed in tails, white tie, and black suede shoes. As he settled into a chair near us, I introduced Judy. He asked about the origin of her last name, Kornfeld, then he told us about his first arrival in the States. "When I came to America, the man at the boat said, 'Stokowski, what kind of name, Stokowski? You must change it!' 'No,' I said, 'I will not!' 'But it must sound American,' he told me. 'That was my father's name and his father's and that of my great-grandfather,' I told him. 'I will always have this name!'"

I related the story of my great-grandfather's arrival at Ellis Island, where officials informed him that his last name, something that sounded like "Vishainsky," was too long and complicated. My great-grandfather then pointed to a prosperous-looking gentleman in line ahead of him and asked his name.

"Goldstein," he was told.

"I'll take it," he said, and that became the family's new name. This elicited a chuckle from Stokowski.

"That's a German name, not American," he responded, either ignoring the fact that it was a common Jewish name or referring back to its origin.

Then he changed subjects. "You will hear a unique orchestra tonight," he told us, emphasizing the second syllable of the word "orchestra." "I hire the players only on a concert basis, not for the entire season. So they play well, or—" he gestured with one large hand "—out! You know, this is not like big symphony orchestras where, after thirty years or more, a man has only three more seasons until he retires and he doesn't care anymore, only about his pension." He mimed the gestures of a bored violinist. "No feeling. The only requirement to play in our orchestra is that you are a good musician. We have every kind of player: Negro, white, Indian, and so on, and many women."

I was very aware that, in the 1960s, most orchestras were employing mostly white, male players; there were only five women—two of whom were harpists—in the Philadelphia Orchestra when I started working there. Stokowski's orchestra was a significant exception, and I wondered about the ramifications of his policy.

"Maestro," I asked, "do you feel that you sacrifice quality to have that kind of diversity?"

"Absolutely not!" he said without hesitating. "They are *all* fine players."

The conversation moved to the growing indifference of the public to great orchestras like the Philadelphia and the New York Philharmonic. "Audiences," he told Judy and me, "are very different in different cities. Philadelphians will come to concerts in any weather. New York is not like that. It's actually many different cities." He surprised me by adding, "Here, I can have an empty house."

"People might appreciate the orchestra only if they're in danger of losing it," I said, and he agreed. "That happened a long time ago, didn't it, Maestro?"

"Yes," he said, "in the twenties, when I conducted in Philadelphia."

"But otherwise," I said, "nothing can be done about it."

"Don't ever say that!" he said, hitting his hand hard against the arm of the chair. "Something can always be done about everything! In my orchestra, at all rehearsals, we have a motto: 'Do better!'"

We talked for at least another fifteen minutes before he glanced at his watch. I thought it was a signal for us to leave, so I stood up.

"We'd better be going," I began to say when he interrupted.

"No, you do not have to go. Sit down! You will come to Carnegie Hall with me." We continued to talk for some time until he finally rose from his chair.

As I sat next to him in the backseat of the car he spoke, nonstop, about buying his sons (then thirteen and fifteen) new coats at Saks Fifth Avenue. He didn't know if he should get black or blue ones.

"Why don't you ask your boys which they'd prefer?" I suggested.

"Yes," he said, pleased with the idea, which seemed obvious to me. "I will do that!" He stared at the scene outside the window—Fifth Avenue and Central Park—and began to talk about how much he hated "society." I wasn't sure if he meant wealthy people or society in general. (I now suspect it was both.) We pulled up at the stage door and entered Carnegie Hall with him.

He had arranged for us to sit in the first balcony, off to the side—the conductor's box, I'd later learn. After the thrilling concert—its final work was no less than *The Rite of Spring*[5]—we went backstage to thank him and say goodbye. His hand shot out when he saw me.

"Don't forget, Maestro," I warned, "you have to play the second half of *American Salute* at the Dell this year."

"What do you mean?" he asked, looking perplexed.

He had obviously forgotten the promise he'd made at his Dell appearance the preceding summer. To end the concert amusingly, he had told the personnel manager to interrupt the final encore—an entertaining work by Morton Gould based on the popular song, "When Johnny Comes Marching Home"—midway through the performance. Holding a large clock in one hand, pointing to it with the other, the manager had stopped the orchestra, gesturing that they had run out of time. As the orchestra and the audience laughed, Stokowski had made a little speech.

Now, backstage at Carnegie Hall, without thinking, I turned away from him to face an imaginary audience.

"*Deo volente*," I slowly began, in his accent, using his gestures, repeating what he had said. "Next year we will all be here and I will play the rest of the piece for you." When I turned back to face him, he was laughing. To my great relief, he hadn't been offended. Then he reached for my hand and held it.

"Write me a letter and remind me. I will start at the very note where we left off."

Suddenly his face clouded with concern. "What train are you taking out of New York?"

---

[5] He had conducted its US premiere in 1922 and in 1930, the first US ballet performance, danced by Martha Graham with choreography by Léonide Massine. The stage sets and costumes were based on the originals by Nicholas Roerich.

"The twelve-thirty," I answered.

"Oh, that's late. You know what you do? When you get to the station, if you have time, go downstairs and have supper. All right?" I didn't tell him that even if we had the time, we didn't have the money.

On the train home that night, I sketched a detailed diagram of Stokowski's apartment. I didn't know I'd soon be spending substantial time there.

I don't remember what prompted the conversation, but one day Jesse and Bill began talking about my future. If I wanted to be a librarian, they said, I should concentrate on playing the cello. Since full-time job openings at major orchestras were rare I might have to audition for smaller orchestras, or orchestras in smaller cities, where librarians also played. They also said I'd have to learn more about music theory.

I didn't want to think about leaving the orchestra, and I didn't want to tell them that I wasn't cut out to be a professional cellist. I just couldn't force myself to practice; after only an hour, it always became torture. Even if I'd wanted to become a professional, starting to play at age twelve is usually too late, particularly for a string player. I also didn't know how I'd leave my mother. I didn't think she'd survive without me to protect her from my father or to care for her when she was ill. I had no idea when or how I'd be able to move to New York, a dream I'd had since visiting there on my twelfth birthday.

My connection to Stokowski was also becoming complicated. In addition to the magnificence of his music and the magnetism of his personality, he was probably a father figure; it didn't seem that way then nor does it now, but I've learned enough about psychology to know otherwise. Considering his reputation, it seems naive for me to have trusted him as I did. I would have been shattered if he had violated that trust. And yet when I was with him, I wore clothes I knew he'd like—favoring those that were a bit provocative; the red knit dress was sleeveless, skin-tight, and short. I desperately wanted his approval.

He never revealed the reasons for his growing attachment to me, which I could sense. It might have been a continuation of his long history with young people: He helped found the Curtis Institute of Music in Philadelphia and conducted its orchestra, and created the vibrant, imaginative Philadelphia Orchestra Children's Concerts—their fame only matched by Leonard Bernstein's televised *Young People's Concerts* a generation later. Also in Philadelphia, Stokowski helped kids form a youth orchestra, a youth chorus, a youth dance group, a traveling youth record library, and youth music clubs. He had the kids suggest programming, write and design the program booklets, sell ads, and help market the concerts. Adults were allowed to attend only as chaperones, and there were stories of childless grown-ups bribing kids to get in. A retired member of the orchestra told me that at one Philadelphia Orchestra Youth Concert, Stokowski had instantly quieted three thousand rowdy children by raising his hands then lowering only his left little finger.

His Philadelphia Orchestra children's programs had been adventurous to the point of being historic. The 1934 US premiere of Shostakovich's First Piano Concerto was given not at the adult concerts, but for the kids,[6] with sixteen-year-old Eugene List as soloist; he waited almost a year to perform the piece for an adult audience. When asked about this, Stokowski commented that children, unlike adults, listened without prejudice to contemporary music.[7]

I heard from many people that Stokowski loved to discuss music with youngsters, always taking their opinions and ideas seriously.

---

6   It was premiered on December 12, 1934, at a Youth Concert.
7   Not everyone recognized the wisdom of Stokowski's actions. An article in Philadelphia's *Public Ledger* in the 1930s announced his intention to broadcast modern music to the children of America "in order to develop a liking for it by them." Conductor Walter Damrosch, the famed, respected conductor and host of music appreciation broadcasts on radio, responded, in all seriousness, "To force these experiments on helpless children is criminal."

Following each of his Philadelphia Orchestra Youth Concerts, teenagers would gather under the windows of his townhouse on nearby Rittenhouse Street, serenading him until he asked for a head count because of limited space. Of course they lied, and when he told them to come in, a much larger group trooped up the stairs. He sat and talked with the kids for hours, and provided pie as a treat. Faye and Natalie, whom I had met at the Dell, had been part of this group. After he left the Philadelphia Orchestra, he formed the All-American Youth Orchestra (AAYO) in 1940, an ensemble that rivaled the sound of the Philadelphia Orchestra at the height of its greatness. He recorded and toured with the AAYO, bolstering America's international reputation while helping to train members of the next generation of musicians. He had to disband the orchestra when many of its members were drafted into World War II.

He was also drawn to youth in his private life, often hiring women in their late teens and early twenties as secretaries and staff members. He seemed to like women in that same age group as lovers. The last two of his three wives were also considerably younger than him: Evangeline Johnson by fifteen years, Gloria Vanderbilt by forty-two years; Greta Garbo was twenty-three years his junior. I wasn't sure where he wanted me to fit into his life, personally or professionally.

I've often wondered if Stokowski, while sincerely enjoying the enthusiasm and imagination of young people, also felt safe with them. They wouldn't challenge his authority nor would they expect him to share his feelings or to reveal the background he wanted to hide. Despite my youth, I had the maturity to understand what he wanted and needed. I was able to "read" him—to judge his moods and behave accordingly—just as I had been conditioned to do with my emotionally fragile mother. This hypersensitivity enabled me to give Stokowski the respect he required and to relax and have fun with him. I also knew about music, particularly *his* music, and about his history. In addition, I had a close connection to his former orchestra. I only wanted to be near him and his music.

Without my knowing it, my timing had been perfect. More than twenty years after his departure from Philadelphia, when he was probably feeling the absence of his old friends, his stature in the city, and the young people who had serenaded him beneath his window, I had appeared at the stage door.

Chapter Six

NO ONE, INCLUDING BILL SMITH—WHO seemed to know everything—knew much about Stokowski's background. "The Maestro's a big mystery," he said. "I think he was born in England, but nobody knows for sure. Some people say his real name is Leonard Stock or Lionel Stokes."

I needed to know more about him. Now, almost six decades later, I realize it wasn't just curiosity. Knowing about his background—who he really was—would help me understand why he was so important to me. Off I went to the main branch of the public library on the Benjamin Franklin Parkway to pore through books, magazines, and newspapers, many published decades before I was born. But the mystery only grew as I encountered constant contradictions. Some stories said he was born in Poland, others in Germany or England; some gave his birth year as 1882, others 1887. I also found five versions of his name—Leopold Boleslawowicz Stanislaw Antoni Stokowski; Leopold Antoni Stanislaw B. Stokowski; Leopold Antoni Stanislau Stokowski; Leopold Anthony Stokowski; and Leopold Stokowski. I know now that only the last two were correct; his birth name was Leopold Anthony Stokowski. The longer Polish names were fictitious, invented by him. The birthplaces other than London were also inaccurate. (Like both his parents, Stokowski had been born in England.) He had purposely misled the public. Although he'd be furious when someone said his name wasn't really Leopold Stokowski, he couldn't offer his birth certificate as proof; that would have revealed his true, non-Polish middle name, his British background, and the correct year of his birth, 1882, five years earlier than he routinely claimed.[1]

It's ironic that the press wrongly accused him of changing his name from Stock or Stokes but didn't bother to verify the false information he gave them. *Time* magazine, under the drawing of Stokowski on its April 28, 1930, cover, identifies him as Leopold Anton Stanislaw Boleslaw Stokowski, and in the article about him, says he was the son of a Polish father and an Irish mother. The *New York Times*, in a 1934 article about his planned resignation from the Philadelphia Orchestra, calls him "the Polish maestro." The *New York Daily News*—in a 1954 story about the breakup of his marriage to Gloria Vanderbilt—reported that Stokowski was "the son of a Polish-born attaché in the Russian government." Even the authoritative *Grove's Dictionary of Music and Musicians*, in a few of its editions, printed the fictitious middle names and the erroneous information about his parents. A later edition (*The New Grove Dictionary of Music and Musicians*, 2001) corrected the name—"Stokowski, Leopold (Anthony)"—but still misidentified his parents' nationalities.

From all my sources—which included older people at the Academy who had known the Maestro in his earlier days—I learned that he had come to America when he was twenty-three to serve as organist and choirmaster of St. Bartholomew's Church, then on New York City's Madison Avenue. In those days—before radio, television, recordings, and sound in films—music could only be heard live. People sang and played instruments at home and attended

---

[1] He trimmed five years from his age as far back as 1907, when he was a twenty-five-year-old organist in New York. On an official customs form that Philadelphia Orchestra personnel had to fill out in preparation for a 1936 tour of Canada, Stokowski—in his distinctive handwriting—gave his birth date as April 8, 1887. He was five years, minus ten days, off. During a live radio broadcast in the 1950s, when an announcer accurately stated the year of his birth, listeners heard Stokowski shout, "That is not correct! It is 1887!" causing the broadcast to be cut off the air. And, according to someone I know who saw his medical records, he told his doctors he was seventy-three, not seventy-eight, when he broke his hip in 1960.

concerts if they could afford to, but they could also hear music in church—sacred works during services and secular repertoire at concerts. Recitals by the organist–choirmasters of prominent New York City churches[2] were major events, and the musicians were highly paid celebrities. With good looks and charisma added to his musicianship, Stokowski quickly built a following—but he also got into trouble. The church's conservative rector disapproved of Stokowski's dramatically staged services, some complete with wandering shepherds, crooks in hand. (I was surprised to hear he hadn't brought live sheep into the church; years after that, he'd fill the Academy stage with livestock for a performance of Saint-Saëns's *Carnival of the Animals* at a children's concert.) During another service, Stokowski played a rousing rendition of Sousa's "The Stars and Stripes Forever." (This did not surprise me. In later years, he often played his own orchestral transcription of this march as an encore.) I also heard stories about his escapades in the choir loft, one involving the daughter of an important church official. (He seemed to like women of relatively high stature. He had broken his engagement to the daughter of the head of St. James's Church, Piccadilly, when he left London for New York.)

I read accounts of his having been a child prodigy—entering the Royal College of Music at thirteen to study piano and composition; becoming organist and choirmaster of prestigious St. James's at twenty; and graduating from Queen's College, Oxford, at twenty-one. He left St. Bartholomew's after three years to become a conductor, and only one year later, in 1909, the determined, brilliant, but inexperienced twenty-seven-year-old became head of the Cincinnati Symphony. He never struggled, never served an apprenticeship because his first wife, Olga Samaroff, was a prominent concert pianist who paved the way for him. They had met in New York in 1906 and were married in 1911, a year before he maneuvered his way out of the Cincinnati contract to come (with Samaroff's help) to Philadelphia. Luckily, he had a gift not

---

[2] St. Bartholomew's parishioners included families such as the Vanderbilts and the Astors.

only for conducting but also for orchestra building, a separate talent. When he became director of the Philadelphia Orchestra, there were a few fine players but it was basically rigid and undistinguished. (He had to rehearse in German, the native language of most of its musicians, which he spoke fluently.) He recruited the finest players he could find, then shaped them into a true ensemble. The Philadelphia Orchestra became famous not only for virtuosity but for hair-trigger flexibility, subtle, nuanced expressiveness and unusually rich sonorities. Only four years after his arrival, the orchestra—and its conductor—achieved worldwide prominence by performing the American premiere of the massive, complex Symphony No. 8 by Gustav Mahler (often called the "Symphony of a Thousand" because of the combined instrumental and choral forces it required; Stokowski employed 1,200). When I heard about the Mahler premiere from a violinist who had played in it, I understood how Stokowski was able to shape the orchestra into a world-renowned ensemble so quickly: I remembered the rehearsal of the high school orchestra I'd heard him conduct in 1962, when he had transformed the sound of the orchestra in minutes.

In my teenaged mind, Stokowski and my other hero, Eleanor Roosevelt, were similar: Both were activists never satisfied with the status quo, and both seemed immune to criticism. I learned that Stokowski, in addition to pioneering contemporary music, had experimented with acoustics and sound reproduction, working closely with Bell Laboratories.[3] (I realized then why his recordings sounded richer—more resonant—than those of other conductors.) He anticipated the future by exploring the "electric orchestra," an ensemble composed solely of electronic instruments, in 1939.[4] And,

---

3   Under Stokowski, Philadelphia was the first orchestra to make electrical recordings (1925); to do the first commercial orchestral broadcasts in the US (1929), a series which included Stravinsky's still-controversial *The Rite of Spring*; to make stereo microgroove recordings (1931); and to make a long-playing recordings. He also worked on developing high fidelity and stereophonic sound.

4   In the late 1920s, Stokowski camouflaged a theremin within the ranks of the Philadelphia Orchestra to enrich the bass line. He stopped the experiments when the musicians became nauseated from the vibrations.

to popularize classical music, he teamed up with Mickey Mouse in the groundbreaking *Fantasia* (1940), the film that introduced viewers around the world to the music of Bach and Stravinsky, in multi-track stereo. He helped take music out of the concert hall.[5]

Being from Philadelphia, I always thought it ironic that this futuristic man had made his mark in a city known for its conservatism. Almost from the time of his arrival, he used the Philadelphia Orchestra as a laboratory for experimentation: developing new recording technology; "auditioning" new scores, some radical, at special Wednesday morning rehearsal sessions; and exploring non-Western musical techniques involving half tones, quarter tones, and one-sixteenth tones. He tried new types of rehearsal seating for himself (including a horse's saddle); burned incense to create an exotic atmosphere while rehearsing Eastern-influenced works; and developed unconventional, changeable seating arrangements for his players.[6] His innovative ideas—many of which became standard procedures in orchestras throughout the world—often met wholesale rejection in Philadelphia.

When I started attending Stokowski's Philadelphia Orchestra concerts in the early '60s, I thought of them as family reunions—but I quickly learned that they were those of a troubled family. His departure from Philadelphia had been bitter. In the late 1930s, the idea of the Philadelphia Orchestra without Stokowski had been inconceivable to concertgoers, but not to orchestra board members. They challenged his authority, saying that decisions involving orchestra policy shouldn't be his alone. The board's concern was mainly about finances: They felt that a contemporary music–heavy repertoire would alienate ticket-buyers (even though it was almost impossible to get a ticket during Stokowski's tenure; the only way to obtain a season's subscription was to inherit it), and that his

---

5   Ironically, Stokowski would have hated the ubiquity of music today. In or out of the concert hall, music, he felt, should be listened to carefully, in quiet concentration, its sound as high quality as possible.
6   His innovation of placing the first and second violins next to each other is now standard.

desire to increase foreign touring would be risky. The musical monarch—perhaps dictator—had entered the age of democracy.

The more research I did, the more inconsistencies I found. The most fascinating involved his democratic philosophy of music making, which matched my own. Although he had gone to extraordinary lengths to cultivate a regal public image, he placed that image at the service of a populist, anti-intellectual approach. No aspect of his work—the nature of his music and how he made it available—was elitist. From the beginning of his career to the end—some seventy-two years—he constantly found ways to bring music to the masses. The title and the content of the only book he wrote, *Music For All of Us*, reflect that philosophy. I can't imagine any other major conductor of his generation—Toscanini, Koussevitzky, Reiner, or Walter—shaking hands with Mickey Mouse onscreen. Nor can I imagine any of them engaging with young people as Stokowski had at his Philadelphia Orchestra Children's Concerts or, for that matter, befriending a teenager like me.[7]

In my late teens, I was becoming a more sophisticated listener, appreciating works from the Baroque and Classical periods, and even "modern music," which at that time focused mostly on serial (non-tonal, non-melodic, mostly dissonant) styles. But I still loved the Romantics best. I didn't share the snobbishness of my friends, who teasingly called me "Tchaikovsky lover!" or "Sibelius lover!" Smiling, I'd tell them they were right.

My friends' attitude was exactly what Stokowski abhorred. In January 1965, when he performed Sibelius's melodic, romantic Second Symphony with the Philadelphia Orchestra, all of us in the audience roared our appreciation. "You were not supposed to like it," he said, after quieting the ovation. "It is the custom these

---

[7] Leonard Bernstein televised his *Young People's Concerts* starting in 1958, decades after Stokowski's Philadelphia Orchestra Children's Concerts.

days of intellectuals to demand music of the mind. That's why the Sibelius symphony is hardly ever played. I am pleased. And this does not mean that you are not intellectual and intelligent. As long as there are real men and women, there will be romance. We need music of the heart!"

In a letter to me a month later, he wrote derisively about intellectuals:

> I…agree with you that the music of Sibelius, Mendelssohn, and Tchaikovsky is sincere and creative and is an expression of the heart.[8] There are persons who do not respond to this music. It is possible that all their vitality is up in their skull, and does not go down below their chin!! Of course they are very intellectual, and also very (?).

The question mark and exclamation points were handwritten, while the rest of the letter was typed. He closed with "Always your friend," then signed his formal, sprawling signature. In a smaller hand, he wrote "Stoki" in the lower right-hand corner.

When Stokowski spoke against intellectuals, he was criticizing a cerebral approach to *anything*, be it art or life. He preferred spontaneity, individualism, impulsiveness, and intensity. He would have agreed with Marc Chagall, who was quoted by one of his granddaughters in a *New York Times* article published in September 2013. Discussing the meaning of his paintings, she said, "He would say to other people, 'What do you feel? Go into your heart.'" Stokowski's philosophy of art is also expressed in a handwritten, signed statement at the bottom of a small 1920s or '30s portrait someone had sketched of him: "Technique is only a means to the end: — expression. Its lack is bondage, its mastery freedom." He often said, "I like anything that makes for self-expression." He said this one day after telling me that he didn't mind applause between movements

---

8   Stokowski underlined the last four words for emphasis.

"if it is sincere."[9] I was, however, beginning to understand that the self-expression and freedom he spoke of pertained only to art. It wasn't what he wanted in interactions with friends, colleagues, or family. I was also beginning to realize that, despite his "music for the masses" philosophy, Stokowski knew that most people in the audience didn't fully grasp the "message" of great music. He unexpectedly revealed this before one of his concerts at the Academy. I'd always walk with him from his dressing room to the entrance onstage and he would invariably be quiet and focused, keeping intact the concentration he'd established meditating in his dressing room. But one evening he peered through an opening between the wall and the doorjamb at the audience, three thousand strong. "How many people out there do you think really understand what we do?" he asked thoughtfully. Before I could respond, he turned to face me. "Only three or four," he answered. Then he added, "We play for *them*," and walked toward the podium.

And yet—there were always contradictions—despite his efforts to popularize classical music, he fiercely championed contemporary works rarely popular with concertgoers. Almost all his programs contained at least one new or unusual piece,[10] and he made no apologies. If the audience booed after hearing a new work, he'd repeat the entire piece. (In 1929, he told an audience that hissed a

---

9   He had changed his mind about that. Decades earlier, when he was music director of the Philadelphia Orchestra, he had angrily silenced applause between movements. At one point, during the 1920s, he had experimented with banning applause altogether. But later, as I witnessed at the Dell in 1963, he had the entire orchestra rise to acknowledge an ovation after the second movement of the Tchaikovsky Fifth and had half a dozen soloists rise between movements of Kodály's *Háry János Suite*.

10 He gave more than one thousand world and US premieres. He conducted the world premieres of Schoenberg's Violin Concerto and Piano Concerto and the US premiere of *Gurrelieder* (Stokowski would conduct Schoenberg's complete orchestral works during the composer's lifetime). He also conducted the world premieres of Rachmaninoff's Third Symphony, Fourth Piano Concerto, and *Rhapsody on a Theme of Paganini*, the latter two with Rachmaninoff as soloist. He gave the US premieres of Mahler's *Das Lied von der Erde* (in the same year as the premiere of the Eighth Symphony); Berg's *Wozzeck*; Falla's *El Amor Brujo*; and works by Scriabin, Richard Strauss, Shostakovich, and Sibelius.

Schoenberg work that they should give their seats to people "who would appreciate great music.") During his Philadelphia Orchestra directorship, he'd often program familiar works at the beginnings of concerts so audience members could leave before the contemporary pieces were played. History has proved him right: Many of the "radical" works he conducted are now part of the standard repertoire. (Strauss's *Ein Heldenleben*, now considered melodic and romantic, was described as "cacophony" in a review of Stokowski's 1913 performance.)

At the time I started going to concerts, audiences rarely expressed displeasure; I never heard any booing (they were either well-mannered or apathetic). The opera house was different, but booing there usually targeted a controversial production or flawed singing. But in the 1920s and '30s, Stokowski's audiences let him know they didn't want to be challenged. He had a running battle with audience members who didn't want new music. He also grappled with the Friday matinee ladies (whose ranks included members of the orchestra's influential Women's Committees). These women didn't hesitate to leave while the orchestra was playing, noisily grabbing their shopping bags to catch the train home to the Main Line. (Eventually, the railroad purposely delayed the departure times of the Friday afternoon trains.) Some of the older orchestra players told me about Stokowski's not-so-subtle reprimand in 1926. He devised a program that opened with Lekeu's *Fantaisie Contrapuntique*, a piece that starts with two players onstage then adds musicians one by one until the stage is full. The concert closed with Haydn's "Farewell" Symphony; its final movement is scored to have musicians leave individually until only two violinists remain. On April 17, 1926, the *Philadelphia Record* wrote an account of the event: "The staid and conservative audience which patronizes Philadelphia Orchestra concerts was treated to a new shock yesterday afternoon, when Conductor Leopold Stokowski staged a rather startling farce by way of rebuke to those music-lovers who annoy him by late arrival and premature departure, with attendant confusion in the auditorium. Stokowski's revenge, perpetrated in a spirit of whimsical irony, took the form of an exaggerated imitation, on the part of the orchestra, of the conduct of his audiences." The musicians, the *Record* reported, "were hurrying in like the late-comers on the other side of the footlights…" Audience members hissed when they realized they were being parodied. At the end of the Haydn symphony, only two violinists were to remain onstage (according to the composer's directions), but Stokowski had them *all* leave. He alone remained, and, playing the satire to the hilt, he turned to acknowledge the empty seats. Audience members were scandalized. "This is outrageous!" they huffed.

It *was* outrageous! He *loved* being outrageous! And I think his audiences (especially the women) loved being scolded by him. It was exciting, and no other conductor had this kind of relationship with them.

Still, his desire for quiet was sincere. "Painters paint their pictures on canvas, but musicians paint their pictures on silence," he'd say. Cartoons, in art deco-style drawing, show Stokowski, the orchestra, and the audience turning to glare at someone who has dropped a handkerchief. His campaign continued until his final concert with the Philadelphia Orchestra, on February 13, 1969, when people noisily began to leave early. "You provide the silence," I heard him say. "We'll provide the music!"

Few artists spoke from the stage in those days (and fewer still in the 1920s and '30s), but audiences enjoyed his impromptu comments. It brought him closer to them. While members of the non-music press seemed amused, reporting on his unusual behavior, music critics didn't hesitate to call him a showman and say he was theatrical. In the conservative, intellectual world of classical music, neither of those terms is ever complimentary. I understood why they wouldn't approve of behavior that would distract attention from the music, but why would a bit of showmanship be bad? Did Stokowski go too far? Some people laughed when they told me about his experiments from those years—banishing applause and stage lighting, having the orchestra play in darkness except for a spotlight focused just on his abundant blond—then white—hair and his baton-free hands. "Serious" conductors are supposed to be concerned only with how the music sounds, not with anything else. And they are *never* to call attention to themselves.[11]

I know Stokowski would have loved being accused of theatricality. If he'd had his way, concerts would have involved all the senses, incorporating color projections (he experimented with this technology) and the scent machines he advocated for movie theaters. But was he theatrical on the podium? Young friends of mine are shocked to see him on YouTube: There's no crouching or jumping or launching himself into the air at climactic moments. The lower half of his body barely moves; his shoes could have been glued to the podium. Nor does he have dramatic facial expressions—no emoting, no grimacing, no looks of torment, pain, or ecstasy.[12] Leonard Bernstein, a far more demonstrative conductor than Stokowski, also didn't escape criticism, but no one ever questioned his devotion to music as they did Stokowski's. Perhaps it was because of what Bernstein said—his insightful commentary during the *Young People's Concerts*—or perhaps it was the difference in the times; Bernstein was thirty-six years younger than Stokowski.

If Stokowski's critics listened with their eyes closed, would they hear theatricality rather than musical drama? Some musicians—fine musicians—still criticize his unabashed romanticism, saying that it's evidence of his theatricality. And, because of those accusations, people who never heard him conduct in person assume that he wanted extreme loudness. In all the years I knew and worked with him, he rarely asked for the fortes and fortissimos[13] that many

---

[11] An article in the *New York Times* on April 1, 2013, noted that Riccardo Muti seemed to have had two spotlights trained on him in the pit in a Rome Opera performance of *I due Foscari*. This might have happened by accident. "Theater officials said they had not noticed, and Mr. Muti said he had nothing to do with the lighting." The implication was that a serious conductor would never have sanctioned such goings on.

[12] This is not to criticize more physically extroverted conductors, such as Leonard Bernstein; what worked for Stokowski wouldn't have worked for them, and vice versa.

[13] Loud and very loud dynamics.

other conductors considered the epitome of drama. Most often, it was lower volume that he sought. That, to him, was essential to the dramatic whole. "Sssssssssssssss," he'd hiss at the entire orchestra or at individual players, or "Sssssssshhhhhh, it's too loud," he'd say almost to himself, shuddering as if he were in physical pain.

To achieve the balance he wanted, he constantly gestured for individuals or entire sections to play at a lower volume so that more important melodic lines could emerge. He usually preferred this approach, rather than asking that the secondary parts be played more loudly. One of Stokowski's most characteristic gestures—a hand turned upward, fingers vibrating—implored strings players to play more intensely but not necessarily more loudly.

In the 1960s, retired Philadelphia Orchestra contrabassoonist Ferdinand Del Negro, still amazed at the phenomenon, imitated Stokowski's gestures from the 1930s and '40s. His eyes almost shut, his shoulders hunched as both hands waved the volume down, Mr. Del told me, "It was already too loud before we made a sound!"

Arthur Berv, who had played first horn in both the Philadelphia Orchestra and the NBC Symphony, was quoted in a 1974 *New York Times* article about the difference between Stokowski's and Toscanini's concepts of how he was to play the horn solo in Brahms's Symphony No. 1: "…subdued, soft, almost like a hunting horn in the distance for Stokowski, and brazen and defined for Toscanini."

Sometimes Stokowski asked that individual instruments or sections be silent—tacet—for reasons other than issues of volume. In an already long letter to me dated August 24, 1965, he had added a P.S.:

> In Wagner's tremendous overture to "The Flying Dutchman" the horns are playing almost all the time, and so become fatigued. I would like to have them rest at certain passages, so that when they have important phrases they will be fresh and can give these phrases great power. I have marked the selected bars in my score. Would you have time on

one of your free days to mark the horn parts where not to play…

He often made such decisions between rehearsals, basing the need for the changes on the strengths and weaknesses of specific players.[14]

Stokowski's transcription of Palestrina's *Adoramus te*, originally a motet (a short, sacred work for an unaccompanied chorus), is thirty-two measures—about three minutes—of chordal blocks of color and texture. It starts with strings (second violins, violas, and cellos *divisi*—each section divided, playing two different lines of notes rather than the more common single line), then woodwinds (with horns), then brass, then combined winds and brass, then just brass, then only strings to the end. All the strings begin muted, upbow, *pianississimo* (*ppp*: extremely soft), *molto sostenuto* (very sustained)—a subdued, prayer-like sound.[15] In the score of the transcription, which I helped Stokowski prepare for publication, he wanted to be certain that other conductors would understand his personal concept of the sound while offering them freedom as well. He indicated crescendos and decrescendos but didn't always specify what dynamics—the degrees of loudness—should be at their peaks. That would be up to the person conducting.

In his transcription of Bach's Passacaglia and Fugue in C minor, the initial statement, for only cellos and basses, is *ppp* and, as per Stokowski's instructions, begins upbow, again asking for a quiet, subdued effect. He does not, however, ask for the distinctive, slightly muffled tone that mutes—devices placed over the instruments' bridges—would provide. When the violins and violas enter eight measures from the beginning, Stokowski specifically asks that they begin at the very point, or tip, of the bow, for the lightest,

---

14 However, even with this reasoning, should he have changed what Wagner had written? Should the horns be silent in passages, even extremely short ones, where Wagner wanted them to play? Was this a reasonable trade-off for having them sound "fresh" in the more important passages?

15 Starting at the base, or frog, of the bow, where it is gripped, would imply that the musicians use more pressure, producing a somewhat stronger, if not louder, sound.

most delicate sound that can be drawn from the instruments. In his attempt to precisely convey the colorations and effects he prefers, Stokowski specifies on which strings certain notes are to be played, as each has its own character.

Even his pianissimos had a broad range of tonal coloration. They weren't always wisps of silky sound; appropriate to the effect he wanted, they could be filaments of spun steel—light but strong. In contrast to these pianissimos, his fortes and fortissimos could seem louder than those of other conductors.[16] But when he did want increased volume, the sound wasn't harsh; it retained his trademark sonority.

When I was alone with Stokowski in his dressing room after concerts, I'd think of people who accused him of being more showman than sincere artist. Still vibrating from the music, not yet tuned in to his surroundings, he'd barely communicate. He told me he'd lie awake all night after a performance.

Bill Smith had been right: Stokowski's background was indeed a mystery, and the more research I did, the more enigmatic he became. I discovered many biographical falsehoods, and realized, from their context, that he had intentionally planted them. The biggest mystery of all was why he'd want—or need—to throw researchers off the trail of his authentic background. Couldn't he have been one of the towering figures of the twentieth century without fabricating an image?

Older players in the orchestra had known friends of Stokowski's during his early years in America. He had, they said, spoken like an Englishman, and with a Cockney accent at that. But around the time he went to Cincinnati (and was developing his conduct-

---

[16] A bonus of having ensemble musicians play more softly is that they may listen even more intently to their colleagues than when playing at higher volume; they need to blend tonal coloration even more carefully. At lower volume, every element of the sound is exposed. There's no place to hide.

ing career), he adopted a kind of East- or Mittel-European accent. Luckily for him, his need to be mysterious served him well. Like Greta Garbo, mystery enhanced his image. His birth name also worked in his favor: In early twentieth-century America, a Slavic or European name was almost a prerequisite to having a major musical career. It would be years before a conductor with a common American name—like Leonard Bernstein—could be successful. Stokowski's first wife, concert pianist Olga Samaroff, was a Texan who had changed her name from Lucy Hickenlooper. From Samaroff, Stokowski had his first lessons in building an exotic image.

In addition to lots of inconsistencies, I found revealing patterns in his behavior. He was obviously drawn to people of distinguished lineage, including the daughters of the heads of the churches where he was organist, and the last two of his three wives—Evangeline Johnson and Gloria Vanderbilt—were both socialites considered American royalty. Royalty, aristocracy, or any bloodline that wasn't "common" appealed to him, and he wanted to claim a similar heritage for himself. He went to great efforts to keep people from knowing that he was middle-class, not royal or aristocratic (his father had been a cabinetmaker), and born in England, not in Poland or Russia or Germany as he often declared.

I encountered his fabrications in media interviews, concert program booklets, and in the biographical information on the cover of his own book, *Music For All of Us*. He even passed along autobiographical fiction to his wives. He misled Gloria Vanderbilt by implying that the Habsburgs figured in his lineage, and gave the name of an aristocratic Polish family, Czartorieska, of no relation to him, as his mother's maiden name on their marriage license (the correct name should have been Moore). Stokowski's second wife, Evangeline Johnson, didn't know his mother was alive until Sonya, the progeny of his first marriage, mentioned her grandmother's existence during a family trip to London. Almost eighty years later, still upset, Sonya told me about the family confrontation she had caused. During her ten-year marriage to Stokowski, Gloria

Vanderbilt never knew that his mother was still alive. To explain his English childhood, Stokowski concocted an imaginative scenario: As an infant, he had been smuggled into London for protection and was raised by a devoted nurse. But the pieces didn't always fit. He'd occasionally tell stories about the grandfather for whom he was named, recalling the Polish clubs in London his grandfather had taken him to and the little violin he had bought him. They're touching stories, but his grandfather had died three years before young Leopold was born.

Members of the press seemed amused, not annoyed, by the Maestro's reluctance to reveal his background. A June 1941, article in the *Philadelphia Record* about his twenty-year-old daughter Sonya, who was pursuing an acting career, stated,

> Leopold Stokowski always kept his origin veiled in mystery, to such a degree that many of his more worshipful admirers have come to think of the glamorous maestro as a semidivine apparition sprung fullgrown from the brain of Apollo…

More recently, a credible music website states that interviews with Stokowski "may not be the best source for biographical information."

Nothing I discovered about Stokowski troubled me or diminished my admiration for him. It only added to the intrigue. Great musicians of that time, like famous movie stars, were expected to be special. They could behave as they wished, exempted from society's rules.

It's hard to understand that kind of star power today, or the willingness of society to overlook what would now be considered bad—even illegal—behavior. Back then, that kind of conduct was more than accepted; it added to a celebrity's prestige.

To protect his secrets, Stokowski would focus on the present and the future, shunning the past as if he was wearing emotional blinders. He'd rarely reminisce; when other people told stories about youthful experiences or milestones, he'd remain silent. If interviewers asked him about his childhood (friends and colleagues were usually too intimidated to question him), he'd vaguely mention an Eastern origin. "The past is gone and cannot be changed," I'd hear him say in answer to a question he deemed as intrusive, or to preclude one, "and the future is unknown. All we have is the present."

Some people close to him—colleagues, even relatives—feel that his behavior reflected the times in which he was born and raised: class-conscious late Victorian England. He was probably embarrassed at his humble background but, equally important, he may have been concerned that he couldn't realize his potential because of his middle-class status. He may have been right, and that may have been one reason why he moved to America. Without the mystery and the accent, he might not have been as successful. His intimidating manner also served him well. It not only added to his impressive stature but acted as a kind of armor, stopping people from questioning him; no one wanted to incur the wrath of the Great Maestro.

His mythmaking and glamorous image, however, also worked against him. Members of the press and music professionals suspected that his accent and his family history weren't authentic, and his compromised credibility threw everything he said and did into doubt. Some music critics and musicologists, in fact, questioned the depth and integrity of his music making because of his behavior off the podium.

Chapter Seven

IN PHILADELPHIA, THE MAESTRO AND I began to develop rituals. At the stage door, he'd hand me his scores—a heavy but thrilling burden I hugged tightly to my chest—then walk beside me, his hand resting on my back or shoulder. Our path to the dressing room cut through the backstage area, where the players dressed and unpacked their instruments. "Good morning, Maestro," they'd call, and he'd nod, smiling slightly in response. Every so often, he'd pause to lightly tease one of them or ask technical questions about his or her instrument, but there was never an embrace or a warm greeting, even for those he'd known for decades. He never inquired about their families or called them by their names.

If he had just arrived for a rehearsal, we'd sometimes chat. But before his concerts—and during intermissions—he liked to be alone to meditate. He had practiced meditation and yoga since the 1920s, traveling to India to learn from the masters. Musicians who had been in the orchestra in the 1920s and '30s told me that if anyone spoke to him on his way to the stage, he'd hurry back to his dressing room and repeat the meditation while the orchestra and the audience waited. They also told me that he spent a lot of time standing on his head.[1]

---

1 These interests were considered bizarre until the Beatles made them acceptable in the 1960s. In a bitter custody battle in the late 1950s, Gloria Vanderbilt cited Stokowski's involvement with yoga as proof of his inability to be a responsible parent to their sons.

Before secluding himself, he'd deal with last-minute changes for the performance or answer questions from the players. I'd stand off to the side in his dressing room as the musicians entered, all of them smiling and visibly in awe. Most of them carried their music and pointed to specific sections: "Do you want each note in this run staccato—separate—or slurred?" "Should I keep this phrase pianissimo, with or without vibrato, to make it more or less intense?" "Would you like me to turn the bell of the horn up toward the ceiling for the entire section, or for just these few notes?" Stokowski explained to each player precisely what he wanted, illustrating by softly whistling each line and conducting slightly with his right hand—a gentle version of what he'd soon unleash onstage.

Even though he was still quite formal, Stokowski seemed happiest and most relaxed at the Dell. There was a populist audience (because of the free admission), warm weather, and the grass and trees he loved (he called himself "the farmer in the Dell"). On the morning of June 20, 1965, I waited for him in the parking lot for more than an hour, not knowing that his car had come through a different entrance. He was to rehearse a program that included Prokofiev's monumental, evocative cantata, *Alexander Nevsky*. He was already on the podium when I ran up the steps to the stage.

"Nancy, come here," he called. "Can you do this?" he asked, turning his score of *Nevsky* toward me. He pointed to horn parts he had bracketed. "I want them to be tacet. Can you mark that into the parts?"

"Yes," I said, taking the score from him. I collected the horn parts from the stands, rushed backstage to the library, and quickly but carefully marked the music. Racing back to the stage, I returned the score to Stokowski and the parts to the players. His pursuit of perfection didn't stop there. Throughout the rehearsal, he kept calling me to the podium, giving me details about additional changes he wanted me to make. During the break between the rehearsals, he asked me to mark substantial new alterations in the brass and string parts. In the midst of making these changes I discovered a discrepancy between his score and the printed parts so I went to his dressing room. There, in the dark, flat on his back on a sofa, hands over his heart, he lay sound asleep. I gently awakened him to discuss which notes were correct. He stared at me when I pointed to the discrepancy, obviously impressed that I had found the error.

I had already marked the parts for another piece on that concert. Weeks earlier, Stokowski had written to me. He had called Jesse, "and he said it would be all right for me to send you the parts of Enesco's 'Roumanian Rhapsody' for the Dell Concert, and that you would do me the great favor of marking the cuts in all the parts." He detailed six cuts, none of them large. He wrote that he had "marked the first desk part of the first violins in blue, and I hope this will be clear as a guide to all the other parts." He was no longer asking my boss to work on his music.

When the second rehearsal ended, I went with him to his dressing room. My mother, a great fan of his, had baked a chocolate layer cake and I had written the iconic five opening notes of *Alexander Nevsky* in frosting on the top. Sitting in front of the cake in his dressing room, he sliced into it with a knife and offered me the first piece. He ignored the plates and forks I had brought and ate with his hands.

He began to talk about the Prokofiev: "Such great music!" he said, nodding his head in admiration. He went on to talk about the challenges of performing it, and I was surprised to hear the former choirmaster complain, "Choruses drive me crazy!" Then he abruptly changed the subject to photographs I had sent him a few months earlier.

During a Philadelphia Orchestra matinee, Bill Smith and I had run up several flights of stairs in the Academy. Through a succession of doorways, we entered an enormous area, like a surreal attic, of wooden planks and catwalks high above the chandelier. From there, we were able to discern the spherical shape that contributed to the hall's magnificent acoustics. Lying on our bellies in century-old dust, peering through a grated circular opening in the floor, we looked through the crystals of the chandelier to the concert hall far below, seeing the tiny figures of audience members as they listened to the orchestra.

I knew that Stokowski, given his long history with both acoustical research and the Academy, would be fascinated by the photos I had taken from the "attic." In a letter to me in March he had written, "What an extraordinary and delightfully unique experience you had above the Academy, both for your eye and your ear." Now, between mouthfuls of cake, he raised the subject of my adventure.

"Nancy, those pictures you sent me, did you take them yourself?"

"I did, Maestro," I said proudly.

"It looks very dangerous," he said.

"It was!" I answered, equally proudly.

Slowly, leaning toward me, he said, "Don't you ever go up there again—*ever*! You'll get hurt!" He paused, and his tone softened. "I need you here," he said. "I don't want to lose you." He paused again, then smiled. "What would happen if I needed a cut in a symphony or a tacet marked?"

"I think Jesse is quite capable of doing that," I answered playfully.

"No," he said, shaking his head and no longer smiling. "I want *you* to do it."

I knew then that I had his approval and perhaps his affection, and I was delighted.

We continued to talk and eat. "Where are you going to school?" he asked. I told him about the Philadelphia Musical Academy and he questioned me about the subjects I was studying. "No shorthand?" he asked, then proceeded to tell me about three different types of shorthand, a subject in which I had little interest. "You know," he added, "it could be useful someday, when we work together." Then he suddenly asked, "What about your future? Are you serious about the cello? Do you want to play for a living?"

"No, Maestro," I told him. "I hope to become an orchestra librarian."

"Good!" he said. "That's what I wanted to hear! Nancy, if there is anything I can ever do to help you in music, please let me know." He reached for my hand and kissed it, and put the remaining cake aside to take back to his hotel.[2]

He didn't meditate during intermission at the concert the next evening, asking me to sit with him instead. The buzz of the massive audience seeped into the dressing room and I offered to close the door, but he smiled sweetly and shook his head, savoring the sound. Suddenly, he turned to me; he cocked his head to the side, as he often did when he was giving something serious thought or being playful.

"Would you consider coming to my home in New York to work with me on my library?" he asked. "You could do this when it's convenient for you." I took a moment to think. I was working for the orchestra part-time, so I'd be able to make occasional trips between Philadelphia and New York. I'd have to keep the arrangement secret from Ormandy, who regarded loyalty to Stokowski as disloyalty to himself. Stokowski was watching me, waiting for an answer.

"Yes," I told him, "I'd like very much to work with you." He smiled broadly. At nineteen, I was now working simultaneously for two of the great conductorial rivals of the twentieth century, Eugene Ormandy and Leopold Stokowski. When the Philadelphia Orchestra members heard that I was working for Stokowski, they nicknamed me "The Sorcerer's Apprentice," referring both to his conducting ability and to the section in *Fantasia*.

Jesse and Bill were delighted about my working with the Maestro. They adored him, too. But they warned me that if Ormandy found out about my double life, he'd probably have me

---

2   A few days later, my mother received a letter from him, sent to our address: "Dear Mrs. Shear, Thank you for the *delicious* cake, it was just perfect in every way, and your daughter made beautiful decorations on the top. She is very talented in many ways, and I think that the development of those talents, and her education in general is very important at this time of her life. If I can ever assist her in any way, please let me know, I shall be happy to do it." My mother read it then handed it back to me. "He wrote this to you, not to me," she said.

fired. Stokowski couldn't have cared less; he couldn't question my devotion and, at eighty-three, was secure about his stature in the music world. I'd spend the day with Stokowski at his Fifth Avenue apartment, working and cooking and eating with him. Then I'd take the train back to Philadelphia for the concert that evening, shaking Ormandy's hand as he went onstage. *If you knew whose hand I just shook…* I'd think as Ormandy grinned at me.

Chapter Eight

OF ALL THE CONDUCTORS I worked with, the one I most disliked, both personally and musically, was Eugene Ormandy. And he was the one I saw—and heard—on a daily basis.

"The Boss," as the musicians and staff called him, always seemed annoyed. Only when he greeted fans after a concert or flirted with an attractive girl would the creases in his forehead disappear and his mouth spread into a smile. The closest he came to conversation was to tease, and his prying questions were complaints in disguise. Nothing about him seemed out of the ordinary: his demeanor, the ideas and opinions he expressed, the conventional lifestyle he and his wife seemed to lead. There's good reason why no one has written a biography of him.

Ormandy's uneven gait (caused by a congenital hip condition) and his diminutive size (not quite five-and-a-half feet tall) did little to generate compassion or sympathy among his players; most resented his cold, vindictive behavior toward them. In spite of that, when his beat became unclear or inaccurate or he cued the wrong instruments, the players rescued him; no one in the audience realized that a mishap, often one of major proportions, had been averted.

Time and history have been kind to The Boss; many music lovers think highly of him, and people are almost always impressed when they hear that I worked with him. But music professionals—even now, decades after Ormandy's retirement in 1980 and his death in 1985—often disagree about his artistry. Some consider his performances—live and recorded—first-rate; others judge him as competent but uninspired, calling him "the best of the second-rate conductors." Thomas Frost, a Grammy award–winning record producer who worked extensively with Ormandy, says that he was an excellent conductor but not a particularly interesting one because his interpretations were always "safe"; he followed the same traditions that other conductors followed. As I knew too well, from hearing virtually all of his rehearsals, concerts, and recording sessions for years, his interpretations were always predictable.

I've always felt that his players imbued their performances with an intensity and expressiveness he hadn't been able to ask for. Max Wilcox, one of the top record producers of that era, agreed. "The players gave Ormandy what he didn't have 'inside,'" Max told me, offering stories to support his opinion. Herbert Light, a retired Philadelphia Orchestra violinist, feels that Ormandy had "plenty inside" but that he couldn't always communicate that to his orchestra. Once, a few years ago, after suffering through the performances of a mediocre guest conductor, Herb quipped, "The longer Ormandy remains dead, the better he looks!" (The comment referred to the guest conductor's weaknesses as well as to Ormandy's strengths, which years after his death seemed magnified.) But Harry Aleinikoff, a violinist in the orchestra from 1915 to 1959, said it best. In a letter to me in April 1978, he wrote,

> Stokie [sic] took a sick orchestra and made it into one of the greatest… an ideal which other orchestras strove to emulate. And then he handed the whole thing to Ormandy who didn't know what to do with it.

I will admit, however, that Ormandy was able to deliver some marvelous performances—works by Richard Strauss, Mahler, and Rachmaninoff among them—and that he was an excellent "accompanist," following his soloists during concertos with sensitivity and flexibility (the great pianist Byron Janis considered him to have been "one of the best in the world"). Ormandy must also be given credit for keeping the sound of the orchestra, particularly the strings, characteristically magnificent (he had been a violinist and the orchestra's opulent string sound reflected that), even though Stokowski's influence was still very much present when I worked with the orchestra. It was a sound, however, that I felt Ormandy couldn't always put to the best use. It reminded me of a moderately talented sculptor having a perfect piece of marble at his disposal. And, under his direction, the lushness of the sound he generated was not always stylistically appropriate: His Mozart could sound like Mahler.

It's ironic that my introduction to Ormandy was so positive. It was he, of course, who had taken me backstage and given me a ticket. Although I didn't know it then, it was out of character for him to have befriended a youngster or performed such an act of kindness. Whether he had ulterior motives, I don't know. He was one of only two people—the other was an orchestra staff member—who later violated the trust of the naive teenager I was. Ormandy cornered me offstage before a concert for a kiss I certainly didn't want. Female members of the orchestra—there were only five when I began working there—and the staff constantly had to find diplomatic ways to fend off his aggressive advances.

Occasionally I had to pick up or deliver scores to Ormandy's apartment in the Bellevue Stratford Hotel around the corner from the Academy. On one of these trips, Ormandy, not his butler, answered the door. Mrs. Ormandy was nowhere in sight. I thrust the package toward him and spoke quickly, to imply that I was in a hurry, but he hesitated. "Come in," he said, "I'll show you the apartment." I felt my heart sink. Now captive, I followed him from one elegantly-furnished room to another. He pointed out fine antiques and artwork that included a magnificent portrait of the Rosé Quartet, the legendary ensemble that had premiered works by Brahms, Reger, and Schoenberg. He chattered on, telling me that, if reincarnation exists, he'd want to come back as "the Ormandys' butler," who yet again had gone back to Europe on some family emergency.

We finally arrived back at the front door. I started to say goodbye but he hesitated. "Here," he said, digging into his pants pocket, "are two tickets for the concert Saturday night." He held them out to me. "I'm not free on Saturday," I replied. Even if I had needed tickets, I didn't want to forge a bond with him, particularly one that included indebtedness. "Take them," he urged, his voice tinged with sadness. "Someday you'll be able to tell your children that Eugene Ormandy, whom you hated, gave you tickets to his concert." I began to protest, but he shook his head knowingly. I thanked him and walked away, empty-handed but filled with relief that he hadn't tried one of his conductor tricks.

"How are your calluses?" Ormandy often asked while reaching for my left hand to feel my fingertips. He knew I was studying cello with Elsa Hilger, the beloved associate first cellist of the orchestra, and that calluses would prove I was practicing. It was not a ritual I enjoyed.

When I wore high heels, Ormandy would point to them with the same finger he used to cue musicians, demanding that I remove them, so I often walked around his office in bare feet, no longer taller than him. For a reason I didn't know, he disliked my wearing sunglasses over my hair on top of my head and he'd order me to take them off. He also didn't allow male orchestra players to have long hair or beards (this was before the union protected members' personal grooming choices). We resented these impositions, knowing they were less about Ormandy's conservative tastes than about his need to dominate people. We had to do what The Boss wanted.

One of the few orchestra players who dared to challenge him was the tall, lanky violist James Fawcett, who sat right under Ormandy's nose. Ormandy had a propensity for malapropisms that always generated snickers, sometimes even open laughter. After each of these gaffes, Jim would glare up at Ormandy, not taking his eyes off of him while reaching under his seat for paper and pencil. As Ormandy watched, Jim would flagrantly write down the quote, replacing his pad and pencil under the seat while still staring up at The Boss. *The Sayings of Chairman Ormandy* became a classic within the orchestra world and we all have cherished copies. ("I wrote it the right way so it was copied the wrong way right—I mean the right way wrong." "I never say what I mean but I always manage to say something similar." "If you don't have it in your part, leave it out because there is enough missing already." "It is not as difficult as I thought it was, but it is harder than it is." "Why do you always insist on playing while I'm trying to conduct?")

There were times when Ormandy, in a rare expansive mood, would try to lighten the atmosphere by telling a joke, but he never did it well; the players would sit stone-faced. A bit later, when he made one of his ridiculous statements, the entire orchestra would break up, shoulders shaking. I remember Ormandy's frustration: "I tell you a joke and nobody laughs, then I say something serious and everybody laughs."

At a post-concert reception in England, violinist William Greenberg expressed the contempt many players felt for their conductor. A large ice sculpture of Ormandy was on display in the center of the room. For a long time, Willie stood staring at it. It was getting late and his colleagues wanted to leave but Willie wouldn't move. "I'm standing here until the damned thing melts!" he declared.

Ormandy's main musical quirk was having a delayed beat—a split-second pause after the baton comes down before the orchestra plays. He said he didn't have a delayed beat. You could have shown him a tape and he would still have sworn that it hadn't happened.

On the rare occasions when Ormandy guest conducted other orchestras, he'd return with reports of how much the musicians adored him. "They loved me," he told Jesse on the phone after conducting the Boston Symphony. "They called me Eugene."

We had fun with that. "Can you imagine calling him 'Eugene' here?" Jesse asked, as a group of us roared with laughter. The orchestra members called him "Maestro" to his face, "The Boss" and other less-complimentary names behind his back. Even though guest conducting is like having an affair and a music directorship is like being married, we all wondered if the members of the BSO had *really* called him Eugene.

It became my job to hand Ormandy the baton as he went onstage, and as much as I disliked him, it was a thrill. I'd stand in the wings of the Academy, look through the ranks of the orchestra to the almost-three thousand people in the hall, hear the tuning dissipate, and, as Bill and Jesse and other staff members looked on, ceremoniously extend the baton to the conductor cork handle first.[1] He'd take the stick, bow to me, bounce lightly on his feet, then turn and walk through the orchestra to the podium, adjusting his cufflinks as he went. I thought Ormandy's constant adjusting of his cufflinks as he walked on and off stage was a nervous tic. Anshel Brusilow told me Ormandy did it to divert the audience's attention away from his limp.

Bill and I took turns timing performances with a stopwatch, noting the durations—each movement, then the total for the complete piece, including pauses between movements—for the orchestra archives and for the engineer taping the concerts for broadcast. Ormandy had the uncanny ability to measure elapsed time as if he had a stopwatch in his head. He'd walk offstage after a performance, point the baton at me, and call out the timing: "thirteen minutes, fifty-seven seconds" for Beethoven's *Leonore* Overture No. 3; he was always accurate within ten to twenty seconds. He could also utilize this skill in reverse: If a record producer needed him to fill a specific amount of time to complete one side of a record,

---

[1] A discussion of batons can irritate orchestra musicians. They are the ones, after all, who actually produce the sound, and often feel that they should be given as much credit as the conductor. Jesse and I went to Erich Leinsdorf's dressing room to return his stick and his scores after he guest conducted the orchestra. By the time we arrived, Leinsdorf had the attention of a dozen or so admirers. He was holding a long, thick baton in the palm of his right hand. "This is good for Strauss and Mahler," he announced in his authoritative Austrian accent, lifting it up and down. He placed the baton on the dressing room table then took a lighter one out of his briefcase. "This is good for Mozart and Haydn," he said, waving it slightly. Jesse, waiting patiently, had had enough. He picked a third stick off the table and handed it to Leinsdorf. "Play me a tune on this one."

Ormandy could alter his tempo to fit the work into that time span. (Without advance warning, he could be asked at the end of a conversation how long he had been speaking and give the timing, accurate within seconds.)

I still wonder if any musician possessing that kind of cerebral control can achieve a high level of emotional involvement, and if Ormandy was ever able to "lose" himself in the music. Whether or not Stokowski was capable of such feats, he would have abhorred the conscious control, the lack of spontaneous feeling.

Both Jesse and Bill were frequently subjected to Ormandy's unreasonable whims and grievances. During a rehearsal, The Boss was not above pointing at Jesse in front of the entire orchestra and accusing him of having marked the parts incorrectly. The first time I witnessed this, Jesse stood impassively behind the first violin section as Ormandy ranted about an error, saying that he had told Jesse what was to be marked and that it hadn't been done. On the library table upstairs, I had seen a memo on Ormandy's official Philadelphia Orchestra stationery—"Office of the Music Director." In his distinctive, bold, vertical handwriting, Ormandy had given specific orders for Jesse to mark the parts as they now were. I was choking back tears of outrage when Jesse returned to the library.

"But that's exactly how The Boss told you to mark the parts!" I exclaimed.

Jesse shrugged it off. "They all know what really happened," he explained.

Never totally secure about his position in the music world and sensitive about his height (Stokowski was six-foot-two), Ormandy had always been in Stokowski's shadow. By the time Ormandy succeeded him as music director, Stokowski was one of the most prominent people in the world.[2]

---

[2] Ormandy was always insecure about his credentials. He had made recordings with a pickup orchestra as "Dr. Ormandy and His Foxtrot Orchestra" and, as a violinist, had played in the orchestra of the Capitol Theatre in New York; he made his conducting debut there in 1924. To his credit, he had successfully led the Minneapolis Symphony (forerunner of the Minnesota Orchestra) from 1931 to 1936.

Stokowski's dismissive treatment of Ormandy hadn't encouraged warmth between them. A veteran member of the orchestra told me that Ormandy, after being given an honorary doctor of music degree by a local college in the 1930s (he was then serving as co-conductor of the orchestra with Stokowski), apparently bragged about it to Stokowski. "Is music so sick," Stokowski responded, "that it needs so many doctors?" He didn't stop there. "Honorary degrees," he told Ormandy, "are not like vaccinations. The knowledge never 'takes.'"

After Stokowski left the Philadelphia Orchestra in 1941, the musicians and the staff knew not to mention him—ever—in front of Ormandy for fear of reprisal. Even official orchestra publications downplayed Stokowski's role in the ensemble's history.[3] This policy persisted for years, even after Stokowski's death in 1977.

Jesse and Bill were well aware of Ormandy's obsessive resentment of his predecessor. "Don't ever let The Boss see you near Stoki," they'd warn, pointing at me for emphasis. But Ormandy usually fled town when Stokowski was about to arrive.

In November 1965, as always, I waited for Stokowski at the Locust Street stage door before his first rehearsal. He handed me his scores and his briefcase and we walked together, talking en route, to Ormandy's dressing room. I opened the door and there stood Ormandy. I had been caught. My job was now at stake, and Jesse and Bill might be implicated in my crime. Ormandy extended his hand to Stokowski and I watched the two, side-by-side, pose for Adrian Siegel, the orchestra's photographer, who was there for the rehearsal. It was a historic moment, representing fifty-three continuous years of the orchestra's music directorship.[4]

Still wearing his full-face smile, Ormandy moved close to me. "Put that down," he hissed out of the side of his mouth, nodding his head toward the briefcase that, frozen with fear, I still gripped.

---

[3] I remember one brochure implying that when Stokowski became conductor of the orchestra, he had inherited a "technically excellent" ensemble—a huge distortion of the truth.

[4] I believe that this is the only photograph ever taken of the two of them together.

My mind jammed with confusion, I uttered the worst possible response: "I don't know where Maestro wants it, Mr. Ormandy." I had never addressed Ormandy as "Maestro," reserving that honorific for the other conductor in the room.

The library phone rang early the next morning. It was Mary Krouse, Ormandy's secretary. "The Boss said for you to tell Nancy to stay away from Stokowski," she told Jesse, who then turned to me, a worried look on his face.

"You're lucky," he said, shaking his head in amazement. "I don't know why he didn't tell me to fire you." Looking back, I suspect that Ormandy might have done just that had he not been concerned that Stokowski, for whom he still had obvious awe and envy, would find out. I never told Stokowski about the incident, not wanting to inflame tension between the two. I avoided anything that might jeopardize Stokowski's return to the orchestra.

Chapter Nine

A FEW TIMES A MONTH, when Jesse didn't need me and I didn't have classes, I'd awaken at 5:30 a.m. to take the train to Stokowski's home in New York. If it was raining, I'd wear a little plastic shower cap under a scarf to protect my hair so I'd look pretty; I was always eager to impress him. After stopping in Macy's ladies' room to freshen up, I'd take the bus up Fifth Avenue—it ran both north and south in those days—to his apartment just down the street from the Guggenheim Museum. Mike the doorman would call upstairs, then give me the signal to enter the wood-paneled elevator. Sometimes the scent of broccoli would grow strong as I rose toward the fourteenth floor. I had always thought of broccoli as just another vegetable but now, because the Maestro liked it, I considered it to be gourmet fare.

His secretary, Jean Leslie, usually answered the door, speaking just above a whisper so that the Maestro, at his desk in the next room, wouldn't be distracted.[1] I'd look past Jean, through a doorway, to see the curve of Stokowski's back as he bent over a score, oblivious to my presence until Jean waved me into the room. "Maestro?" she'd say tentatively. Startled, he'd turn his head then stand up. If he was in a lighthearted mood, he'd grasp my hand and playfully turn it back and forth. I liked when he did this because it meant that he'd probably be in a good mood most of the day.

---

[1] I still admired the Monet on the wall, but differently. Jean had told me that Stokowski had noticed it in the window of Lamston's variety store on Madison Avenue, and had bought it—a cardboard reproduction—for $1.95.

Jean would take my coat, then disappear into her office as he'd motion for me to sit in the ladder-back chair across from him. "How is the Philadelphia Orchestra?" he'd always ask, and I'd reply truthfully but cautiously: "It's still a great ensemble, Maestro, but not as great as it was when you were there." He seemed pleased with both assessments. I thought of him as a caring parent who had given a child up for adoption; he wanted the orchestra to thrive, but I also knew he wouldn't want any other conductor to match the impressiveness of what he had done.

"What have you heard?" he'd ask, leaning toward me, and I'd recount details about concerts I'd recently attended, the works performed and the musicians involved. (I was always careful to run the names of the musicians quickly through my mind. I didn't want to mention anyone with whom he'd had any tension.) Although I was only nineteen—it was 1965—and I was hearing many works for the first time, he seemed intensely interested in every opinion and insight I shared.

"How about *you*?" I'd ask, and then it was his turn.

"I went to Carnegie Hall and heard the Beethoven Ninth," he told me one morning, "but it was not a good performance," he said, shaking his head in disappointment. "I sat in the back, and during the concert, I looked at all those heads in front of me and thought, 'They think *this* is how the symphony is supposed to sound!'" He seemed to find the situation almost tragic. In his hands, it would not have unfolded in the pedantic blandness he went on to describe.

He then went into detail about another mediocre performance. "All the bows were going in the same direction," he said, amazed at this foolishness. "You would have laughed!" He knew I fully subscribed to free bowing, one his most controversial practices.

Another day when I arrived he wasn't studying a score but was looking through his audition book, a meticulously-kept log of information about musicians who, hoping to be engaged for the American Symphony, had played for him. He seemed sad and frustrated. "I want so much to have more Negroes in the orchestra, but the quality isn't there." It wasn't a matter of talent, he said, but of education and training. The opportunities were not adequate for people of color.[2] He then raised the subject of female conductors. They were as capable and talented as men, he said decisively. I disagreed, telling him that I wouldn't feel confident having a woman on the podium. Conductors were dominating, powerful figures, and I couldn't imagine a woman successfully filling that role. "You're prejudiced against your own sex! There is no reason why a woman can't be as good a conductor as a man!" he almost shouted. In years to come, I'd learn that he was right. Today, women are on the podiums of the world's great orchestras, just as they hold positions as presidents and prime ministers.

We often discussed concerts I'd recently heard him conduct—what had moved or impressed me most. "The Stravinsky was remarkable!" I'd say, going into detail about what he had done to bring out the music's evocative power.

A program he had conducted at Carnegie Hall the day before one visit had included a Haydn symphony. Music of the Classical period—leaner and more restrained than that of the Romantic era—was not Stokowski's strength. I mentioned all the works on the program except the Haydn. Hoping he wouldn't notice the omission, I quickly rose from my chair to go into another room. I felt his eyes following me. Then I heard the question I'd hoped to avoid.

"What did you think of the Haydn?"

I hesitated then slowly turned to face him. I had no intention of lying, but I didn't want to risk insulting him or losing his affection. "It wasn't my favorite, Maestro," I cautiously replied.

I saw his eyebrows rise to the top of his forehead. He was accustomed to compliments.

---

2 I remember only a handful of Black players in the ASO—perhaps five or six—which was still more than most orchestras. This included the magnificent timpanist, Elayne Jones, who was a longtime member of the American Symphony. The orchestra also had a number of Asian players, also a rarity at that time.

"Oh, so you don't like that music?" he asked. I was becoming uncomfortable. If only the phone would ring.

"It's not that I don't like it…" I let my voice trail off.

"All right, Haydn Hater," he replied, and, for the rest of the day, he called me "Haydn Hater." He placed the reason for my feelings on my opinion of the composer, not on the quality of his performance.

Sometimes he'd tell me amusing stories about concerts I had attended. In April 1965 at Carnegie Hall, he had conducted the world premiere of the Ives Symphony No. 4, a work of multilayered complexity. It was an artistic and personal triumph—the most difficult piece he said he had ever conducted. The symphony contains ensemble-within-ensemble juxtapositions—marching bands, distant instrumental choirs, chamber groups, and a chorus—often sounding simultaneously, as background and foreground, and fragments of hymns and popular songs evoke a panoply of moods and associations. The performance required a main conductor plus two subordinates to help coordinate, refine, and unify it stylistically.[3] After the Carnegie Hall performance, Stokowski had just turned toward the audience to speak when a sneeze exploded throughout the hall. "That was not in the score!" he said. The audience cheered. A day or two later, I arrived to spend the day with him. "Do you remember that sneeze after the concert?" he asked, grinning.

"Of course!" I answered, joining him at his desk.

"I received a call from the person who sneezed. It was Ives's business partner, Julian Myrick!" Stokowski explained delightedly.

---

[3] I often saw Theodore Seder, head of the Edwin A. Fleisher Collection of Orchestral Music, in the Free Library of Philadelphia. Ted had deciphered Ives's almost-unintelligible scrawl in the manuscript of the symphony. I remarked to Ted that it was fortunate to have a great conductor like Stokowski give the world premiere. "He's not my first choice, not the ideal one to conduct this," Ted answered. Shocked, I asked whom he would have preferred. "Howard Hanson," he replied, saying that a born-and-bred American like Hanson, who was also a composer, would have been better equipped to recognize American folk melodies and bring out those themes, which appear whole and fragmented and can easily be hidden within the work's thick textures.

The *New York Times* had reported the sneeze and Stokowski's comment, but didn't know the identity of the sneezer.[4]

I never arrived at his apartment empty-handed, always bringing him some small gift. If its shape was long and rectangular, he'd shake it slightly, his ear close to the package. "Does it gurgle?" he'd ask playfully, knowing that I sometimes showed up with a bottle of tawny port in winter or May wine (and strawberries) in spring. Once, like a child, he snatched a gift box from my hands. "I shouldn't have done that," he said, laughing but visibly embarrassed. Months later, for his birthday, I brought him a thick, powder blue pillar candle on a round wrought-iron stand. He carefully removed the candle from its wrapping and stood beside me while I demonstrated how the sides of softened wax could be bent down like wings, to curl as the candle burned. He watched intently, as if it was a matter of great importance. "Thank you for your good wishes for my birthday," he wrote soon after. "I wish the same for you." Following this, by hand, he wrote: "The blue candle & stand is [sic] delightful—(so are you)." In tiny handwriting in the lower right corner, he signed "Maestro." He didn't shop for presents for me but, at Christmas, told me to choose any book I'd like from his library. The first was *The Wisdom of Laotse* edited by Lin Yutang, in which he wrote, "Happy Christmas '65 para Nancy" then his signature. I asked for the companion volume the following year.

During my initial visits to 1067, I'd have lunch with Jean at the counter in Lamston's. One day, when she began to put on her coat to leave for lunch, I rose to go with her. She shook her head and smiled. "You're going to eat with Maestro today," she said.

I heard the elevator door close behind her. A moment later, he appeared. "Come with me," he said, and we walked down the main hallway, peering into seven or eight rooms as he explained what they were used for. Most, including those of his two young sons, were sparsely furnished—only bare necessities. The tour ended in the kitchen. I wasn't surprised, or disappointed, that he hadn't

---

4   Ives had composed music in his spare time. He and Myrick had co-owned an insurance company.

shown me his bedroom. I thought that would have been too personal for a great conductor to share.

He had planned ahead. He took shrimp and vegetables out of the refrigerator then began to arrange pots, pans, cooking utensils, and containers of seasonings on the counter. "Put salt here," he said, gesturing conductorially with his arm extended, finger pointing. "Cut this into small pieces." He worked with focused concentration; after adding salt and sugar to the shrimp-milk-egg mixture in a saucepan, he wordlessly handed me the spoon. "Stir this." As I did so, he came up behind me, gently put his hand over mine, and we continued to stir together. It was a sweet, affectionate gesture but not a romantic one, and I felt close to him at that moment. Apparently, it was mutual. When we finished cooking and began to carry the food out of the kitchen, he looked at me. "You are home now," he said.

We ate at a small table in one of his sons' bedrooms, talking first about the food then about the Philadelphia Orchestra and my classes at school. In the midst of conversing, he reached across the table for an empty wine bottle and I watched as he brought it to his lips and blew across the top, reacting with childlike glee at the fog-horn sound it produced. This was the first of many meals together. After half an hour or forty-five minutes, he'd usually become impatient at the slowness of my eating. "Eat, don't talk!" he'd command, and long periods of silence, except for the sounds of chewing, would follow.

One of my favorite moments often occurred in late morning when he'd phone a fish store around the corner to order the ingredients for our lunch. After listing small quantities of sole or shrimp or other seafood, he'd confidently say, "This is Leopold Stokowski." Pause. "S-T-O-K-O-W…" Stifling laughter, I didn't look in his direction.

The room next to his studio had a wall of metal bookshelves that held scores, oversize books and, most intriguing, record albums that were not commercially packaged. "They are recordings I made that were never released," he explained when I asked about them.

"I did not feel that they were of high enough quality." I wonder now if he was referring to the quality of the recorded sound or of the performances. I was fascinated that his speakers, in the living room bookcase, weren't the size of walk-in closets nor were they expensive; he said he wanted to hear what the average person would hear listening to his recordings.

Stokowski was constantly making records. I was in the apartment one afternoon, and answered the phone when the producer of his next album called. Producers had to be prepared to fill both sides of an LP (now a complete CD) by having all the repertoire ready in advance of the recording session. "Please ask the Maestro what his timings are," the producer requested. This would have been a reasonable request for most conductors, whose tempi for specific works never varied greatly (Ormandy's hardly varied at all). I relayed the question to Stokowski, in the next room.

"I do not know what my mood will be," he replied. His tempos depended completely on his emotional state and could vary widely from performance to performance, even for a program repeated on successive nights with the same orchestra in the same hall. His behavior was as unpredictable on the podium as it was off.

Occasionally, as we sat at his desk, he'd share interesting correspondence he had received. But it was Jean who showed me some of the most amusing letters—including those from a man who claimed to be the progeny of his relationship with Greta Garbo. "Dear Dad," they began. Less amusing were notes from his third ex-wife, Gloria Vanderbilt, whose harsh tone seemed to perplex him. "Do you want to hear the latest 'love letter' from Gloria?" he'd ask, his voice reeking with sarcasm, then read excerpts as I listened and commiserated. Palms up, shrugging, he seemed perplexed by her hostile tone. He seemed to have forgotten that six or seven years earlier, in a heavily publicized court battle, he had sued her for custody of the boys. (I didn't remind him.) But talking about Gloria's childhood nurse, "Dodo," who had cared for her like a mother, Stokowski bitterly commented, "Gloria loved her so much that *I* had to pay for her when she needed help!"

He began to refer to events that had happened before he and I met as "B.U."—"before you"—and I soon realized that this most private of men would hold telephone conversations, while I was in the room, that seemed highly confidential; I wondered if he had waited until I was present to make the calls. By the end of one day, I had heard conferences with his doctor; his son's doctor; and his financial advisor. I knew the names of companies in which he had invested, the balance of his checking account, and had learned about the benefits of pie charts. I loved hearing these conversations, finding the tiniest details about his life fascinating. But more importantly, I took them as evidence of a growing trust between us.

Near the end of one visit, I reinforced that trust. He asked me to give his regards to three members of the Philadelphia Orchestra. "They don't know that I come here," I said. He seemed not to understand. "I've never told them," I explained. "They might ask personal questions about you so I thought it best not to say anything." I wanted him to know that I was aware of, and honored, his penchant for privacy. But in spite of our growing closeness, I knew that he might greet me as if we'd never met if we saw each other backstage after a concert or at a public function. I had seen him behave that way with his second ex-wife, Evangeline, with whom he had remained friendly. In the Carnegie Hall Green Room, I saw him kiss or shake her hand then dismiss her. If that had happened with me, I'd have been disappointed, but I also loved sharing that kind of secrecy with him.

He didn't, however, want everything that happened at 1067 to remain confidential. Working at his desk one afternoon, he shouted down the hallway: "Nancy, come here!" The urgency in his voice was alarming and I feared he was ill. I raced into his study where I found him sitting with his head in his hands, a rare posture for a man of imperial bearing.

"Sit down!" he commanded. "I must tell you why I left the Philadelphia Orchestra!" His voice rising with outrage, he told me about being denied the authority to program substantial amounts of contemporary music and to take the orchestra on foreign tours.

"They dared to tell me what I could and could not do!" he said, frustration and fury burning their way through the decades. I listened to what he said but didn't reply. I didn't want to say what I was thinking, that whether he knew it or not, he had probably been ready to move on. He'd been in Philadelphia for more than two decades and had new worlds, including Hollywood, to conquer. He probably thought he'd become the monarch of another world-class ensemble, but that never happened.[5] After his impassioned account, he pointed at me. "Someday," he said, "you will tell people about this!" Apparently I was to keep personal confidences private but eventually, decades later, to set history straight on his behalf.

I didn't even share details about my visits to him with my friends, who knew I was working with him. When they questioned me, I'd answer vaguely. But he was their favorite conductor, too, and I knew they'd love to meet him in a more personal way than just in the Green Room after concerts. "How'd you like to have dinner with Stokowski when he's in Philadelphia?" I asked a few of them after a concert. One person began to laugh, thinking I was joking. Although I was frequently with Stokowski, I put the invitation in writing. He wrote back saying that he already had commitments during his next trip, giving specific details to show that he really was busy. He ended the letter, "Please ask me again, because I would very much like to meet your friends and be with you all." I did ask him again, and in August 1965, he accepted: "I would so much like to meet your friends and talk about everything!"

Three months later on Thursday, November 18, at 7 p.m., Allen, my conducting-student boyfriend, and I waited for Stokowski in the lobby of the Barclay Hotel. "My heart's pounding!" Allen whispered as the elevator door opened and Stokowski stepped out. The three of us walked through the exit onto 18th Street where

---

5 After leaving Philadelphia, in addition to making guest appearances, Stokowski held positions with the All-American Youth Orchestra (which he founded); NBC Symphony; New York City Symphony; Hollywood Bowl Orchestra; New York Philharmonic; Symphony of the Air; and Houston Symphony. His final music directorship was with the American Symphony, which he founded.

Allen's borrowed Buick was double-parked. Then the Maestro took charge, directing us to our places in the car as if he was directing a performance. He sat in the front passenger seat; I was between him and Allen. As we drove the dozen or so blocks to the restaurant in the Society Hill section of town, he repeatedly remarked about the car's "wonderful suspension"—"WAHNerful," as he always pronounced it.

The Tony George restaurant occupied a brick townhouse on Bank Street, one of the charming, narrow, colonial-era passageways for which Philadelphia is known. It was the kind of atmosphere I knew Stokowski would enjoy. Allen and I had gone there a few weeks before to check the private room, and had made a reservation without revealing who would be coming for dinner. In early afternoon on the day of the dinner, following his rehearsal, I had waited with Stokowski outside the stage door for his car to arrive.

"How many are we tonight?" he asked.

"Four boys and four girls," I answered.

"And me," he said.

"No," I corrected him, "you're one of the boys."

That set the tone for the evening. We climbed the stairs to the second floor where a long table had been set. Relaxed and happy, Stokowski perched on the edge of the table swinging one leg, reaching over to nibble from a dish of condiments. Then he sat himself at the center so that he could converse with everyone. I was to his left, Allen to his right. A bowl of fresh daisies blossomed in the center of the table. "They're too pretty to be real," I joked.

"That's decadent!" he admonished.

The waiter delivered our drinks, moving Allen's Brandy Alexander in front of Stokowski. "What is *that*?" he asked.

"It's brandy, cream, crème de cacao, and some nutmeg," Allen told him.

"Oh, that looks very good," Stokowski said, obviously wanting a taste.

"Please take it, Maestro," Allen implored.

Stokowski demurred: "No, no, that is yours." But Allen insisted.

"This is *wahnerful*!" Stokowski exclaimed after a sip.

He also seemed to enjoy his platter of baked fluke. The rest of us had lobster, steak, veal scaloppini, and Baltimore crab cakes; this was a major occasion for us. Allen said it was like having the president of the United States to dinner, but I thought it far more special than that.

During our meal, Stokowski generated a stream of conversation, intuitively knowing what was important to a group of music students. At one point, talking about expressiveness in music, he instructed, "When you get home, look at your scores of *Le Sacre*," and referred to a specific point in the piece. I was amazed. *The Rite of Spring* was the only score that every one of us had saved for and bought.[6]

Because his temper could flare unpredictably, I had advised my friends not to ask him personal questions, particularly about his sons. Of course Candy Bliss, a French horn student, immediately asked about the boys. He answered as if it was the most natural subject to discuss, and he clearly adored them. About an hour and a half later, when we finished dinner, he said he had to go back to the hotel to call them, which he did every evening.

As we were leaving the restaurant, Stokowski spotted the black iron hitching posts used to tie up horses in colonial Philadelphia and, once again, I saw the boyish enthusiasm he so often hid under authoritative dignity. "Look at those!" he yelled, commanding us to run to both sides of the street to examine them. Then we piled into the car for the trip back to the Barclay.

Stokowski wasn't the only musician I introduced to my friends. Mostly because of *The Rite of Spring*, Stravinsky was our hero composer. We referred to him as "The Old Man" and to his works as "Old Man music." There was no disrespect implied; it was our way of establishing intimacy.

---

6   We purchased our scores from Henri Elkan, a dealer who had been a violist in the orchestra years before. Whenever we told Henri the name of a score we wanted to purchase, he would exclaim, in his Belgian accent, "What a coincidence! That is on sale today!" He knew, as students, we had limited funds.

Half a century after its premiere, the piece was still considered radical—dissonant, melodically fragmented, rhythmically savage—lacking much for casual listeners to hold on to. To us, *The Rite* was a miracle of originality. It was dangerous music and we loved it. While we all regarded Stravinsky as an exalted figure, Jack Heller, a talented composition student, worshipped him.

I brought my friends backstage to meet Stravinsky after the Philadelphia Orchestra's performance of his *Perséphone*, introducing each of them. Jackie was overcome with emotion. Towering above the diminutive composer, Jackie addressed him: "Mr. Stravinsky, you are the last of the great old masters." Peering up at Jackie through his spectacles, clasping his hands to his waist, Stravinsky quietly replied, "I hope so."

Chapter Ten

WORKING WITH STOKOWSKI BROUGHT ME inside his musical thinking. We'd discuss the rationale for the way he wanted the parts marked—and not marked—and how his interpretive concepts could be supported by these indications.

For all its prestige, working for him was easier than working for other conductors. They usually needed more extensive markings to help communicate their wishes to the players; Stokowski communicated almost solely by gesture, rarely speaking during rehearsals, rarely even needing the descriptive metaphors relied on by other conductors.

Because he seldom wanted the effects of synchronized, or "uniform," bowing, I didn't have to bother with the time-consuming task of marking bowings into the string parts. Occasionally, in Classical repertoire like Mozart or Haydn, he'd want specific, short passages to have the clearly defined articulation of uniform bowing; but only rarely would he use it in Romantic music. However, all the markings in his sets of parts had to be clear and unambiguous; musicians had to be able to keep undistracted eyes on his often impetuous, unpredictable gestures.

Orchestra parts often look cluttered, containing the printed notes and directives the composer wrote; bowings, phrasing marks, and rehearsal numbers and letters written by the librarian; and directions penciled in by the musicians during rehearsals. Because Stokowski would announce a rehearsal number or letter and, without hesitating, begin to conduct, musicians wouldn't have time to eyeball the page to find the place to start. A solution was to write the numbers and letters in the left-hand margin next to the lines in which they appeared, so that the eye could zip down to locate those lines then move inside to the starting places.

I always loved coming to the final page of an orchestra part. At the bottom, after the final measure, musicians often signed their names, the names of their orchestras, and the dates of performances; some of the great names in orchestral music appeared on those pages. Many players also expressed their feelings about the conductor inside the parts. In a first violin part for the Beethoven Seventh, one musician drew a profile of Stokowski, the face beginning on page one and the nose continuing on to page sixteen or seventeen. I erased like mad before Stokowski came back into the room.

There was a rule in the business that parts be marked only in soft black pencil, never in color, because markings in color could be distracting as well as difficult or impossible to erase. Stokowski, however, liked colored crayon for his scores and colored pencil for the parts. Occasionally, when he was out-of-town guest conducting, I'd work on his music at my home. Rather than giving me his score (which he needed to study), he'd sometimes send me one part from each string section—first and second violins, viola, cello, and bass—that he had marked in blue pencil. In a letter to me dated September 23, 1965, he wrote, "I suggest you use blue or green pencil for the brackets of the music not to be played, reserving red for dynamics, etc." As the owner of the sets, only he would be conducting from them, so the markings would rarely have to be changed.

There were also inserts, which had to be handwritten, cut out, and taped over the original notes. Unless it corrects an error, virtually any change to a composer's original can be questioned. Stokowski was known for making changes, sometimes small, sometimes substantial. He would often "double" winds or brass—two players to a part instead of one as the composer had written—to increase the volume and/or thicken the texture of the sound.

He'd also sometimes request that a single instrument or section of instruments double the notes of a different instrument, to fortify them. Stokowski was, of course, altering what the composer had asked for, and this is another controversial aspect of his music making. Many musicians—and critics—complained that if a composer had wanted two flutes or two oboes or two clarinets rather than one, he or she would have written it that way. Also controversial were cuts that eliminated what, to Stokowski, were unnecessary repetitions. "Say it once, well, and it will have more effect," he said. I never felt guilty about making these changes. From my conversations with Stokowski, I knew that he was trying to realize the composer's intentions. Whether he did or not is still—to this day—hotly debated.

Initially, I had refused to charge Stokowski for my work, accepting only reimbursement for expenses. It would have been sacrilegious to accept payment for the honor of working for him. "You must let me pay you," he announced one day, in a determined voice.

"If Bach or Mozart asked you to do something for them, would you have given them a bill?" I asked.

But he was adamant. "In the end, one would feel used," he told me.

In a letter in October 1965, he wrote,

> The score and parts have just arrived, and thank you for helping me so much. Please be a good girl and send me a bill, because then I can take advantage of your kindness and ask you to help me with some other musical projects. But if you don't send me a bill, I never can ask you again, and this would cause me great and lasting disappointment. So be a good girl.

Following this, by hand, he wrote, "(but not too)!" A few days later, he sent a check for fifty dollars (more than $450 today), folded into a letter in which he wrote, "I enclose a little present with which perhaps you might like to buy a little present for your mother."

Stokowski was becoming two entities in my mind—the man and the musician. I was happy and comfortable with him at his home but, in the concert hall, he remained a god. While I chatted with him in his apartment one sun-filled afternoon, a housekeeper walked across the room carrying the black suede concert shoes I had often seen on the Carnegie Hall and Academy of Music podiums, and I suddenly became nervous.

He, however, began relaxing more with me, becoming less the Great Maestro. Late one afternoon, I was lying on the floor studying one of his scores as he worked at his desk a few yards away. Engrossed in the music, I felt something stir nearby and found him reclining on the floor beside me. "What score do you have?" he asked, leaning over on one elbow to look.

"The Mahler Eighth," I replied, closing the aged volume to show him the cover. This was the work that had brought both him and the Philadelphia Orchestra to world prominence in 1916.

"When I was in Germany and had to leave quickly because of World War I," he recalled, "I slept on a bench in a railway station with the score under my head like a pillow." He had heard Mahler himself conduct the world premiere. After ten or fifteen minutes of lying on the floor talking, I had to get ready to leave. I got up but didn't look down at him. I didn't know if he'd be able to get off the floor easily because of his reconstructed hip, but I didn't want to risk embarrassing him by offering help or by witnessing any difficulty he might have. If he needed assistance, he'd let me know. But by the time I was ready to leave a few minutes later, he was sitting comfortably at his desk.

Sometimes we talked about specific works of music, other times about preparations for historic performances. One afternoon, when we began to discuss *The Rite of Spring*, he moved his chair to the middle of the room, sat down, and re-enacted his meeting with Stravinsky (in preparation for the piece's US premiere). "Stravinsky and I sat side-by-side with the score open over both our laps, and he started to sing the opening…" Stokowski whistled a few bars of the high bassoon solo, then continued. "He sang the entire score, beginning to end, for thirty minutes, and beat out every tempo with his hand…" He imitated Stravinsky's right hand, pumping the complex, constantly changing rhythms.

But when we referred to his score of *The Rite*, I saw something on the cover I didn't understand: "LE SACRE DU PRINTEMPS d'Igor Strawinsky et Nicolas Roerich."[1]

"Who is this?" I asked, pointing to the unfamiliar name.

"Roerich was a Russian set designer, painter, and mystic whom I knew, and who worked with Stravinsky on *Le Sacre*. The concept for the ballet had been his idea, and the original story and setting was supposed to be American Indian, not pagan Russian. There's an interesting museum on One Hundred Seventh Street that has Roerich's paintings, and you should go there. Call and ask for Sina Fosdick and tell her I sent you." Months later, guided by Ms. Fosdick, Roerich's disciple and biographer, I saw the spectacular designs for *Le Sacre* and other Stravinsky ballets, painted in tempera, giving the effect of light shining through brilliantly colored transparencies.[2]

Stokowski also told me about the young Shostakovich coming backstage after a concert in Russia to hand him the score of his First Symphony. "I looked deep into his eyes and saw great sadness," Stokowski said with intense feeling. Stokowski conducted the American premiere of the work with the Philadelphia Orchestra in 1928.

Most conductors didn't talk about other conductors unless they'd been dead a long time, so it wasn't a subject I would have

---

[1] His score had been published in France by ÉDITION RUSSE DE MUSIQUE, hence the French spellings.

[2] The stage designs for the original 1913 production are not in New York; we saw the ones done in 1944 for a 1948 production. All are in tempera.

raised. But one afternoon, after lunch, he began to discuss conductors who had influenced him. Because of Stokowski's dynamic stage presence, people assumed that his model had been Arthur Nikisch. Nikisch, the dramatic, late nineteenth- and early twentieth-century Austro-Hungarian conductor, was one of the most influential musicians of his time. Like Stokowski, Nikisch was known for his orchestras' expressive string sound and for the plasticity of his tempos.[3] "People think that Nikisch was the strongest influence on my conducting, but they are wrong," he said, refuting statements that remain in print to this day. "It was Hans Richter, who conducted many concerts I heard in London."

Stokowski continued. "I very much like Leonard Bernstein"—he pronounced it "BAIRN-shtine"—and volunteered that the legendary competition between himself and Toscanini hadn't existed. "Everyone thinks that Toscanini and I were rivals, but we got along *very* well," he said, nodding his head. "That whole story of our rivalry was invented by the press. I greatly admired him, and often attended his rehearsals," he explained, as proof of the good feelings between them. I couldn't believe what I was hearing.

"You attended Toscanini's rehearsals?" I asked, incredulous.

"Oh, yes!" he answered. Then, to my delight, he stood up beside his desk and began to imitate Toscanini, conducting an imaginary orchestra with an imaginary baton. "Toscanini is always criticized for his fast tempos," he added, starting to beat time. "But he would start at one tempo and I would watch his beat get faster and faster." His hand churned the air in front of him. "I think it was a kind of nervousness," he commented, and sat down.

---

[3] Tchaikovsky said about Nikisch: "He does not seem to conduct, but rather to exercise some mysterious spell…" Many musicians have said the same about Stokowski. Nikisch was known for the communicative quality of his eye contact, and I wonder now if Stokowski had known about that aspect of Nikisch's technique, which paralleled his own. Like Stokowski, Nikisch was charismatic and controversial, often taking interpretive liberties. Stokowski heard Nikisch conduct, and in May 1912, Nikisch was present for at least one of the thirty-year-old Stokowski's concerts with the London Symphony, Nikisch's own orchestra.

"Do you mean that Toscanini's tempi were not always what he really wanted?" I asked.

"Yes, I think so," he answered.

Stokowski didn't know that his charitable feelings toward Toscanini were not reciprocated. His Italian colleague had written him a letter (replete with misspellings) after hearing his radio broadcast of the César Franck Symphony in D minor:

> My dear Stokowsky This afternoon you have vitrolized Franck's Symphony… Never in my long life I have heard such a brutal, bestial, ignobil, unmusical performance like yours—not even from you. The Divine Art of Music too, has its own ganster like Hitler and Mussolini… Believe me, you are ready for madhouse or for jail… Hurry up!!! Toscanini.

Toscanini gave the letter to his son, who never mailed it. (It was reproduced in Harvey Sachs's book, *The Letters of Arturo Toscanini*,[4] and is now owned by the Italian government.)

During another relaxed afternoon, Stokowski again talked about conducting technique, this time focusing on John Philip Sousa, "The March King."

"Every few measures, Sousa would conduct the first beat behind him. He'd bring the baton down, then up in the back," he said, standing to face me. He started to conduct a march—two beats to the measure—with his right arm, on some of the downbeats, extending all the way down then up behind his back, then coming up again in front. Stokowski greatly admired Sousa's marches, which he had transcribed for both organ and for orchestra. Then we started discussing people who were "natural musicians." He surprised me by saying that one of the most intuitive musicians he had ever worked with was Harpo Marx.

---

4   *The Letters of Arturo Toscanini*, compiled, edited, and translated by Harvey Sachs, Alfred A. Knopf, 2002.

When he was in an especially good mood, he'd talk about his early days in Philadelphia—driving his hand-crank Model T Ford along an unpaved Broad Street—and about the city: "It was so dirty!" he told me delightedly. He recalled the orchestra's first recording sessions, in 1917, when he and the musicians traveled across the Delaware River to the Victor Talking Machine Company (which later became RCA) in Camden, New Jersey. He mimed the vigorous motions of string and wind players who had to crowd around and lean into the big wooden "horn" that captured their sound. The result was the twelve-inch 78 rpm of Brahms's *Hungarian Dances* Nos. 5 and 6, full of color, personality, and surface noise.

Laughing, he impersonated the ladies of the Main Line who, before his outrageous parody of them in Lekeu's *Fantaisie Contrapuntique* in 1926, placed their shopping bags along the edge of the stage then noisily grabbed them when they left. It didn't matter to them that the orchestra was still playing; they couldn't be late for the Paoli Local. The passage of more than four decades allowed him to smile at the memory.

In late afternoon, Central Park and the reservoir softened into watercolor hues and the light in the apartment deepened into gold. Stokowski would put his scores aside and we'd drink cups of tea and talk. I'd sit across from him at the narrow desk, the long fluorescent light focused on us from above. During one of our discussions he shared an insight that would guide me over the years, in art and in life: "I learn more," he said, "from bad performances than from good ones."[5] One afternoon, when the golden glow had lulled us into quiet conversation, there was a loud *pop* then a *whoosh*. Fireplace embers, dormant from a fire the evening before,

---

[5] The conductor and composer José Serebrier, who served as Associate Conductor of the American Symphony Orchestra from 1962 to 1967, told me of asking Stokowski for advice about becoming a conductor. "Go around the world and watch all the bad conductors," Stokowski told him. "Learn what not to do." Other than that, he offered the young conductor no advice. "Conducting cannot be taught," Stokowski often said; one had to have natural talent, a quality he called "X."

had spontaneously ignited. Stokowski stared past me at the blaze. "That's a lot like life," he said.

There were times, I realize now, when the intimacy between us almost crossed into romance. Standing by his desk one afternoon, waiting for him to finish a phone call, I felt a beam of sunlight, streaming in through the window, illuminate my long blonde hair and warm my shoulders. I was aware that he was staring up at me but I looked down, not in his direction. This continued for several minutes, until he finished his call. A few weeks later, he began to stare at me again. Finally, he came close and, squinting in concentration, began to arrange my hair with his fingers, pushing a curl one way, moving a wave in a different direction. He seemed lost in my hair. Suddenly he stopped and looked at me. "Don't ever make it shorter," he implored.

"All right, Maestro," I quickly agreed.

"You must promise," he insisted. I hesitated. Would I want to have long hair for the rest of my life?

"I promise," I said. I've never broken my word.

I was delighted when this happened. If he cared about the length of my hair, I thought, he cared about me, and it seemed to be evidence that our bond was growing stronger. I see it differently now. I suspect that, at eighty-three, having a young woman do as he wished fortified his ego and satisfied his need for control, even with something as trivial as the length of her hair. I think the same was true about his insistence that I wear the white jacket for him.

When we were together, Stokowski often revealed a caring, gentle side of his nature rarely, if ever, seen in public. But that didn't always guarantee a happy experience for me. I foolishly mentioned that, as part of my degree program, I had to take singing lessons. I didn't possess even basic vocal talent. "Come in here," he said, gesturing for me to precede him into the room that housed the music library and a piano. "I'm going to teach you vocal exercises I developed," he said. "They will help you."

"Oh, no, Maestro!" I told him, horrified at the thought of singing for him. "I'm not a singer!" He ignored what I said. I kept protesting but he sat down at the piano, just as I'd seen him do in the movie *One Hundred Men and a Girl* with Deanna Durbin. He began to play arpeggio-based exercises, explaining how I should vocalize up the scale as he played. He gave me advice about sustaining my breath between the notes, moving smoothly from one to another. The lesson didn't last long; I was no Deanna Durbin. I was relieved when he rose from the piano and we went back to his studio.

His concern, however, seemed to go too far when I sustained a small paper cut from a sheet of music. To get a bit of sympathy and attention, I showed him my finger, expecting to be offered a bandage I would have refused. When he saw the nick in my skin, he jumped up, rushed to the bathroom, and returned with a larger bandage than the cut warranted. He wrapped it tightly around my finger and repeatedly checked to see if I was all right. His reaction mystified me. Years later, Curtis W. Davis, while writing a biography of Stokowski he wouldn't live to complete, told me that Stokowski's younger sister Lydia (whom Stokowski never mentioned) had died from a lung embolism on safari in South Africa in 1911. Shortly after her death, local thieves apparently severed her swollen fingers to steal her rings. Curtis said that one of Stokowski's wives, during dinner, cut her finger slightly when a paring knife slipped, and her husband passed out cold. Lydia's death, I believe, left him with a phobia about knives and blades. I never saw him use a razor, only an electric shaver. And Rosamond Bernier, in her book *Some of My Lives: A Scrapbook Memoir*,[6] recalled being in Morelia, Mexico, when Stokowski was to guest conduct a local orchestra. A strike had cut off the town's electricity. "He stormed. No electric razor, no concert. The organizers were appalled. The concert was sold out. Total impasse." In the hotel's bar, she met engineers working on a new highway and was able to convince them to install a portable

---

[6] Farrar, Straus and Giroux, 2011. Bernier, the writer and art lecturer, had known Stokowski since childhood. Her father, Samuel R. Rosenbaum, was on the board of the Philadelphia Orchestra. He married the renowned Philadelphia Orchestra harpist Edna Phillips when Rosamond was nine years old.

generator outside the hotel. "It was turned on just long enough to produce the current to feed Stoki's razor." That wasn't reasonable behavior even for a temperamental conductor.

The ambiance at 1067, quiet to the point of being almost somber, always brightened when I arrived. I wanted to bring him happiness, not problems, so I never told him about the turmoil I was enduring at home. When I arrived at his apartment the morning after a brutal argument between my parents, he asked how I was. "I'm fine," I told him, then walked across the room toward the music library. He followed me, gently turning me around, his hands on my shoulders.

"What's wrong?" he asked.

"Not a thing," I answered, and changed the subject. In spite of my studied equanimity, he told me one afternoon, "You are so intense!" His jaw was set, his eyes narrowed, his right hand turned upward in the same gesture he used to make an orchestra play more ardently. I realized then how sensitive he could be to people's moods and thought it sad that he so rarely used that ability to bring happiness to others.

I now attended Stokowski's Carnegie Hall concerts as his guest, sitting in the first-tier, stage right box. He'd mount the podium, look upward, make eye contact with me, and bow. It was heady stuff for a young woman.

He still insisted that I wear my white jacket. I had outgrown it psychologically—it seemed like schoolgirl attire—but I did as he wished. One evening, my friends and I attended a performance at the last minute, purchasing our tickets and surprising him backstage after the concert.

"This jacket, I cannot conduct without this jacket!" he announced to everyone in the room as he pointed to it and hugged me to his side.

"You did very well tonight and you didn't know I was in the hall until now!" I challenged.

"I get a *feeling…*" he said dramatically, closing his eyes and shaking his head, to the amusement of everyone in the room. I walked out of the dressing room with Stewart Warkow, general manager of Stokowski's orchestra, whom I had come to know well. "You can get away with *anything*," he remarked, amazed at the good-natured way Stokowski reacted when I teased or confronted him.

About a month later, a group of us drove to New York to hear him conduct the Philadelphia Orchestra at Philharmonic Hall. Half an hour before the concert, while my friends took their seats, I headed backstage to see Jesse. In the world of professional music, nothing was—or is—more important than a New York performance; it never occurred to me to bother Stokowski before the concert. Jesse greeted me with an amused smile. "You'd better get in there," he said, gesturing toward the conductor's dressing room. "He's been asking for you."

I quickly made my way down the hall and knocked on the door. In white tie and tails, Stokowski looked handsome but worried. "Where have you been?" he asked sternly. "I have been concerned."

"I drove in from Philadelphia with a whole bunch of friends. We stopped and had something to eat on the way," I explained.

"All right," he said, his voice softening. "I will see you later."

Backstage after the performance, my friends and I pushed through the crowded reception room to where he was standing.

"Hello, whole bunch!" he greeted us loudly, smiling and shaking hands all around. "Who is driving?" he asked, and Allen stepped forward. "Come here," Stokowski instructed, and the two of them moved to the side of the room. I watched the pantomime: Stokowski did a lot of talking; every few seconds Allen would nod his head and swallow. Finally, they walked back to where the rest of us were waiting, and we all said goodbye to the Maestro.

"What did he say to you?" I asked Allen eagerly.

"He told me to drive carefully," Allen said, "that I had precious cargo."

Between visits, I'd eagerly wait for the small white envelopes with the rubber-stamped "L S APARTMENT 14" on the back. In addition to musical matters, we corresponded about faith: "I agree with you that organized religion is necessary for many persons but some individuals do not need it, but have a religious inner life. I am glad you are like that." He constantly spoke of one's "inner life" (probably referring to both spirituality and to private, unshared feelings), and of the "divine." That seemed to refer to a mysterious spirit that might have been God but might not have been connected to an organized religion. Not all of his letters, however, dealt with serious subjects. "I wish I had been there with you when you had the accident with your shorts. Could you ever do it again?" he asked, commenting on my report that my pants had split up the back when I helped move the Philadelphia Orchestra library. Following his typed comment, he had handwritten a question mark and two exclamation points. Occasionally, he'd ask me to kiss his former Rittenhouse Square neighbor, the bronze statue of the goat, for him.

"Thank you," he wrote in 1965, "for your letter of November 2. I am afraid Jesse does not understand women. (Nor do I.) Never mind, he is doing his best. (So am I.) Looking forward to seeing you next Thursday." The letter was spiced throughout with handwritten punctuation.

"Dear Nancy," a typed December 1965, letter began, "Wishing you Good Health and Well-Being in the New Year, and thanking you for your great assistance to me. With friendly thoughts, Leopold Stokowski." Then a handwritten note begins on the side, curves all the way around the top, and ends upside down: "Please more -- & be good girl." He often asked to be remembered to "my friends in the orchestra." And yet, had he seen them in person, he would have been no more than cordial.

Chapter Eleven

THE PHILADELPHIA ORCHESTRA'S HAPPY-FAMILY ATMOSPHERE was shaken in September 1966, when contract negotiations sputtered then stalled. The musicians' union and the orchestra management could not find common ground. On September 19, the musicians went on strike.

Every morning, a group of players formed a picket line around the Academy, and I sadly watched these distinguished artists carry placards pleading their case as one concert after another was canceled. I delivered coffee and cake to the picketers, commiserated with them, then went to the back of the Academy to cross their picket line. Whenever the strike was settled, the orchestra would go into rehearsal the following morning so the parts had to be marked and ready for performance. It would have been too risky for Jesse and Bill, both union members, to do this work.

My position was complicated. Since I was paid by the Philadelphia Orchestra Association and wasn't yet a member of the musicians' union, I was technically aligned with the management. I'd sneak in and out of the library, preparing the music for the next scheduled concert and place it back on the shelves as each performance was canceled. In one sad moment, Bill pointed a finger at me. "And one of your friends," he said sarcastically, referring to a member of the orchestra, "brought up your name to the union, telling them that you've been working in the Academy." I had been accused of being a strikebreaker. I don't know why Bill told me about this betrayal, but I'm grateful that he didn't identify my accuser. Shortly after the strike was settled, Jesse told me to join the union.

At the time, I was working simultaneously for the Philadelphia Orchestra and for Stokowski, but only a few of the players knew about my double life. I was in Stokowski's apartment one afternoon when the phone rang. "Three-six-eight-nine," I said, stating the last four digits of Stokowski's phone number, as he preferred.

"May I speak with the Maestro, please?" a familiar voice asked. It was Joseph Primavera, a violist who was head of the strike concert committee. I had known Joe for years.

"Just a moment, please," I said, without revealing my identity. The committee was organizing a strike benefit concert to raise money for the musicians, and they were asking Stokowski to conduct. He said yes. The event was set for October 14, 1966, the day when the first of his rehearsals for the Bach *Magnificat* and the Mahler Symphony No. 2, postponed because of the strike, was to have taken place.

Joe Prim, as we called him, organized his colleagues into a construction crew. They bought gypsum board, two-by-fours, hammers, and nails to construct an acoustical shell (which Stokowski always referred to as a reflector) that would convert the barn-like acoustics of Convention Hall[1] into those of a concert hall.

The night of the concert, I waited on the loading dock for Stokowski's car to arrive. The women I had met at the Dell two years earlier, Faye and Natalie, had driven him from New York. Emerging from their black Cadillac sedan, waving and smiling radiantly, he looked younger and handsomer, I noted in my diary, than ever before.

Everyone was excited. We all had a sense of participating in history: The famed former music director would conduct the orchestra during its long, controversial strike.

---

1   This building was demolished in 2005.

Stokowski went directly to his dressing room, and I helped Jesse place folders on the stands, answer musicians' questions, and smooth out logistical issues. When I heard the orchestra finish tuning and the crowd go silent, I dashed into the hall. At that moment, Stokowski walked onstage and nine thousand people jumped to their feet, cheering. I watched his eyes move slowly over the audience, taking in the prolonged display of gratitude and affection.

The crowd was noisy, almost rowdy, before and after each work on the first half—David Diamond's Overture to Shakespeare's *The Tempest* and Beethoven's Symphony No. 7—but utterly silent during the performances. There was more work for Jesse and me to do than at Academy concerts, so I didn't see Stokowski during intermission. Ten minutes before the break ended, Jesse called to me, "It's time to get the Maestro."

Still in high spirits, Stokowski followed us down the hall to the elevator. At one point, he asked about the gold ring on the pinky of my right hand, a sweet-sixteen gift from my parents four years earlier. He stood behind me in the elevator, encircling the base of my neck and my shoulders with his hands, rocking me gently from side to side. "And this one asked for my autograph!" he laughingly told the others. I had not, and I didn't know what he was referring to, but I suddenly realized that he now felt we were too close for me to seriously request his signature.

The concert continued with the mysterious, majestic Entr'acte from Act IV of Mussorgsky's *Khovanshchina* and a Stokowski specialty: the brilliantly orchestrated, dramatic suite from Stravinsky's ballet, *Petrushka*.

At the end of the concert, Stokowski quieted the audience. "We are very sorry that the program is finished and that you all must go home," he said, not revealing that he and the orchestra had prepared four encores. They shouted their disappointment. Turning to the orchestra, he began to reward his adoring audience, first with his transcription of the Bach E-flat minor Prelude from *The Well-Tempered Clavier*, then the prelude to Act III of Wagner's *Lohengrin*, his transcription of the Haydn Divertimento, and the fierce "Sabre Dance" from Khachaturian's ballet, *Gayane*. "Could you be persuaded to hear…" he'd ask before each piece, then turn back to the orchestra. Between encores, he asked "two favors" of audience members: "Make every effort to solve this condition, which is so sad. We cannot lose the great Philadelphia Orchestra. It has a great past and, I hope, a more distinguished future. Do something about it!" and to do what they could to save the "reflector" so that the children of Philadelphia, "rich and poor," could enjoy concerts there. Proceeds from the event were estimated at $15,000, substantial money in 1966 (more than $140,000 today).

Even then, I realized that Stokowski was an ironic hero. It was behavior like his years before—openly embarrassing the players, firing them at will—that had necessitated the protection of the musicians' union, strengthening it to its level of power then and now.

I planned to see him off at 30th Street Station the morning after the concert. At the final rehearsal, without his knowledge, I had told the musicians when his train would depart for New York, hoping some of them would show up. I met him on the main level of the station, near the information booth, and he took me to a counter in the corner of the terminal where he bought orange juice for us both. Sipping from cone-shaped paper cups in silver metal holders, we talked about the concert the night before and, yet again, about my education. I looked at him standing there—tall, in his pin-striped suit, white hair swept behind his ears—a commanding figure at the orange juice counter.

As we walked down the stairs to the platform where his train would depart, I spotted a mouse on the tracks. I might not have pointed it out to someone else, especially an adult, but I couldn't resist showing it to him. His distinguished demeanor vanished. There we were, pointing and laughing like two gleeful kids, watching the mouse scamper about. Then the musicians began to arrive, each one a surprise for him. His dignity restored, he vigorously shook each person's hand, nodding in response to expressions of gratitude for his efforts the night before. About a dozen of us stood chatting when the train roared into view. Stokowski quickly turned toward us, opened his arms wide, and using his body, pushed us away from the tracks. It was as close to an embrace, I remember thinking, as he could give his musicians.

At eighty-four, Stokowski was surprisingly naive. He participated in the strike concert to help the musicians financially, but orchestra officials perceived his actions as anti-management. The event had generated a huge amount of publicity, and that publicity had been polarizing: Stokowski's involvement had weighted public sympathy to the players' side. I remember being horrified when Joseph H. Santarlasci Jr., assistant manager of the orchestra, standing in the library, expressed his anger at Stokowski. I had asked about his returning in future seasons. "He's just another guest conductor," Santarlasci replied. The orchestra's management, however, was contractually obligated to have him conduct the canceled concert. In November 1967, a year after the strike, he led searing, transcendent performances of Mahler's monumental Symphony No. 2, "Resurrection," at the Academy and in New York.

When the fifty-eight-day strike finally ended on November 15, the day before the orchestra's sixty-sixth birthday, thirty-five concerts had been canceled. Bill Smith was scheduled to conduct the next set of performances. His program had originally included Beethoven's music from *The Ruins of Athens* but he quickly replaced that with the more optimistic Symphony No. 4, "The Inextinguishable," by Carl Nielsen.

During the strike, I once again saw the lack of loyalty I then considered to be a Philadelphia trait (the city was famous for booing its own sports teams). Anshel Brusilow, the orchestra's brilliantly talented, charismatic concertmaster, had decided to leave to form and conduct his own ensemble, the Chamber Symphony of Philadelphia, and its debut concert took place during the strike. I was in the ladies' room at intermission and overheard a conversation between two well-dressed matrons. "What do we need the Philadelphia Orchestra for?" one asked. "Now we can have this on Saturday nights."

The orchestra survived the strike, but the experience left me shaken. Some of the players had been offered positions with other ensembles and, had the strike continued, they would have been forced to leave Philadelphia. "This orchestra can fold," more than one player told me during the strike. The most stable part of my life, I suddenly realized, wasn't stable. I also had no idea what part Stokowski might play in my future. But for the time being, all seemed to be well. As long as the orchestra existed, I would be safe. It didn't occur to me that you could be fired from your family.

Chapter Twelve

I NEVER KNEW WHAT I'D find at home—my father in a rage or my mother gripped by panic. In a vastly different way, I never knew what I'd find at the Academy—remarkable music I'd never heard and great conductors I'd never heard of: Hermann Scherchen (in his American debut), William Steinberg, Jean Martinon, and Rafael Kubelik; the young conductors István Kertész, Seiji Ozawa, Lorin Maazel, Claudio Abbado, and Colin Davis, all in their thirties; and Daniel Barenboim, who was in his early twenties. And there were soloists whose names I was just beginning to associate with specific sounds and styles: Emil Gilels, Arthur Rubinstein, Rudolf Firkušný, Yehudi Menuhin, and Jacqueline du Pré.

I'd rush to finish my work in the library then sit in on rehearsals. Sometimes I'd make a game of studying the musicians, reducing their actions to the most basic physical movements. The process could seem ridiculous—men and women sawing away at little wooden boxes that had strings stretched across them, or blowing across or into intricate machines of wood or metal. Why, I wondered, was I so moved by the sounds they produced? Why did they generate such intense feelings? They were, after all, only vibrations. Even now, no one—including scientists and psychologists—can solve the mystery of why most people are hardwired to react emotionally to music. But I didn't respond only to the nobility of Beethoven, the struggles of Mahler, and the elegant, profound humanity of Mozart; I also reacted to a single isolated chord, perfectly tuned, beautifully blended, removed from the context of a piece of music. It was a thing of beauty and power that could evoke a thrilling, even ecstatic, physical and emotional response. I felt a reaction to it deep in my stomach and in the part of my chest that holds my heart.

Placing importance on the quality of an ensemble's sound—pure sound independent of other details of interpretation—is sometimes regarded as decadent or superficial, particularly if that sound is colorful and expressive. It appeals, some people say, to our baser instincts and not to our intellect. While I often hear music lovers and critics comment on the quality of sound systems—speakers, headphones, or earbuds; on the acoustics of concert halls; and on the qualities of individual instruments (the sound of a Strad or a Steinway, for example)—rarely do I hear people comment on the blend and color of an orchestra's sound (or on the absence of those qualities).[1] Would anyone observe a beautifully designed and crafted garment and ignore the fabric from which it's made? Or disregard the colors in a painting, paying attention only to the subjects' shapes and forms and their relationships to one another? I often wondered, while working with various conductors, if they didn't possess the technical ability to generate colorful, balanced sound; if it didn't exist in their imaginations; or if it just wasn't important to them.[2]

---

[1] Some ensembles, particularly from poor countries, do not have instruments that can produce the sonorities that would enhance their performances, particularly of late Classical or Romantic music. And some conductors admit only players who have high-quality instruments into their orchestras.

[2] Herbert von Karajan was one conductor who did pay attention to pure sound. I never worked with him. When I was orchestra librarian at the Curtis Institute, he was supposed to conduct a rehearsal but had to cancel. Because of Karajan's Third Reich associations, I told the Institute director that I would restrict my contact with him only to musical responsibilities: if he wanted a score, I'd get it for him; if he wanted a glass of water, I would not.

Sometimes, when Stokowski conducted, I'd study him just as I did the players, reducing his gestures to the purely physical. I began to realize that whether you liked music or not, or whether you liked *his* music or not, Stokowski could serve as a fascinating subject for scientific study. What enabled him to communicate specific directions to his orchestras with only the slight lifting of an eyebrow or the raising of his little finger? How did he generate his trademark sound within minutes of working with any orchestra he conducted? Did he hypnotize his players without their knowing it? Were they under some kind of spell? He embodied proof that human beings are able to communicate non-verbally on a highly sophisticated level. But while we're fascinated with dog whisperers and horse whisperers and people who talk birds out of the sky, we don't trust people who have the same sort of power with their fellow humans.

"I never knew I could play like that," I constantly heard veteran musicians murmur as they came offstage after a Stokowski performance. But no one could completely identify what he had done to affect them, and through them, the audience. Even today, knowledgeable, articulate musicians resort to talking about "some sort of magic," hypnotism and the paranormal, describing his ability to transmit something like electrical current. John Carabella, who played horn with the New York Philharmonic for thirty-three years, shrugs helplessly when I ask how Stokowski got the effects he consistently achieved: "I don't know how he did it." I make my questions about gestures more specific. "ESP [extra sensory perception]," he says.

Ellen Taaffe Zwilich, a violinist in the American Symphony from 1965 to 1972 (before she became a prominent composer and the first woman to win the Pulitzer Prize for a musical composition), says that Stokowski "invited" the orchestra to play. "Something emanated from him. He conveyed great love and understanding of the music to us," she said, her hands making a sweeping gesture toward an imaginary orchestra. It wasn't, however, love for his musicians. They often felt that they were only a means to his end, serving his purposes, completely expendable. And although they gave him what he wanted musically, she made it clear that they didn't necessarily like him personally any more than he seemed to like his players.

At the Dell in June 1965, I had been able to see—not just hear—how he influenced his musicians. A hot breeze carried the heavy scent of mimosa into the Friends of the Dell area, where I watched and listened to him rehearse. A half hour into the session, I realized that the door at the back of the stage had been opened for ventilation, so I tiptoed up the stairs at the side of the stage, then around to the doorway. Now, for the first time, standing directly opposite him, I could see Stokowski conduct from the front. His hands moved poetically, like a dancer's or a mime's, drawing his trademark intensity and voluptuousness from the ensemble. But I saw something I hadn't been able to see from the audience: He was conducting with his eyes—intense, focused beams that signaled an entrance for an entire instrumental section; flashed a warning to an individual player not to make a tricky entrance prematurely; and, narrowing slightly with a raise of his eyebrows, conveyed to the hundred-plus musicians to play so softly that the sound was barely perceptible. While facing forward, he was able to communicate to the players on both sides of him the way he wanted an entire line to be phrased.[3]

I stood brazenly in front of him, too fascinated to move. He looked at me; his eyes met mine, then he looked away. I stayed where I was. He started and stopped the musicians, making mostly minor corrections, but, as I had seen from the hall, a few moments after starting a section, his head would tilt back slightly, almost

---

[3] Allen Halber, my conducting-student boyfriend who was also a bass-clarinetist, was a member of the All-Philadelphia Senior High School Orchestra when Stokowski conducted the rehearsal I attended in 1962. Fifty-one years later, when we spent a day reminiscing, Allen recalled, "You knew what to do by looking at his eyes. You knew exactly how to phrase. You didn't have to see his hands at all." Jayn Rosenfeld, a flutist in Stokowski's American Symphony, said he seemed to have eyes like a whale, somehow visible from the sides. "Every player," she told me, "thought he was looking directly at him or her."

locking in place; he seemed to go into a trance even though he continued to shape phrasing and adjust balance and cue the musicians' entrances. At times, he stood stone still; no part of his body visibly moved, yet the pulse was somehow transmitted. Then his right hand, index finger pointing skyward, signaled a change in mood or texture of sound. The left hand, fingers curled upward, stimulated the players to infuse the music with intensity and urgency. But his eyes, more than his hands, implored the musicians to give him what he wanted.

I had seen those penetrating, sky-blue eyes at close range. They could be encouraging and understanding, but they could also be cold and reproachful. They could invite you to come close or warn you to keep your distance. Often, they suggested that he had a secret he wouldn't share. When Stokowski looked into your eyes with his gaze unbroken, it was impossible to look away.

When the rehearsal ended, I raced back to his dressing room. "Maestro!" I called out, as he sat quietly. "I never saw you conduct from the front before!" He didn't wait for me to continue.

"Everyone always talks about my hands," he said, raising them in front of him, then looking at me. "I really conduct with my eyes."

"Some people say what you do is a mystery, a kind of magic." I was asking him a question by making a statement; one had to be cautious about questioning him.

He looked up at me. "Oh," he said, smiling shrewdly, "I know exactly what I am doing."

Indeed he did know what he was doing, in ways I was just beginning to understand. I had always thought that music was supposed to be beautiful, but he was more concerned with its dramatic power—its expressiveness—than its musicological or traditional "correctness" or its being "beautiful." This was key to his concept of the art. At a Philadelphia Orchestra rehearsal I attended, he stopped the players when he felt they were playing too prettily. "Music is not always beautiful!" he said passionately. "Sometimes it is ugly!"

In Richard Strauss's tone poem *Till Eulenspiegel's Merry Pranks*, there is a fast, descending run that an orchestra he was rehearsing played with perfect clarity—each note beautifully articulated. "No!" he yelled at the musicians. "No! You are playing each note too clearly! This is Till falling down! That is the effect we must have!" I heard evidence of the same aesthetic in the earthy, raw tones of his performances (and recordings) of Manuel de Falla's *El amor brujo*.

But in Stravinsky's *Firebird Suite*, there is a run—a sequence of notes going from low to high—that lasts only a second. Rehearsing the Philadelphia Orchestra in November 1965,[4] Stokowski stopped the musicians. Conducting almost in slow motion, he stretched the run to five times its normal length. Over and over, the orchestra played every note separately until each had a different color and character. Only then did he take the run "up to tempo"—back to its split-second length. It was no longer a blur but a multicolored, breathtaking rainbow of sound. He was using tonal coloration and texture as an artist uses paint. He wanted to place an endless palette of hues and effects at the service of the expressiveness of the music.

The seamless, flowing line—one of the most identifiable characteristics of "the Stokowski sound"—was achieved not only through his gestures but by the use of a technique called "free bowing" or "staggered bowing." Because string players bowed as they wished, they didn't all change the directions of their bows at the same time.[5] This remains the most controversial aspect of Stokowski's art. A former organist, he might have wanted to replicate the unbroken, sustained line he could produce by keeping his fingers on the keys or his feet on the pedals.

As liberating as it sounds, free bowing wasn't always easy or gratifying for the musicians. As I learned from my cello lessons, students are taught to follow the bowing indications in the music

---

[4] This was the 1919 version of the piece.
[5] The corresponding technique he asked for in the winds and brass is called "free breathing" or "staggered breathing," where musicians take breaths at different times from their section mates so that there is no perceptible gap in the sound.

from the time they begin to study; it becomes second nature. So Stokowski's practice went against the musicians' training.

In traditional "uniform bowing," all the musicians within a section have the same markings as well as notes; all bows move in the same directions. This provides the clear articulation that many musicians prefer, or at least are accustomed to. Musicians—and audiences—sometimes favor uniform bowing not just for its sound, but for its coordinated, choreographed look. Free bowing, where bows travel in different directions, can look bizarre, even chaotic.[6]

When a bow changes direction, there's a very slight "gap" in the sound, and when an entire section changes bow directions simultaneously, that gap is magnified. Stokowski often compared free bowing to chorus members taking breaths at different points (which he often asked choruses to do), so that there wouldn't be a break in the sound except when that effect was desired. I remember many rehearsals when, in a tone of childlike disappointment, he'd tell a string section bowing in sync, or members of a wind section taking breaths simultaneously, that they had "made a hole in the legato!"

While it's certainly possible for synchronized bowing to produce a flowing, singing line, it can't produce the distinctive, seamless sound that Stokowski favored. Except for the movies he was in, he didn't care about the coordinated look. To encourage that seamless effect from the orchestra, his left arm, hand, and fingers would move smoothly, gracefully. Simultaneously, his right hand—providing the pulse and delivering cues—moved in a fluid manner, turning slightly between the beats to keep the sound flowing. And, of course, his eyes somehow conveyed that he wanted continuity of sound. It's part of the mystery of conducting (and of non-verbal communication) that other conductors, using free bowing and breathing, wouldn't be able to produce the effect Stokowski achieved.

---

6   Austrian conductor Herbert von Karajan, influenced by Stokowski, was also known at times to employ the free-bowing system. But it's never become a commonly used technique.

Individual bowing, of course, gave the musicians freedom to express themselves, not to simply follow the markings in their music. Characteristically inconsistent, Stokowski was both a dictator and a liberator. He imposed iron discipline on his players but offered them great freedom of expression. This was true not only with bowing and breathing, but in the occasional solos that appear within many orchestral works.[7] It's not unusual for conductors to impose their interpretations on these solos, but I always saw Stokowski give his players freedom. Using minimal gestures, his hands barely moving, he'd provide the pulse (so that musicians who were not playing could keep track of where they were in the piece) or adjust the dynamics for balance (so that musicians who were playing as background to the solo wouldn't be too loud or soft). The solo players made their own decisions about phrasing, tempo, and tone quality. He'd follow their lead.

A 1970 NET documentary about Stokowski contains rehearsal footage of Beethoven's *Leonore* Overture No. 3. At one point, he tells members of the American Symphony, "*Camera! Camera!*" using the Italian term for an intimate, chamber music style. "Start with three desks, then more come in, *ad libitum*," he says. Only six players—three desks—are to start the section, with the others gradually joining in. "You will know when to come in by instinct," he tells them. This is not a dictator speaking; it is a trusting colleague giving his players the responsibility to decide, through *feeling*, what the music needs. "Feel it!" he'd often implore at rehearsals, moving his hands from his heart toward the players.

In his struggle to get his musicians to express their individuality, he sometimes resorted to sarcasm. During an American Symphony rehearsal I attended at Carnegie Hall in January 1966, he sat back on the high stool and looked at his players. "You know," he said, "acting on impulse is not good. Now, in modern times, one must act like everyone else, talk like everyone else, dress like everyone

---

[7] I am not referring to concertos, which feature a soloist throughout the work, but symphonic pieces that contain solo passages.

else, and think like everyone else. Acting on impulse is *very dangerous*! *Only in music* is it allowed. But don't worry, I will protect you!"

Conditioning, however, is difficult to overcome. After many of his concerts, Stokowski would laughingly comment to me, with a tinge of amazement and annoyance, that he had offered the musicians an opportunity to express themselves, but being creatures of habit, they were unable to bow or breathe differently from their section mates. "I offer them freedom, and they insist on doing what their neighbors are doing!" he'd complain.

There are, however, opposing opinions; few conductors have followed that practice. Most conductors and instrumentalists feel that the free bowing technique doesn't provide the clear phrasing and articulation the composer intended. It certainly goes against the styles of the Baroque and Classical periods. It could even work against what Stokowski wanted. "There were times when you felt the best way to express yourself, and to serve the music, was to bow in sync with your neighbor," Ellen Zwilich said. "But Stokowski would see the uniformity in the bowing and become annoyed!"

In all of our discussions about sound, Stokowski rarely spoke about "blend" or "sonority," words frequently used by other musicians. More often, he spoke about "balance" and "clarity"—"a certain clarity"—and talked about instruments being "in good proportion" to each other.[8] But no conductor can produce a performance that has good balance unless a composition is well orchestrated. If an orchestration is too "thick"—has too much going on simultaneously—important instrumental lines (often called voices) will be buried. Stokowski referred to this in a June 1968 letter about my education, advising me to listen carefully: "I am glad you are going to study orchestration, harmony, and theory. Have you a good teacher? Much of orchestration you can learn by listening to orchestration that is balanced or unbalanced." (He assumed that

---

8   There is a difference between "blend" and "balance." "Blend" refers to the combination of instruments playing together—the colors that are produced. "Balance" refers more to the relative loudness of the sections that are playing together—whether the proportions are correct, or if certain sections are too prominent, burying others.

the conductors of those performances would be competent; otherwise, an unbalanced performance could have been their fault.)

To maintain the correct balance, Stokowski encouraged specific sections or individuals to play out while he subdued others, shifting with both hands among the sections of the orchestra. In a video of him conducting Tchaikovsky's *Romeo and Juliet* Overture-Fantasy, his left hand turns upward toward the first violins, fingers vibrating, while the right hand, palm held out at a right angle to his arm, subdues the brass at the right rear of the stage. Suddenly he looks annoyed; his head shakes from side to side and his eyes shoot warnings to the timpani to hold back. His gaze then shifts and his eyebrows rise, signaling the woodwinds to play out. During all of this—through a subtle, almost imperceptible, pulse in his body—he keeps the beat going and, nodding his head, cues entrances for solo instruments and entire sections. Like all conductors, he doesn't physically produce the sound—he must influence others to generate the sounds he wants—but because of the fluidity of his gestures, he seems to "play" the orchestra almost as one would a theremin.[9]

Conductors are supposed to hear everything that's happening in the orchestra, even in thickly scored pieces. The scores in front of them show what notes *should* be played, not necessarily what notes *are* being played. I'm still amazed, during rehearsals of a complex piece, to hear a conductor call out, "Third horn, you're playing an F-sharp! It should be a D natural!"

In addition to being able to hear what's happening at the moment, many musicians have the ability to keep sounds accurately stored in their memories. In his dressing room after a concert in the Academy of Music, Stokowski told a few of us that he had heard a bell close by, its sound resembling one he remembered from his youth. That bell, he said, had been cast in Croydon, England.

---

[9] The theremin, developed in the 1920s, was one of the first electronic instruments. The pitch of its eerie, otherworldly sound is determined by the distance of the player's hands from the theremin's antenna. They do not make physical contact with the instrument.

Orchestra's Pert Lady Librarian

By JAMES FELTON

WANNA GET a job with the Philadelphia Orchestra? You can try sitting on the steps near the stage-door to the Academy of Music, although this method isn't recommended.

But that's what Nancy Shearer did when she was 13. Now she's working for the orchestra's librarian, Jesse Taynton, and she just became the recipient of the first grant ever made by the Martha Baird Rockefeller Fund to help anyone become a professional music librarian.

Nancy, now 20, pert as pie, confesses that she still has the cringing feeling of a sneak-in whenever she comes to work through the stage-door. She plunked herself there after hearing the orchestra for the first time. She went to the concert on a free ticket supplied by the orchestra's Van Rensselaer fund, established to help schoolchildren, like Nancy, experience the thrill of coming to the Academy for the first time in their lives.

For Nancy it was love at first sight—and sound. She loved the building, idolized the men who made the gorgeous music that thrilled her. She sat on the steps of the stage entrance for months, hoping that someone would notice her and take her in.

When she heard that some of the players ate lunch in a delicatessen near the Academy, she saved enough pennies until she could afford a few sandwiches there. She nibbled away in a booth, hoping for a word of recognition from the men, all of whom were heroes in her star-struck eyes.

THEN, one day back on her perch at the Academy, she felt a friendly pat on her shoulder. It was conductor Eugene Ormandy himself, asking if she had a ticket to the concert. No. Of course she didn't. It was impossible.

But yes, it was possible. The maestro waved a magic wand, making her immune to the scrutiny of ushers and stagehands. Suddenly she was plunged into the glamorous world she craved. That was the beginning of a daffy affair between her and the Philadelphia Orchestra that is stronger now than the day it started.

"It seemed like a crush at first, but I never got over it," Nancy recalled recently, ensconced at her desk in the library backstage at the Academy. Surrounded by rows of green lockers that gave the place the look of a sedate gym room, she was mending a piece of torn music. The pin on her sweater had the shape of a G-Clef.

"When the men get excited, they often slap the page over with their bows or bend the corners. That's where the mending comes in," she said, explaining a large part of her job.

Jesse Taynton laughed when she asked for her assistant's job three years ago. She wanted to replace a young man who had just left. Taynton said he couldn't picture her carrying large bundles of music to the post-office for mailing, etc., etc. The job wasn't for a girl, but he said he'd call her if she was ever needed.

That call came the very next afternoon. Nancy could hear the sound of the orchestra in the background, and she flipped as hard as she had the first time she was ever in the Academy.

* * *

NANCY works full-time at her part-time job in the library. As apprentice and mascot, she commutes daily to the Academy from her parents' home at 7036 Kindred St., in the Oxford Circle area. During her explorations of the building she once had the wierd privilege of crawling across the ceiling to hear the orchestra from above the chandelier.

When seats were replaced in the Academy's amphitheater last year, Nancy asked for a plaque attached to one of the seats, as a souvenir. Instead, the stage-hands ripped out the whole seat and presented it to her. It now sits in her studio at home, along with some hand-made nails that were once part of the Academy's original structure. There are also stacks of program notes dating back to 1900, the year the orchestra was founded.

Nancy collects the autographs of every guest conductor, and has 50 of them framed on her wall. Besides her chores at the library she writes program notes for the Senior Student concerts of the orchestra.

Other items: she ushered free at Robin Hood Dell to hear the orchestra play there; she studied the cello with

Continued on Page 9, Col. 2

The Sunday Bulletin
PHILADELPHIA
Sunday, December 4, 1966

KEEPING SCORE—Nancy Shearer, 20, is library helper at the Philadelphia Orchestra. She has a Rockefeller grant to study orchestra librarian work.

Musical Librarian

Continued From Page 3

Elsa Hilger, a member of the orchestra; she plans to become the first trained orchestral librarian in the country.

* * *

WITH HER grant, Nancy expects to take special courses at Temple University. Marketing, cataloging, mending and filing musical scores requires a skill peculiar to a big, busy, modern symphony orchestra like the Philadelphia.

No less than 1,077 full scores lie in the filing cabinets of the orchestra's library. They must be ready at an instant's notice for use, and, usually, corrections made by the conductor. The corrections must be carried out on each part of the score (parts can run as high as 110 to each score) by the librarian, who has to know how and where to make them.

Asked about her cello, Nancy joked: "I play it well enough to want to be a librarian."

It's an odd job, but she hopes to make it full-time and professional. To her it's thrilling enough to make the slightest contribution that might help the orchestra play a little better and more easily.

"Isn't it a wonderful chance to help something you've always loved?" she asked with a twinkle. With the blessing of conductor Ormandy, librarian Taynton, and the Martha Rockefeller Fund, it will be, some day soon.

The editors of the *Sunday Bulletin* in Philadelphia felt that a seventeen-year-old working for the Philadelphia Orchestra was unusual enough to warrant a story. (Unfortunately, they misspelled my name.)

Two of my mentors, Jesse C. Taynton, Librarian, and William R. Smith, Assistant Conductor, at the green linoleum table in the Philadelphia Orchestra library. Photo by Adrian Siegel

The entire Philadelphia Orchestra celebrated my twenty-first birthday (two days early) backstage at the Robin Hood Dell, June 29, 1967. I wish I had a recording of them singing "Happy Birthday"! Photo by L. Shear

My perfect world: backstage at the Academy of Music. Photo by Adrian Siegel, courtesy of the Philadelphia Orchestra

Generations of music lovers and filmgoers know about Stokowski from *Fantasia* (1940). Here, he and Mickey Mouse congratulate each other. Photo by Walt Disney/Photofest

Stokowski conducting the Philadelphia Orchestra in the Academy of Music in the 1960s. Photo by Adrian Siegel

Stokowski insisted that I always wear my white jacket for him. Here, we are onstage at the Academy of Music. Photo by Adrian Siegel

Two music directors of the Philadelphia Orchestra, spanning a period of fifty-three consecutive years. I wasn't able to fully appreciate this historic moment—the first known photo taken of the two of them together—because I was terrified I'd lose my job! (November 19, 1965) Photo by Adrian Siegel, courtesy of the Philadelphia Orchestra

Eugene Ormandy in action. Photo by Photofest

Eugene Ormandy during a photo session in the Academy of Music reception room, 1966. Photo by Nancy Shear

Arthur Rubinstein and Ormandy (with Mrs. Rubinstein in the foreground), in 1968, listening to playbacks at the recording session for Chopin's Piano Concerto No. 2. This was the first major recording project that Jesse asked me to work on. Minutes after I took this photo, the usually good-natured Rubinstein stormed out of the room, telling Ormandy that all he could hear were the strings, not the piano! Photo by Nancy Shear

Stokowski wearing the straw hat he had brought from France, August 1975. Photo by Nancy Shear

In England in August 1975, I mentioned to Stokowski that the Philadelphia Orchestra members hadn't seen him in more than six years. "Let's take a picture for them!" he said, then he sweetly smiled into the camera. Photo by Nancy Shear

Stokowski during dinner, Nether Wallop, England, August 1975. Photo by Nancy Shear

The usually impeccably-dressed Stokowski became chilled and put on his pajama tops instead of a sweater (Nether Wallop, England). Photo by Natalie Bender

Stokowski and his daughter Luba in The South of France, 1974. He began to joke and laugh when he saw me with my camera. Photo by Nancy Shear

The South of France, December 1974 (left to right): me; Stokowski; his daughter Luba; Natalie Bender; and Luba's daughters Diana and Laila. Photo courtesy of the Stokowski family

LEOPOLD STOKOWSKI

23 February 65

Dear Nancy

I enjoyed very much your visit and your letter, and agree with you that the music of Sibelius, Mendelssohn and Tchaikovsky is sincere and creative and is an <u>expression of the heart</u>. There are persons who do not respond to this music. It is possible that all their vitality is up in their skull, and does not go down below their chin. Of course they are very intellectual, and also very (?)

I agree with you that organized religion is necessary for many persons but some individuals do not need it, but have a religious inner life. I am glad <u>you</u> are like that.

Thank you for reminding me about Gould's "American Salute". We must keep our promise to play from the time Robin Hood stopped us.

Always your friend

[signature: Leopold Stokowski]

In only two paragraphs, Stokowski expresses his philosophies of art and religion.

LEOPOLD STOKOWSKI

14 June 65

Dear Nancy

Thank you for the DA CAPO YEAR BOOK,* and for the wonderful quotation you made. I cannot believe I wrote anything so good, (did you forge it yourself?) ?!

Have you been able to finish all the cuts in Enesco's Rhapsody?

If you go for long walks in the parks, be careful that Robin Hood does not catch you.

I am greatly looking forward to being with you all for the rehearsals and concert in his Dell.

Your friend

1067 Fifth Avenue
New York, New York 10028
ATwater 9-3689

* May I receive the negative of the foto — for a few days?

The "DA CAPO YEAR BOOK" Stokowski referred to was my college (Philadelphia Musical Academy) yearbook. It had been dedicated to him, and included an excerpt from his book, *Music for All of Us*.

LEOPOLD STOKOWSKI

Dear Nancy   30 September 65

Would it be convenient for you if you picked me up at the Hotel Barclay at 7:00PM on Thursday the 18th, so that we could start our evening half an hour _earlier_?

October 4 I will take the Wagner score and parts to Carnegie Hall, arriving there about 7:10. Would it be convenient for you if I gave you the material then in my dressing room? Another way would be _after_ the concert in my dressing room.

I wish I had been there with you when you had the accident with your shorts. Could you ever do it again? ?!!

Looking forward to seeing you on the 4th.

                                              Your friend

1067 Fifth Avenue
New York, New York 10028
ATwater 9-3689
                                              [signature] Leopold Stokowski

Almost every letter I received from Stokowski contained some element of humor. This letter referred to the fact that my shorts had split up the back when I had helped move the Philadelphia Orchestra library to a new location.

LEOPOLD STOKOWSKI

                                              19 October 65

Miss Nancy Shear
7036 Kindred Street
Philadelphia, Pennsylvania 19149

Dear Nancy

The score and parts have just arrived, and thank you for helping me so much. Please be a good girl and send me a bill, because then I can take advantage of your kindness and ask you to help me with some other musical projects. But if you don't send me a bill, I never can ask you again, and this would cause me great and lasting disappointment. So be a good girl. *(but Not Too)!*

                                              Sincerely
1067 Fifth Avenue
New York, New York 10028
ATwater 9-3689
                                              [signature] Leopold Stokowski

At first, I didn't want to charge Stokowski for the work I did for him—I considered it an honor—but he insisted on paying me. "In the end, one would feel used," he told me. He seemed to be protecting our relationship.

In April 1967, I attended Mstislav Rostropovich's rehearsal with the Philadelphia Orchestra. It was the first time I heard his unforgettable artistry. Photo by Nancy Shear

When Rostropovich saw that I had my camera, he began to clown around, switching the cello from his left side to his right (April 1967). Photo by Nancy Shear

The master of his instrument in every way. Photo © Steve J. Sherman

Conductors must influence others to create the sounds they want. Here, Rostropovich is doing just that. Photo © Steve J. Sherman

Slava, holding his beloved little dog, Pooks; Juri's daughter, Carolyn; and me having dinner at Juri's home in Chevy Chase, MD, January 20, 1979. Photo by Juri Jelagin, courtesy of Carolyn Jelagina Falb

On June 11, 1992, Steinway & Sons produced a gala concert at Kennedy Center in Washington, DC, featuring the world premieres of three works for piano and orchestra. Slava conducted the National Symphony Orchestra, and I was working as Steinway's national press representative. He and I celebrated backstage after the concert. Photo courtesy of Steinway & Sons

A serious virtuoso onstage, having great fun backstage. Robin Hood Dell, July 1976. Photographer unknown

Lorin Maazel, a brilliant musician who maintained a serious, distinguished demeanor, showed up at his rehearsals with the Philadelphia Orchestra wearing a Beethoven sweatshirt! (A Beethoven concerto was on the program.) The members of the orchestra were shocked and delighted. Lorin posed for this photo in his Academy of Music dressing room (1966). A few years later, he asked me to work for him privately. He was a kind and respectful colleague, always asking me if I agreed with his musical decisions. Photo by Nancy Shear

I took this photo in April 1967 during the rehearsal for a videotaping with Byron Janis as soloist with the Philadelphia Orchestra. Janis was the only one of my hero musicians I seldom spoke to backstage. I attended as many of his concerts as I could, but, like the images of the Romantic composers whose music he played so beautifully, Janis seemed to be of another time and sensibility–introspective, thoughtful, brooding. But in the 1980s, when I went to his home to interview him, he and his wife, Maria Cooper Janis (an artist, author, producer, and daughter of Gary Cooper), became cherished close friends. I discovered–and delighted in–Janis's warmth and robust sense of humor. Photo by Nancy Shear

I had been broadcasting on WNYC-FM for about five years when they asked me to host the inaugural broadcast from the new studios in the Municipal Building (in downtown Manhattan). We invited many distinguished guests, and the studio became, in effect, an open house–an hours-long party that included Mayor Edward I. Koch and singer/actor Theodore Bikel, pictured here (December 11, 1985). Photo by Linda Naklicki Karten, WNYC

The one near the Academy was atop the Philadelphia National Bank building. Samuel R. Rosenbaum, a prominent attorney and a member of the Philadelphia Orchestra board when Stokowski was music director, checked into the history of the bell. It had indeed been cast in Croydon.

I, too, was starting to develop a trained ear. During rehearsals, Bill Smith or members of the orchestra who weren't needed onstage would sit about halfway back in the hall to listen for balance. This required a highly developed ability to hear which of the orchestral sections or individual instruments were either too prominent or were being buried; the podium is too close to the orchestra for conductors always to know how the acoustics in the hall are reacting. In the middle of one rehearsal, Stokowski stopped the orchestra and turned toward the hall, his left hand gripping the brass rail of the podium.

"Can you hear the cellos?" he asked. No one answered. I turned to see who was in back of me. There wasn't anyone there. He was speaking to me!

"Yes," I said, "but they could be brought out just a bit more." (This exchange was a rite of passage—an act of confidence on his part—that thrilled me.) All he had to do then was to signal the cellos to play out more, or to subdue the other instruments. But if the problem had been caused by the characteristics of the hall, Stokowski—more than any other conductor—would have known how to solve it.

Recognized as an acoustical expert, Stokowski was able to adjust to the characteristics of halls new to him, or to deal with problematic venues. I'd often see him walk around the stage before a rehearsal began, clapping loudly and listening to how the sound reverberated. That would enable him to adjust the dynamics during the rehearsal.

It was fascinating to watch him solve problems. He never stopped experimenting with orchestral seating and other acoustical issues. At a rehearsal the day before I got my job in February 1964, concertmaster Anshel Brusilow and principal cellist Lorne

Munroe had a duet in Gabrieli's Canzon Quarti Toni a 15. The Maestro didn't like what he was hearing. Stopping the orchestra, he asked Munroe if he thought sitting closer to Brusilow would improve the effect of the duet. When Munroe said yes, Stokowski, without hesitating, ordered the specific rearrangement of seats and stands throughout the stage. Munroe ended up wedged somewhere between the first violins, second violins, and the podium. Now, when they played the duet, the sound blended and resonated throughout the hall.

However, no matter how great a conductor may be, or how much he may know about acoustics, there are limits to what he can do in an acoustically poor hall. In November 1965, I was standing at the podium with Stokowski during the break in a Philadelphia Orchestra rehearsal at Philharmonic Hall,[10] which had infamously problematic acoustics.

"I could make this hall sound excellent," he said, looking above and around the stage.

"What would you do?" I asked. He pointed to the baffles—the panels that reflect sound—hanging above the orchestra.

"I would lower those panels as far as they could go, all the way down. But they wouldn't do it."

"Why do you say that?" I asked.

"Because," he said with a touch of bitterness, "the wires would be exposed, and they are more concerned with how the hall looks than how it sounds!"[11]

For decades, I'd heard that New York Philharmonic officials had called Stokowski shortly before Philharmonic Hall opened. They knew that there were serious acoustical problems and they wanted his advice about correcting them. Members of the orchestra board

---

10   Philharmonic Hall would be renamed Avery Fisher Hall in 1976, and David Geffen Hall in 2015.

11   In 1970, when Stokowski conducted the American Symphony in the Ives Symphony No. 4 on that stage, Donal Henahan, in a review in the *New York Times*, wrote: "Philharmonic Hall gave off a rich and wonderfully colored sound that one would never have expected of it, perhaps because Mr. Stokowski had arranged his double basses against the back wall, with cellos in front of them, circling of [sic] to the left."

and staff were scattered throughout the hall, and the full forces of the Philharmonic were onstage. They were to play Beethoven's Symphony No. 3, "Eroica." For the purposes of the experiment, Stokowski had the trombones, which don't have parts in the symphony, play in the opening of the piece; he wanted to hear what the complete orchestra would sound like. Stokowski brought his hands down and the two strong, iconic chords sounded. He stopped the players and had them begin again. He went no further than those two chords. Without saying a word, he stepped down from the podium and put on his coat. Philharmonic officials rushed to his side. "Maestro, what do you think?"

"You called me too late," he somberly told them, and left.

The story seemed to be one of those apocryphal tales that float around the music business.

"I've heard that story for years," I once said to the horn player John Carabella. "It certainly seems like a characteristic Stokowski response."

"It's true!" he said, grinning. "I was there!"

There are situations, however, where acoustical deficiencies can produce benefits. The relatively dry—non-reverberant—acoustics of the Academy of Music encouraged, if not forced, the musicians of the Philadelphia Orchestra to play out, projecting the tone and filling the hall with the orchestra's trademark richness.

Some of Stokowski's Philadelphia Orchestra concerts were repeated in New York, Baltimore, and Washington—"run-outs," as out-of-town concerts, where the orchestra makes the round trip in a day—and each venue had very different acoustics. During the rehearsals, Stokowski would instruct the players about altering the dynamics of each work for the individual halls: forte in one, fortissimo in another, a bit less in the third. At one point, he hesitated, smiling. "It's like a man with three wives." One brave brass player shouted, "You ought to know!" and Stokowski joined in the laughter.

As I had seen and heard at the first rehearsal he allowed me to attend, there were obviously sounds in his imagination he was working to replicate. A veteran member of the orchestra told me that in the 1930s, for one of his Bach transcriptions, Stokowski wanted a specific tone quality from Saul Caston, the orchestra's remarkable principal trumpet player. He had Caston try every mute available, but none produced the exact color and texture he wanted. He asked Caston to aim his trumpet up toward the ceiling, down toward the floor, then at the back of the stage, but nothing worked. Then he spied the carrying case for Caston's trumpet. "What's that?" Stokowski asked, pointing to a crumpled canvas bag on the floor. "Put that over the bell of your horn," he ordered, and Caston played through the fabric, producing the exact color Stokowski had in mind. Two Curtis students attending that evening's concert were baffled. What instrument had produced that sound? Was it brass or woodwind, high bassoon or muted horn? The two boys who came backstage to solve the mystery were Samuel Barber and Gian Carlo Menotti. They'd become two of the most prominent composers of the twentieth century.

"I prefer rehearsals to concerts," Stokowski would often tell me. Then, with a glint in his eye, he'd add, "But for some reason the management insists on our doing the concerts!" He wasn't completely joking. He loved the plasticity and experimentation rehearsals allowed, even though his concerts had more spontaneity than those of any other conductor I've encountered. In Stokowski's rehearsals, every repeat of a section embodied change: a tonal shading, a curve of phrase, an emphasis on a note or group of notes, a subtle rhythmic shift.

As orchestra members know too well, not every great conductor knows how to run a rehearsal. There's often wasted time—too much talking, repeating sections that don't need repeating (unless, of course, the conductor needs to learn the piece). Unlike many conductors who constantly use imagery or metaphor to convey their wishes in rehearsals, Stokowski mostly used gestures; he became more verbal when there was a discrepancy between the score and the parts, when he was in front of a less technically proficient ensemble, or if he became frustrated. (He'd also talk more when a rehearsal was being filmed.) When he did speak, the effect was powerful. "Violins," he said, at one point while rehearsing the overture to *Die Meistersinger*, "there is tremendous emotion in that music! Each note is a tear, and must fall like a tear!" In an excerpt from *Götterdämmerung*, he wanted a trombone entrance to be "like the sun coming up." (Occasionally in his scores, as a note to himself, he'd write the word "sunrise.") And in one burst of frustration, he suggested to a mostly male orchestra, "Gentlemen, buy the record!" But initial rehearsals, even with the Philadelphia Orchestra, could frustrate him. "You know how to play pianissimo!" he would shout, hitting the palm of his hand against the top of his music stand, "Do better!" They had not yet made the shift to Stokowskian dynamics, where a pianissimo was barely audible. Occasionally, however, he'd articulate his concept of phrasing: "In every phrase, there is one note—the keynote—that is most important. It's like the keystone in a building." His hands would trace the curve of an arch to illustrate how he wanted the phrase shaped—"spinning a phrase," as musicians say. The intensity and connectedness of the notes would lean toward that keynote, reaching it then curving away, giving each phrase an architectural shape. Each movement had its own, related architecture, fitting into and shaping the totality of the work.

As I had learned in 1964 (when he called the library asking if I'd help him write out music at the Barclay Hotel), even after a dress rehearsal he'd replay in his mind what he had last heard, thinking of ways to improve it—precise issues of color and nuance and balance. This would continue until the moment the concert began.

At the tops of memo sheets bearing the logos of the Ritz-Carlton in Boston or the Barclay Hotel in Philadelphia, in a more delicate hand than he used for writing letters or signing his name, Stokowski would note "before con" at the top; then he'd list last-minute changes he'd ask the musicians to implement.

For a 1969 performance of his *Boris Godunov*: "Symphonic Synthesis" with the Philadelphia Orchestra, a note reminded him to ask, backstage just before the performance, that in two places, only "two desks" of double basses should play pianissimo, the rest of the section would be tacet (silent). Also in *Boris*, there were places where he wanted the cellos not only to play pianissimo but to use mutes for additional muffling of the sound. As I learned from working with him, Stokowski might not have marked these last-minute changes into his score. They could have been solutions to problems presented by individual players or by the acoustics of specific halls. He might not have needed these changes for future performances with other orchestras or in other venues.

Sitting in his dressing room before concerts, where I had arrived early enough to give him time to meditate, he'd ask me to fetch one player after another so that he could refine the effects he wanted. When he used Ormandy's dressing room, he'd write memos on the official Philadelphia Orchestra stationery that bore Ormandy's name at the top, invariably turning the sheet upside down. He wanted to avoid any reminder that his rival was now at the helm of his former orchestra.

Chapter Thirteen

FOR CLOSE TO A DECADE, in his home, concert halls, and hotel rooms, Stokowski touched me lovingly but not romantically. But perhaps I was too young and inexperienced to pick up cues. I think now about the time we had first prepared lunch together in 1965, when I was eighteen. He had come up behind me and placed his hand on top of mine as I stirred food in a saucepan. When I looked back at him, we had smiled at each other. I suspect now that he would have liked me to have turned and embraced him.

He had, however, rejected a possible opportunity in 1966. Early one evening, I stood under the archway between his study and the secretary's office, looking with sadness at the time on the hand-painted wall clock. Leaving him, and New York, was always difficult. "It doesn't make sense for me to go all the way back to Philadelphia then come back here," I explained as he sat at his desk. I had, on occasion, made the round trip journey on two successive days. "It would save time and money if I just stayed in New York." His apartment was huge and, except for him and occasionally his two young sons and a housekeeper, the rooms were unoccupied.

He stared at me intently, then, with a little smile, clarified my request. "So you want to stay in New York?"

"It would seem reasonable," I replied. He continued to stare at me as I leaned against the arch. Then his smile disappeared.

"No!" he said, shaking his head and turning away from me. "You go home to your family!" (When I made the suggestion, I was being naive. I did not imagine sleeping with him.)

I also think about standing at the window near his desk one afternoon, gazing at the beauty of a Central Park sunset. Quietly, he came up behind me and gently enveloped me in his arms, holding me tenderly for a long while. But he didn't move forward to press against me, nor did I want him to. He was still an exalted figure, and sex with him was unthinkable.

Studying photos of myself at that age, I see a five-foot-two, blonde-haired young woman, perhaps cute but not glamorous—not someone who held the promise of a passionate encounter. My closeness to the Philadelphia Orchestra might have deterred him, but I doubt that. I probably looked at him with an innocent adoration he didn't want to violate; he might have sensed that any sexual move on his part would have been an abuse of trust. I like to think that his reticence was a way of protecting me, and our relationship. The intimacy between us was strongest when we sat and talked, listened to music together, and worked side by side. But years later, after he'd moved to Europe, it was I who wanted the relationship to change and he was more than willing.

I wish I knew the reasons for Stokowski's legendary libido. Did he have something to prove? Had there been childhood trauma? Sexual abuse? No one, including his family, knows for certain. Sex might have provided human contact without his having to reveal himself psychologically or talk about his origins. Despite his behavior toward me, I suspect that he had a form of sexual addiction. In Donna Staley Kline's book, *An American Virtuoso on the World Stage: Olga Samaroff Stokowski*,[1] Madam Samaroff, the first Mrs. Stokowski, is quoted as having told a friend that her husband's dalliances were not altogether his fault "…because if you continually put liquor under the nose of a man who loves to drink, no matter how strong he wants to be, he will eventually take a drink.

---

[1] Texas A&M University Press, 1996.

...He loved women, and they were continually there throwing themselves at him." I doubt if Stokowski had any interest in being "strong." Or perhaps he was simply doing what many men can only fantasize about.

I knew he was involved with other women during the time I was working with him. For a while in the 1960s, a diminutive, English-accented woman in her forties or fifties had a room in his Fifth Avenue apartment. She served as his housekeeper but I suspected that there was a romance in progress. (When she was out, Stokowski would sneak me into her room to see her adorable Siamese kittens. He always seemed anxious that we leave before their owner returned.) Stewart Warkow, a friend of mine who had worked for two of Stokowski's orchestras (the American Symphony and the Symphony of the Air), and later as executive director of Carnegie Hall, said he knew Stokowski was having affairs in the 1960s; characteristically, the Maestro kept them secret.[2] One of Stokowski's associate conductors at the American Symphony told me that he discovered, to his chagrin, that he and his boss had been sharing a girlfriend.

"How did you deal with that?" I asked.

He shrugged at the inevitability of the answer: "I gave her up."

A member of the ASO confirmed for me that Stokowski had romantic relationships with some of the women in the orchestra, and I recently learned that around 1970, when he was in his late eighties, he frequently shared a bed with Natalie, one of the women I had met at the Dell in 1964.

Many writers have portrayed him as a playboy and a womanizer, but not everyone was that kind. In her memoir, Rosamond Bernier described him as a "notorious lothario [sic]." The description seems apt: a man who obsessively seduces and deceives women. He clearly wasn't seeking lasting relationships. I suspect that, after sex, his goal—conscious or not—was eventually to leave his part-

---

[2] I think he liked having some "secrets," particularly those about his relationships with prominent women, revealed. On occasion, he'd mention having had a "Swedish girlfriend"—an obvious reference to Greta Garbo.

ners. Never content, he was always looking for the next object of interest, romantically and artistically.[3]

The intimacy these women shared with him seemed to be more physical than emotional. Gloria Vanderbilt, in her book *It Seemed Important at the Time: A Romance Memoir*,[4] wrote,

> No, I never did break through to him—except in passion. There he was free and unedited, giving me all of himself in wordless intimacy. But it wasn't enough. Afterward I would be alone once again and living with a stranger, the glass wall impenetrable…

None of his lovers knew where he was just before or after their liaisons, and none of them (except his first wife, Olga, who met his parents) knew the truth about his background.

Even today, when I tell a musician that I knew him, I see a glint in the eyes and a knowing smile. In October 2012, I mentioned to pianist Leon Fleisher that I had known and worked with Stokowski. "So you were able to escape his clutches?" he quickly responded.

"That's a complicated question," I told him, but nothing more. He probably wouldn't have believed that the Maestro had been quite the gentleman with me.

I still wonder about that reticence. I wasn't a world-class beauty or a member of society, but that wouldn't have mattered to him; his lovers—not his wives—included the less attractive and the socially undistinguished.

I wonder, too, about the cause of his temper and his need for control. His music was free and flexible, but his interpersonal rela-

---

[3] He wanted to marry Garbo in the late 1930s, even telling the press that they had wedding plans. I don't know if he loved her or if he coveted her as a prize that would boost his image and his ego. I don't doubt that he loved Gloria Vanderbilt, but I wonder if he would have married her if she hadn't been from a renowned, wealthy family. Unlike Stokowski, Ms. Vanderbilt didn't have to invent a distinguished family history. Nor did Evangeline Johnson.

[4] Simon & Schuster, 2004.

tionships were not. As I'd often seen, he could become angry and withholding without warning. A few of his children told me that they loved him but were frightened of him (I heard this from the offspring of many famous musicians), and they obeyed his edict not to ask about his family in England (which, of course, was their family, too). Everyone followed his wishes as if they were visiting a country he ruled. Otherwise, they risked banishment. While this could be frightening to a devoted friend like me, it probably seemed like the threat of annihilation to a child.

Everyone had to be cautious with him. There were times when he wanted to talk and times when he wanted silence, times when he wanted attention and times when he didn't even want to be looked at. He and I, and others who might be present, would be engulfed in awkward silence as we sat together, not acknowledging each other's presence. If someone asked a question he didn't want to answer, he'd ignore it—and the person—completely. Those of us who enabled this kind of behavior were, I thought, making a contribution to his art. Stokowski's biographer Oliver Daniel, during a conversation with me, suggested that Stokowski's narcissistic behavior might have stemmed from feelings of inferiority—possible "dissatisfaction with himself." This might also explain his need to reject his humble ancestry, but no one really knows.

Intimidation was a tool many conductors used at that time. Whether their musicians worshipped or hated them—the great majority I knew respected them musically, if not personally—most feared them. And they weren't always benevolent dictators, even though they might have perceived their actions as beneficial to the quality of the music. As I witnessed, even Stokowski's beloved Philadelphia Orchestra wasn't spared his wrath. I saw this first at his rehearsal of Ravel's *Boléro* at the Dell. The musicians were in a happy, playful mood, stamping their feet and cheering as each instrument came in on cue to state the famous theme, and the Maestro seemed to have no problem with their antics. Debussy's *Prelude to the Afternoon of a Faun* was next, and as the sensual, impressionistic piece began, the rowdiness resumed. With one powerful kick, Stokowski suddenly sent his music stand flying into the players in front of him, his score landing in the violin section. A stunned silence prevailed. "You should consider yourselves fortunate to play the music of Debussy!" he shouted. But moments later, his mood changed again. A bird landed on top of the shell over the stage and, accompanied by the orchestra, sang its heart out. Stokowski stopped the musicians, cocked his head upward and, with a smile, repeatedly implored, "Quiet, little bird," until it finished its solo.

Members of the Philadelphia Orchestra when Stokowski was music director, and later in his American Symphony, had more to fear than just his temper; they could lose their jobs with little or no notice. When I worked at Settlement Music School during my studies at Temple University, I met a sweet, gentle member of the violin faculty who had played in the Philadelphia Orchestra when Stokowski was music director. Stokowski, I heard, had singled him out during a rehearsal and pointed offstage. "Out!" he said, and suddenly the man was unemployed, in spite of the fact that he'd done nothing wrong and had a family to support. Colleagues told me that the musician never fully recovered. Lawrence Foster, who became music director of the Houston Symphony a dozen years after Stokowski's departure, told me another characteristic story. Stokowski had arrived early for a concert. After listening to one of the violinists practice in an adjoining dressing room, Stokowski called the personnel manager. "Who is that?" he asked. The manager told him the musician's name. "Fire him," Stokowski said.

He pretended not to know the names of longtime members of his orchestras—"You, violin," he'd address someone whose name he knew well. It was a way of diminishing people, of keeping them off balance. Such tactics also worked well for Toscanini, Szell, and Reiner but were not necessary for the likes of Mitropoulos, Munch, and Walter. Stokowski never would have sweetly welcomed his players as Walter had on my recording of the rehearsal of Beethoven's Ninth. Stokowski's gestures, not his words, invited and encouraged his players to make music.

I admit that I had loved his anger about the Debussy at the Dell. While I wish he had communicated kindly, I knew his annoyance evidenced his devotion to the music. I'd often see him express displeasure, through anger and humor, to musicians who didn't show total dedication to their art.

He'd become infuriated with players who weren't doing their best. "No!" he'd yell. "You must watch! You must do better!" while the musicians froze in their seats. Sometimes he told them that they played "like babies" or "sissies," but his harshest criticism came when they weren't playing with enough emotion: "You're too intellectual!"

His behavior toward his musicians might be understandable within the context of that era, but why did he impose strict rules on friends and family? He would become annoyed if someone used the word "love" if it did not involve a living thing. (You shouldn't say that you loved a certain type of food, for example, because it couldn't love you back.) Another forbidden word was "more" when one was offering additional helpings of food or drink. He said that could imply that someone was greedy—eating or drinking too much. "Would you like some tea?" he'd ask, offering someone a second or third cup. To this day, I never ask guests if they'd like "more" of something I'm serving.

I was able to gain a bit of insight into his psychology one evening when the phone rang at home. "It's Maestro!" my mother announced, and I picked up the receiver.

"Hello, Maestro," I greeted him.

A stern voice responded: "This is *not* Maestro!" I didn't know what was happening but played along.

"Oh, I thought it was. Who is this?" He gave a fictitious name, using Mister, not a first name.

"What are you doing?" he asked. I told him I had been listening to "Stokowski's" new double recording of Stravinsky's *L'Histoire du Soldat*, one with the narration and spoken roles in English, and one in French. "Listen to the French one," he advised. "That is the more authentic, because Madeleine Milhaud and Jean Pierre

Aumont are speaking in their native language." We chatted about the recordings and the piece, then said goodbye.

"Why did Maestro call?" my mother asked, thrilled to have spoken with him, but I had no idea. I didn't occur to me then that he might have been lonely.

Stokowski's demeanor—on and off the podium—was the result of a highly complex, obviously fragmented psychology. He believed in psychotherapy (I was with him once when he called a psychiatrist, enthusiastically arranging an appointment for a family member), but he would never have submitted to the process, even if he had allowed himself to recognize the need. Music lovers should be grateful that he never gained self-knowledge. His audiences were—and through videos and recordings remain—the beneficiaries of whatever demons he exorcised through his art.

Hearing about Stokowski's demanding behavior, a friend of mine recently asked why I wanted to be close to him, why it was worth the effort. I could have attended his concerts, even worked with him, but not shared a close relationship. I showed my friend photos of him, but they only hinted at the power of his personality; his movie clips provided only a bit more evidence of his charisma.

The desire to be close to him obviously resulted from my own psychological wounds. And because his arrogance hinted at his emotional unavailability, he was both a challenge and a perfect subject for obsession. From the time we met, I knew instinctively what he wanted and needed; I had developed highly sensitive antennae by coping with my emotionally ill mother (who could be plunged into panic by a single word or comment) and an abusive father. I could almost read minds. But I also realized that I couldn't let Stokowski know that I was consciously aware of what he needed. This wasn't a game; it was essential to having a relationship with him.

And the sixty-four-year age gap? Strange as it may sound, I never thought about it. Backstage in 1964, Stokowski had asked my age. When I said eighteen, he had responded, "You are eighteen going on thirty-five!" But if I was eighteen going on thirty-five, he was eighty-two going on thirty-five—not an average octogenarian.

He behaved and thought like a young man, and moved with the vitality and grace of someone decades younger. People who knew him described him as "ageless." I've always thought of him as a stone in a stream, the generations moving past him, others growing old while he did not.

An example of this vitality involved his performances of the brutally difficult Ives Fourth Symphony. He was eighty-three in 1965 when he premiered and recorded it with the American Symphony in Carnegie Hall, and eighty-eight when he repeated the work in Philharmonic Hall. The recording sessions had taken place from 2 a.m. to 6 a.m., 10 p.m. to 1:30 a.m., and midnight to 3 a.m., the last of which was filmed for broadcast. In a review of the 1970 performance, the *New York Times* had written,

> "Could Leopold Stokowski, at age 88, be at the peak of his powers?... with a concentration and energy that would have seemed astounding in any conductor, let along [sic] one nearing 90."

Even his tempos didn't slow as they often do when conductors age. He stayed healthy and youthful by supplementing his good genes with yoga (when it was still relatively unknown in the West), a healthful diet, optimism, and a love of change and innovation.

He abhorred the traditional and the habitual. I witnessed an amusing example of this one morning when Stokowski, his secretary, and I were having tea at her desk (he filled the cups by dipping them into a pot of tea he had prepared). After several minutes, Jean rose and said she'd be right back.

"Where are you going?" he asked.

Jean looked at him in amazement. "I'm going to get the mail," she sputtered, baffled by his question.

"Why must you get it now?" he challenged.

"I always get the mail at ten-thirty," Jean replied, a bit defensively. I could see that she instantly realized she had given the wrong response.

"Sit down," he commanded. "Why must you get the mail at the same time every day? You must have a better reason for doing something than just doing it that way every day!"

I think part of his dislike of routine—artistic and personal—was related to his awareness of the unpredictability of life (he also wanted to keep things interesting). He often talked about this, particularly when I told him about plans I'd made. "Look at your watch!" he'd order, pointing to my wrist. "What time is it?" I'd tell him the time. "You don't know what will happen in the next five minutes of your life!" His aversion to routine included any sort of repetition, one of the reasons that he rarely conducted the works of Bruckner—with their frequent repeats—and why he'd occasionally cut sections of works (even in standard repertoire) he considered redundant.

Our goodbyes, however, were always the same. I'd put on my coat and make my way to his desk, where he was engrossed in a score. Sensing me standing there, he'd break his concentration, adjusting to the room around him like someone awakening. Then he'd stand up and clear his throat or cough slightly, shielding his mouth with his hand, his forefinger resting across the space above his upper lip.

"Do you have your train ticket?" he'd ask.

"I do," I'd answer.

"Do you have enough money?" he'd inquire, watching me intently.

"Yes, Maestro, I do."

He'd hesitate, looking concerned. "Are you certain?"

"Yes, Maestro, I am."

"What if you see something at the train station that you'd like to buy?"

"I have enough money," I'd keep repeating, until he was reassured. Sometimes he gallantly kissed my hand. Most often, he'd take my face gently in his hands, turning it to kiss each cheek then lower it to kiss my forehead. Then, with a wave of the great hand, he'd send me on my way. Sitting down at the desk, he'd immediately become absorbed in a score as I stood in the foyer waiting for the elevator. I always hoped it wouldn't come too quickly as I looked at him through the doorway, seeing the curve of his back as he leaned over the desk, the light of the overhead lamp illuminating his hair. Sometimes, in the concert hall, among thousands of people who had risen en masse in a standing ovation, I'd picture him quietly alone at his desk.

Chapter Fourteen

"DON'T LET ANYONE LOOK AT these!" Stokowski would order as he handed me his scores in his dressing room after a concert. "Don't put them down! You hold them!" I did as I was told. We both knew that soon, as he greeted people backstage, musicians who had been in the audience would approach me, smiling and reaching out for the scores. I'd always smile back, press them tightly to my chest, and shake my head "no." These musicians—and occasionally music critics—were eager to see the changes Stokowski had made to the scores.

What did he want to hide, and why did he want to hide it? Those questions raise issues that are at the heart of classical music interpretation: how closely an artist should adhere to a composer's wishes; the kinds of changes a performer may implement; how much interpretive leeway he or she may have. Because Stokowski was famous for taking liberties, the continuing controversy about his career raises compelling questions about the responsibilities of *all* performing artists, particularly musicians, to deliver what the creator of a work intended.

What were his intentions? I constantly heard Stokowski speak about wanting to convey what the composer wanted—what he said was "in the soul of the composer"—and he assumed that was maximum expressiveness. So he'd take liberties, departing—sometimes slightly, sometimes considerably—from what the composer had notated. He'd change, add, or omit notes, or, through gesture, would alter what the score had asked for. This didn't necessarily indicate that he thought the composer hadn't done his job adequately but that a particular "message" could be enhanced.[1] He certainly wasn't the only conductor who took liberties but he did so more frequently than others. Was he justified in doing what he did? Was he playing co-composer?

I remember sitting with Morton Gould in Carnegie Hall as Stokowski rehearsed one of his works. Even with the composer present, Stokowski wasn't completely sticking to what was written. But Gould leaned over to me and whispered, "I'm listening to what he's doing and wondering why *I* didn't think of that!" Gould looked up at Stokowski on the podium and signaled his approval. But, as I'd learn a few months later, Stokowski was well aware that the liberties he took might not be gratefully received by *all* composers. We were alone in his dressing room after a concert when he astounded me by making a confession. Grinning like a naughty boy, he said, "When I get to heaven or hell, I don't know what Bach, Beethoven, and Brahms will do to me!"

And yet—there were always inconsistencies—he was respectful enough of the written note to be adamant about fixing errors in scores and parts. I knew this because it was one of my responsibilities to correct mistakes in the materials in his library, as well as in the scores of his transcriptions that I helped prepare for publication.

It is, of course, critically important for every note in a piece of music—and there can be hundreds of thousands of them in large orchestral works—to be correct in the scores and parts and to be played accurately in performance. In the case of an unclear manuscript or of a conflict between two versions of a manuscript, there can be endless debate among musicians and musicologists

---

[1] Some of the changes he made reflected the increased power, range, and facility of modern instruments due to improvements in design and materials. For example, he felt it was obvious that Beethoven wanted some lines for wind instruments to go into a higher register, but the instruments of that time weren't able to produce those notes. Having modern instruments at his disposal, Stokowski rewrote the original notes for the higher register.

about accuracy, particularly if the original manuscript is compromised—illegible or incomplete. A discrepancy between notes in different manuscript versions, or the correctness of a changed note in a manuscript, might require a good deal of sleuthing: Who made the change? The composer? A copyist? The conductor or soloist in a premiere performance?

Stokowski's concern for accuracy in performance materials was revealed in a letter he wrote to Bill Smith in 1965. He asked Bill if he'd share a list of mistakes he had discovered in a Stravinsky score, writing: "Sometimes in the loudest tuttis[2] it is difficult to hear all the details which, nevertheless, are important to have correct." And Oliver Daniel, in his massive biography *Stokowski: A Counterpoint of View*,[3] writes about the preparations for the premiere performance of Arnold Schoenberg's complex Piano Concerto. The soloist, who was a close friend and colleague of Schoenberg's, prepared a twelve-page list of mistakes he had discovered in the parts during the initial rehearsals. At the next session, Stokowski had the orchestra correct every error. However, had the composer not been as prominent as Schoenberg, who was alive and listening (and had a colleague as soloist), Stokowski would have corrected the errors but might have felt more freedom with his interpretation. But he dared to challenge Rachmaninoff about the interpretation of one of his works. A 1930 *Time* magazine cover story about Stokowski reported that he and Rachmaninoff, at a recent rehearsal, "almost came to blows over the tempo of a Rachmaninoff concerto which Stokowski felt he knew better than the composer." A similar situation had occurred in a 1926 rehearsal of Rachmaninoff's *Three Russian Songs*, Op. 41, dedicated to Stokowski and the Philadelphia Orchestra. Despite emotional pleas from the composer, Stokowski refused to slow the tempo to the speed Rachmaninoff wanted.

At 1067, I became Stokowski's accomplice, making changes to the scores and parts as he instructed. His apartment became my classroom: I learned from every change I marked in the parts—

---

2   Sections in which all the instruments are playing simultaneously.
3   Dodd, Mead, 1982.

added notes that enriched an orchestration's color or reinforced dramatic effects; cuts that removed sections he considered redundant; eliminated notes that preserved the musicians' strength for more important sections or clarified the orchestral balance. By comparing the original with what Stokowski wanted, and understanding the differences that resulted, I learned about harmony, theory, orchestration, musicology, and music history. I also learned about musical ethics, because the changes he made were so controversial. Although I questioned whether I was doing the right thing, I admit that I loved the results.

Many knowledgeable people, particularly the "purists" and musicologists Stokowski regarded with disdain, were aghast when he altered composers' notes and when he took interpretive liberties with whatever notes were there, altered or original. A musician's right to take such liberties, and what the limitations of those liberties should be, remain hotly debated issues. Can the brass, for instance, legitimately be asked to play a phrase in a register higher than what the composer had asked for, to heighten the dramatic effect? Can more than the originally assigned number of instruments be asked to play a given section, to intensify the emotional impact? Should a clarinet or an English horn be asked to double a viola part, providing a different coloration? Should several measures, or even a few notes, be omitted to make a work more "effectively" concise? Stokowski thought so, but he wouldn't have admitted it publicly.

When I made even a small change to what a composer had notated, I knew I was in dangerous territory. If one note could be changed, why not two or two hundred or more, until the composer's work would no longer be recognizable? Where was that line to be drawn? And even if notes aren't changed, the style in which they're played can be questioned. When judging how emotional or sensual or controlled a performance "should" be, are all the guidelines to be found in the score, or should performance traditions play a role? Musicians know that those traditions, accumulated over a period of years, often drift from the composer's intentions. In a radio interview I did with the cellist-conductor Mstislav Rostropovich in the 1980s, he said a work of music was "like a ship": Over time, it would accumulate the "barnacles" of incorrect performance practices. One must, he said, return to the score to clearly see what the composer originally wanted. (Stokowski, commenting about things musical and non-musical, often told me that he considered following tradition "a form of laziness.")

However, given the ubiquity of live performances and recordings, it's difficult for musicians to delete memories of performances they've heard. And when they return to the score, how do they know how fast is fast, or how slow is slow? Metronome markings noted by the composer—which provide an actual, set speed for the music—don't appear in every work, and the tempos of sections that are not marked become relative. These musicians, of course, have studied music history and performance practices and know what's "correct" to the era of the piece they're performing. But musical notation, while providing a huge amount of information, blessedly embodies a lot of ambiguity, allowing for what we call "interpretation." Otherwise, all performances would basically sound alike.

Musical notation, I'd often hear Stokowski say, was "just black marks on the page." The notes were static until they were brought to life in performance. This was also his way of saying that a composer's wishes could never be fully communicated. He also referred to notes as being "imprisoned within the bar lines," speaking as if he had sympathy for the notes. He wanted as much flexibility and expressiveness as he felt the drama of the music demanded.

This philosophy formed the foundation of his musical identity. The now-defunct magazine *The Musical Leader*, in its February 19, 1925, issue, wrote about Stokowski conducting the Curtis Institute orchestra. One young player held a note longer than Stokowski had indicated because "it was a quarter-note on the paper." Stokowski told him that there were enough "paper musicians" in the world, and that "murder has been committed for less than that, young man."

I witnessed a similar situation at a Philadelphia Orchestra rehearsal in the mid-1960s. In one work, the cello parts had a quarter note—a single, short beat—held over from the previous measure, then a three-beat rest, noting silence. The cellos played the one beat and stopped. Stokowski leaned sideways toward the cellos, his upturned right hand vibrating, asking for more. But they had played what was written.

"Why did you stop?" Stokowski challenged. Lorne Munroe, the principal cellist, looked up at him, amazed. "We have a quarter note then rests, Maestro."

Stokowski stared at him. "If you stop at a traffic light and a policeman waves you on, what do you do?" The quarter note grew in length. But purists would have said that Stokowski had no right to hold the note longer than the composer had indicated.

He had the imagination—the vision—to understand how even small details can produce powerful effects. The memory of his Mahler Second Symphony with the Philadelphia Orchestra in 1967 still gives me chills. In other conductors' performances of that work I have experienced, the chorus (which sings only in the fifth, final, half-hour-long movement) is usually onstage from the beginning of the symphony. The chorus members stay seated until the opening of the final movement, or until it makes its initial entrance—about midway through—and then remains standing until the end. But Stokowski instructed the singers to stay in their seats as they sang their soft, prayer-like entrance, and through the thunderous music that builds to the climax, close to the end of the symphony. At that point, when they triumphantly sang the words "Aufersteh'n, ja aufersteh'n" ("Rise again, yes, rise again"), the organ entering with the chorus, Stokowski had them stand *as they started to sing*, and the sound of the 150 voices soared upward.[4] Those performances were unforgettable. Even nature seemed impressed:

---

4 Stokowski penciled those directions into his score: "chor sitting" at its initial entrance, then "chor stand" at the beginning of the powerful section. Another detail was a bit more controversial: at the jubilant ending of the symphony, Mahler wrote eight measures of strings playing tremolo—moving their bows rapidly back and forth to produce an exciting, tension-filled effect—but had them change to regular, sustained bowing for the final four measures. Stokowski had the strings continue the tremolo until the very end.

During intermission in New York's Philharmonic Hall, I stood at a window looking up Broadway as thick snow began to fall and bolts of lightning shot through the sky.

When he spoke of the "clear message, in tones, of great music," Stokowski was referring to its expressiveness; any philosophical meaning would be conveyed through that. "I am trying to get to the spirit of the music, how it *feels*," he would say in rehearsals, often pressing both fists to his heart. He meant, of course, how it felt *to him*. The changes he made not only helped facilitate and intensify what he felt the composer wanted to convey, they allowed him to conduct these works with the fullest emotional involvement.

Whatever his intentions may have been, Stokowski sometimes went too far even for his admirers. In April 1971, I sat in one of the first-tier boxes in Carnegie Hall for his rehearsal of Tchaikovsky's Symphony No. 4 with the American Symphony Orchestra. The work opens with a bassoon and horn fanfare which, about fifteen seconds in, has an upward leap from one note to another. Most conductors perform this in a straightforward manner, as it's written, with no strong emphasis on the higher note and the tempo remaining steady. Stokowski not only added a slur that had the instruments swoop up to the higher note—which he wanted considerably louder than the first—he added trumpets and trombones (which are supposed to come in a few beats later) to the horns and bassoons. He also pulled the tempo like taffy, stretching and elongating it to the point of distortion. I looked down at Stokowski in his navy blue shirt, his hair unruly, his feet several inches apart on the podium, and watched his right hand pull back behind him then surge forward. I wondered what he could have been thinking. But the idiosyncrasies softened for the performances and mostly disappeared for the recording. (One reviewer, in *Music and Musicians* magazine in July 1971, called the recording "a tremendous performance…very improvisatory in approach.")

When he handed me his scores in his dressing room after concerts, he was concerned about others actually seeing the changes he had made. Knowledgeable people who knew the original could hear what he had done, but for some reason he didn't want anyone to see the evidence in the scores. I was shocked that he bequeathed his entire collection of scores and parts to the Manhattan School of Music; later, with my help, it went to the Curtis Institute, then to the University of Pennsylvania. I never thought he'd want anyone, even after his death, to see evidence of the alterations he had made.

Back then I couldn't understand why Stokowski's overtly emotional interpretations didn't appeal to everyone. Musicians, of course, may have thought that they weren't what the composer had had in mind. Or they may have made some people uncomfortable. But for Stokowski, a man loath to reveal himself personally, the abstraction of symphonic music may have been the safest medium of expression. Like other performers, he was expressing *his* emotions, not just those of the composers.

In all the performing arts, emotion is most often ascribed to the psychology of the creator. While people frequently seek parallels between a playwright's life and the content of his plays, rarely will anyone say about an actor, "He must have experienced all the emotions and situations presented in the play. His performance is so convincing that, on some level, it must be autobiographical." We just say that he or she is a great actor. The angst in Mahler's music, we assume, is a reflection of the composer's state of mind; but doesn't a performance of searing emotional power reveal something about the psyche of the performer? Is it possible for a musician to extract emotion from a score if he or she hasn't experienced those feelings? Stokowski spoke to me about this many times. "No one can take out of his pocket what is not already there," he'd say. By his own admission, this austere, controlled man had tremendous turbulence inside of him.

But there were also charming, childlike traits in many of his interpretations. I had seen this playful part of him when he had impishly blown across the top of a wine bottle during our first lunch together in New York. I also saw it when I opened many of his scores. Like a schoolboy, he had pasted photographs and drawings of the composers, cut out of magazines and newspapers, inside the front and back covers. There were also program notes, letters from composers, and pictures of musicians whose interpretations he admired.

I saw this playfulness again one evening when I hadn't needed to rush back to Philadelphia for a concert. We were relaxing at his desk when he excitedly asked, "Do you want to hear the gong?" "Yes!" I answered. "That would be wonderful!" He had an extensive collection of percussion instruments that included magnificent Asian gongs molded from mixtures of rare metals, purchased when he traveled to places like Bali. "Meet me in the hallway!" he ordered. He showed up a few minutes later, his hair falling in front of both ears, holding a large, flat, circular gong with thick black Oriental characters painted near the top. The instrument was suspended from a rope he held in his left hand. Happy as a kid, he began to "warm," or prime, the gong, hitting it slowly and softly near its edge with a double-headed wooden mallet to get its body vibrating. He then struck it more forcefully, just off center, to make it "speak." He hit it repeatedly until the sound roared at me like an oncoming train—a terrifying rush that soon would have become physically overpowering. When he saw me back away, he placed his hand on the front of the gong to still the vibrations. Then he held up the large wooden mallet. "Look," he said proudly, "this was made especially for me!" and pointed to the "L" on one side and "S" on the other. For a fleeting moment, I wondered if they actually stood for "loud" and "soft."

One afternoon he ran down the long hallway of the apartment to the back room where I was working. I was startled by his sudden arrival. "Look at this!" he ordered, thrusting a score of the Beethoven Seventh in front of me. "Look at this violin part! I never noticed this before! Isn't it remarkable!" I was working on the parts to the symphony, and later that day, he looked over my shoulder, reaching down to pick up a part for a different instrument. I watched his eyes narrow and his forehead crease with concentration as he held the music in his left hand and began, almost imperceptibly, to conduct with his right. He started to whistle the part softly, then sing it, most likely hearing the full orchestra in his imagination. His gestures became increasingly animated until he was fully conducting, as if there was an orchestra in front of him. Abruptly, he stopped, realizing that he was in his home. He looked at me, cleared his throat, and left the room. After six decades of conducting it, the work still thrilled him. Perhaps it was the child in him, and his sense of wonder, that allowed him to appreciate—without prejudice—the music of his own time and of other cultures. He had instinctively known that his children's concert audiences, when he performed contemporary music for them in Philadelphia, would do the same. I wish he hadn't worked so hard to hide this delightful part of his personality from public view.

Many people have said that Stokowski was spoiled by success—that it was the strongest influence on his complex personality—but I think it was the opposite: that his personality was shaped by the failure of not being able to successfully compose. Being "just" an interpreter and not a creator had to have been the defining disappointment of his life. There are clues, musical and personal, pointing to who he really was.

Stokowski had conducted an ensemble for the first time when he was twelve; he later said he decided at that time to become a conductor. I suspect that he wanted the combined career of conducting and composing, not unusual in those days. Composer-conductors like Mahler, Strauss, and Rachmaninoff had prominent double careers, and there were many other conductors who composed but whose works were not of high enough quality to enter the standard repertoire.

His transcript from the Royal College of Music shows piano as his "Principal Study," and organ as his secondary subject. But even though he played those instruments (and some tuba and violin), his eye was probably on the podium. However, for the Christmas term of 1903, when Stokowski was twenty-one, his Principal Study was "Composition only." In 1908, when he was organist and choirmaster at St. Bartholomew's Church, "Sto," as he signed the letter, wrote to his former teacher and mentor Walford Davies. He didn't mention his work at the church or his plans to be a conductor. He told Davies that he had written "an oratorio, a number of smaller things, and for the last nine months have been engaged on an opera."[5]

As a wedding gift for Stokowski's first bride, Olga Samaroff (whom he married in 1911, when he was twenty-nine), Stokowski's father handcrafted an elaborate wooden jewelry box. He inlaid into its top not a theme from one of Bach's great organ works—which his son had performed at both St. James's Church and St. Bartholomew's—or a theme from one of the orchestral masterworks that the young Stokowski had begun to interpret in his new career as a conductor, but, instead, he quoted a section from one of Stokowski's original compositions. His self-identity at that time was as a composer. It also might have represented what his parents expected him to be.

The most revealing insight into Stokowski's feelings about his own artistic identity is buried in Gloria Vanderbilt's book *Black Knight, White Knight*, where she wrote about her ambition to be an actress. Her then-husband supported her efforts and even made contacts on her behalf. But, she wrote, "Of course L. thinks acting can't be compared to painting and writing because it's an interpretive craft…"[6]

In addition to satisfying his own creative impulses (and perhaps the expectations of others), Stokowski might have wanted the immortality accorded to creators, not re-creators. He was well

---

5 His daughter Sadja—the younger of his two children with Evangeline Johnson—told me that when she was born, in 1930, he had identified himself on the birth certificate as a composer, not a conductor or a musician.
6 Alfred A. Knopf, 1987

aware of the ephemeral nature of conducting: An unrecorded concert lives on only in memory, and performance styles, recorded or not, pass out of fashion.

Retired members of the Philadelphia Orchestra told me that Stokowski occasionally played through his own compositions at private rehearsals. He always used pseudonyms; only later did the musicians learn that their conductor was also the composer. One work of his called *Reverie*, possibly dating from his student days, was first credited to "Slavici," but by the time I reworked the catalog, he was claiming credit for it. He did not, however, perform it often, nor is there any record of him ever performing his own symphony. In those closed sessions, Stokowski was testing the quality of his work but not doing so publicly. He didn't want to risk being judged by audiences, critics, or members of his orchestra, particularly in light of his success as a conductor.

Many great conductors have been mediocre composers—Stokowski, Klemperer, and Koussevitzky among them; they never achieved the double careers that others had. While they could recognize weaknesses in their own compositions, they weren't able to improve them. (Even if the pieces were well-crafted, they might have been uninspired.) Like other gifted conductors, Stokowski was able to judge the basic quality of a new or unfamiliar work by looking at the score and hearing it in his mind. I'd sit with him as he went through stacks of unsolicited scores submitted by hopeful composers. He'd read through the works using the extended forefinger and little finger of his right hand, moving them vertically down the page. "Right here," he'd say, halting the movement of his hand, "it will not 'sound.'" The word "sound," said with an emphasis that conveyed its importance, meant that the music wouldn't ring, or blend; the color would be unbalanced—too thick or too thin. But even he needed to hear a work live to know what the actual sound would be. Stokowski wrote about this in a 1939 letter to C. David Hocker, then manager of the Philadelphia Opera Company. Stokowski had apparently been asked to judge new scores but didn't have time to study them, as his letter stated:

> My experience is one never knows how good a symphony or an opera is until after one has performed it. I don't think one can judge completely from the score. One can evaluate technical things very completely from the score, but the emotional qualities and the deep beauty of the music can only be known through performance, in my opinion.

I saw evidence of this at a Dell concert on June 21, 1965, when Stokowski performed Vincent Persichetti's *The Hollow Men* for Solo Trumpet and Strings. In his dressing room afterward, Stokowski told me that the piece had disappointed him. "It didn't sound as I had expected," he said.

Whatever weaknesses that existed in Stokowski's own music had to have involved thematic and formal structure more than orchestration; his transcriptions (and his own symphony) were evidence that he was a highly gifted orchestrator. He was not, however, able to compose a high-quality piece from beginning to end. As transcriber and orchestrator, he was able to put flesh and features on a skeleton of someone else's creation or do aural plastic surgery on features that already existed. That's probably the main reason why transcribing was so important to him: It was the closest he could come to composing.

There are strong parallels between the work of a musical transcriber and a literary translator. Both must consider the intention of the original creator—the composer and the author. A transcription is, after all, a type of translation. When he transcribed works for the forces of the full symphony orchestra, Stokowski took the composers' perspective. "In giving this sublime melody orchestral expression," he writes in the Foreword to the score of his transcription of Bach's *Komm süsser Tod*, "I have tried to imagine what Bach would do, had he the rich resources of the orchestra of today at his disposal." Transcribing was also another way for him to bring great music to the broadest possible audience. When he was a church organist—years before radio and recordings made music widely available—he transcribed orchestral works by the likes of Wagner, Mendelssohn, Schubert, and Tchaikovsky for the organ; when he became a conductor, he transcribed organ works for the orchestra.

Today, transcriptions are less controversial than they were years ago; it's no longer incriminating for musical sophisticates to admit that they like or approve of transcriptions. I remember the debates in the 1960s about the validity of a version of a work that wasn't done by the original work's creator. It's an argument I've never understood. Is there any reason not to "reimagine" a work of art? If a painter is inspired by a centuries-old Venetian sketch and wants to represent the same scene in oil, should anyone object? One wonders why a musical transcription or any new conception of a work of art can't be judged completely on its own, independent of the original.[7] But even now, nothing will identify someone as a second-rate intellect more quickly than his admitting his preference for a transcription over the original; it's not unlike someone preferring the movie version of a book to the book itself. Today, the discussion is more about the quality of a transcription than its right to exist.

People have often asked me if the transcriptions were products of Stokowski's ego. I learned, a bit painfully, that they were not. He didn't, in fact, always want credit for creating them. (He was originally outed in a December 1930 *New York Times* story: "Stokowski Admits Writing Orchestrations of Bach.") In the mid-1960s, I began to write program notes for the Philadelphia Orchestra's student concerts and in late 1968 I brought a program booklet with me to Stokowski's apartment. He paged through it and saw my byline. "How long have you been doing this?" he asked, but made no other comment. (I wondered if he was annoyed that I hadn't shared my writing with him before this.) He then turned to the back page and saw the announcement of his February 13, 1969, concert. He had programmed four of his transcriptions; one was listed as "MOUSSORGSKY-Stokowski .... Symphonic

---

[7] If, however, a work is based on or derived from another work and isn't just influenced by it, its debt to the original should certainly be acknowledged.

Synthesis from Boris Gudounov." (They hadn't identified him as transcriber of Palestrina's *Adoramus te*, Victoria's "Jesu dulcis memoria," or Bach's Chaconne, just of the Mussorgsky, using the French spelling of the composer's name.)[8] He fumed. "I told them *not* to print my name as transcriber for *any* of these works! I told them to list only the composers' names, *not mine*!" He was in no mood to hear my opinion: that omitting the fact that the works were not the original versions would be misleading, if not untruthful. He must have then spoken up—loudly—to the Philadelphia Orchestra management. His credit was omitted from the huge poster advertising the concert outside the Academy and from all successive concert programs (including for the concert itself). And, because it was a special event to benefit the orchestra's Pension Fund, the program didn't contain background notes on the pieces. There was no way for anyone to know that the composers hadn't written exactly what they heard that night.[9]

His motivation for wanting these omissions might have been uncharacteristically self-effacing. In the foreword to the published score of his transcription of the Passacaglia and Fugue in C minor, he wrote: "This passacaglia is one of those musical conceptions whose content is so full and significant, that its medium of expression is of relative unimportance." He seemed to be downplaying the role of the transcriber more than trying to fool people into thinking that the later version had been created by the composer. In the Foreword to the score of his transcription of Bach's Fugue in G minor ("The Shorter"), he writes: "In its orchestral form," not "In *my* transcription for orchestra of this fugue…" At no point in

---

8   The terms "arrangement" and "transcription" are sometimes used interchangeably even though they should not be. A transcription usually refers to the transferring of a work from one medium to another—a piece for an instrument or instruments, chorus, and so on, reworked for other instrumental or vocal forces but otherwise kept intact. An arrangement can refer to use of the same or different forces but could involve structural changes in the work, perhaps re-juxtaposing the sequence of its sections, or otherwise significantly changing the form or nature of the original.

9   He also must have spoken up about the spelling, "Moussorgsky," which was changed to what Stokowski always preferred: the more Russian transliteration, "Musorgsky."

this foreword does he mention that he orchestrated it; the reader might think that Bach had composed a version for orchestra in addition to the one for organ.

Characteristically, there were inconsistencies in his attitude. In a letter dated May 21, 1968, he wrote,

> Dear Nancy, I have a letter from the house in Eisenach, Germany where Bach was born. They would like to know dates and receive programs of all the music of Bach we performed in Philadelphia when I was there. Would you do me a great favor and send me a list of the compositions of Bach showing date and title. I presume these are in the programs for the period I was Music Director with the Philadelphia Orchestra. I realize this will take much of your time but I shall be most indebted to you and so will the house in Germany where Bach was born. It is now a museum and the custodian is very anxious to receive these records of performance.

I supplied him with the information. A month later, another letter arrived. After thanking me for the Bach list, he wrote, "Forgive me if I have another thought. How about all the other composers we performed in orchestrations I made. There were many others and often very beautiful. Am I asking too much? Am I greedy? Do you have the time?" He was obviously pleased to receive credit from an important institution. It's possible that future generations may know Stokowski more as a transcriber than as a conductor.

Chapter Fifteen

EVEN AS STOKOWSKI AND I grew closer, he'd need to pull back, to maintain distance. He was scheduled to guest conduct the Baltimore Symphony and I wanted to attend one of the rehearsals. The repertoire included the dramatic, voluptuous "Prelude and Love Death" from *Tristan und Isolde*, and Stokowski's transcription of the Passacaglia and Fugue in C minor. He sent me a letter that listed the dates and times of his rehearsals, adding, "You will be most welcome at any of them." He later told me which train he'd take from New York but didn't invite me to travel with him. I boarded in Philadelphia, greeted him at his seat in the parlor car, and went to my coach seat a few cars away. When we arrived in Baltimore, I saw him leave the train and walk ahead on the platform with the stationmaster, who had come to meet him. He didn't wait for me or look to see where I was, and I had to run to catch up with him, arriving breathless at his side. He introduced me to the stationmaster as if I had accompanied him on the trip and took me with him in the car to the concert hall. I wished he had been warmer toward me, but I attributed his behavior to a bad mood.

His mood, however, didn't affect his conducting. As I'd heard at all his rehearsals, whether he was conducting a professional orchestra or a group of high school students, the "Stokowski sound" blossomed within minutes of the initial downbeat. When the session ended a few hours later, I walked with him through the backstage area. As we neared the exit, a stagehand ran to catch up with us. He didn't know that Stokowski was famous for not using a baton.

"Maestro! Maestro!" he shouted, and Stokowski stopped and turned around. "Did you leave this in the dressing room?" he asked, hoisting a bandmaster's long wooden baton.

Stokowski stood tall and looked disdainfully at the stagehand. "I don't need one of *those*," he answered, turned, and walked out of the building. I thought the scene was comical but he was visibly annoyed. I said goodbye to him and made my way to the train station. He had been the Great Maestro that day, dignified and aloof. My affectionate cooking partner and dining companion hadn't been present, but I didn't take it personally; my feelings weren't hurt, nor was I concerned about our relationship. I just hoped he'd be in a better mood the next time we were together.

He sometimes maintained distance in less obvious ways. As I was leaving his apartment one evening, he asked if I'd get information for him from someone in Philadelphia. "Say that," he hesitated then continued, "an acquaintance of yours requested this." He would not, or *could* not, call himself my friend. I wasn't really sure what the word meant to him. He signed most of his letters "Your friend," or "Always your friend," whether they were written to me or to dignitaries. (I recently saw a copy of a letter he wrote to Blanche Knopf, asking her to consider Gloria Vanderbilt's love poems for publication. It was signed in his usual manner, and neither the tone of the letter nor the way he ended it gave any clue that he and Knopf had been lovers.)

One year, in early autumn, he asked if I'd come to his home on Thanksgiving. Mom always cooked special meals on holidays but I didn't want him to think that I preferred anything to being with him. "Of course you should go," Mom said, touching my arm reassuringly. But I had seen her face cloud with disappointment. I would spend the day with Stokowski, excited about having holiday dinner with him, not knowing if we'd cook together or go out to eat. At about three o'clock, he appeared in the living room doorway, dressed up, bottle of wine in hand. He was off to the home of Sam and Cyma Rubin, supporters of the American Symphony Orchestra. "Have a good evening," he said, as the door closed behind him. A bit stunned, I worked for another hour then took the train back to Philadelphia, too late to eat with my parents. I wondered if he had asked me to be there that day to ensure that he wouldn't be alone, then—at the last minute—had received the Rubins' invitation. I assume he hadn't told them that he had a guest at home. (I now suspect that he didn't want to risk damaging his image by showing up with a young woman who wasn't a fashion model or a socialite.) Years later, I told Ellen Taaffe Zwilich, the composer and former member of Stokowski's orchestra, about this incident. She said that Stokowski had once invited one of his assistant conductors, Ainslee Cox, to visit on Christmas, probably for the same reason. Ainslee, however, hadn't lost out to a last-minute better offer.

Stokowski also kept people at a distance by avoiding personal subjects during interviews and speeches. I'd hear him talk about global issues—world peace, an end to hunger, racial equality—and I knew he sincerely cared about them.[1] But discussing these subjects also helped him avoid more personal commentary. He'd speak in platitudes and generalities, rarely referring to his family or his own experiences. His propensity for irony or sarcasm served the same purpose. I'd watch, amused *and* horrified, as awed reporters recorded as fact something he had said sarcastically. Amazed at what I was hearing, I'd look at him. Just his eyes, locking with mine, acknowledged the mischief. (Only once did I hear him tell a gullible interviewer, "Print that in pink-colored ink, please, to show that it was said humorously or ironically.") He also feigned anger to intimidate interviewers and keep them off base. He seemed to scare the hell out of Dan Rather by starting to rise from his chair

---

[1] He had made news in Houston in 1959, as music director of the orchestra, by planning to engage a mixed-race chorus and, as a soloist, the black mezzo-soprano Shirley Verrett-Carter. (Ms. Verrett-Carter later dropped the name Carter and began to sing soprano repertoire.) At that time, Houston was still somewhat segregated. The board of the Houston Symphony eventually allowed the chorus to perform but not Ms. Verrett-Carter. Shortly after that, Stokowski invited her to appear as soloist when he returned to the Philadelphia Orchestra for the first time in nineteen years—a high-profile, historic event.

prematurely to end an interview on the TV program *Who's Who* in January 1977.

He loved fooling people, having the upper hand. In his memoir, *Agitato: A Trek through the Musical Jungle*, Jerome Toobin, a well-known music business and broadcasting executive, wrote, "Stoki wasn't the man for put-ons generally; his humor, what there was of it, didn't lie in that direction." It's a tribute to Stokowski's skill as an actor that Toobin didn't realize what was happening. Depending on his mood, Stokowski could react with humor instead of anger or sarcasm. (His sense of humor was more obvious onstage than off.) During one American Symphony Orchestra (ASO) rehearsal, he abruptly stopped the orchestra. A lone violinist, not paying attention, continued to play at full volume. "Stewart," Stokowski shouted to the orchestra's manager, "double his salary! He's playing solo!" (It was at another ASO rehearsal that Stokowski heard one of the musicians address Stewart as "Stew" and referred to him thereafter as "Ragout.") At the end of a Philadelphia Orchestra rehearsal I attended, one player loudly told his colleagues, "Play well tonight! The Maestro's parents will be in the audience." I thought the musician was taking an awful chance but Stokowski, then past eighty, laughed as much as the musicians.

His personal interactions, however, were rarely as lighthearted. To maintain his aloofness, he'd often keep a straight face when others around him laughed—even when I'd gently try to goad him into smiling. He was able to hide any emotions he might have had, and no one I knew felt free to challenge or question him. When American pianist Jerome Lowenthal (who performed as soloist under Stokowski) first met Stokowski, he was asked about his teachers. "Olga Samaroff," the pianist responded. "The Maestro didn't move a muscle," Lowenthal told me. Lowenthal also knew someone who was with Stokowski when he received the news of Samaroff's death. Again, he said, there was no visible reaction, no comment. At home, Stokowski would often tell me, "I'm a good actor!" followed by a soft chuckle, as if he was taking satisfaction in fooling the world.

Stokowski's cold treatment of people was well known in the business. Bill Smith's admiration for him bordered on worship but he warned me about the Maestro's egocentricity: "Be careful," he said. "He'll suck out your blood then throw away the bones." I often thought about Stokowski's comment to me in his Academy dressing room shortly after we'd met. We had been talking for several minutes when he suddenly stopped and looked at me. "I'm a mean man, Nancy," he said with great intensity. I didn't know then if he was bragging, confessing, or issuing a warning. I realize now it was all three, but his comment didn't scare me off, nor did his inscrutability. I might not have been as attracted to him if he had been open and gregarious.

Only his two sons, Stan and Chris, seemed to have his total devotion. (The older boy was born when Stokowski was sixty-eight, the younger when Stokowski was almost seventy.) He hadn't been an attentive father to his three older children, all girls (one from his marriage to Olga Samaroff, two from his marriage to Evangeline Johnson). When the boys were young, Stokowski left the thirty-foot-long central hallway in his apartment uncarpeted so they could play ball and ride their bikes. It was where he broke his hip in December 1960, playing football with them. In his identity as Stan and Chris's father, Stokowski seemed to be at his most empathetic. In a letter to me in May 1965, he said that he had just heard on the radio that a boy had been stabbed and beaten to death in Philadelphia, and asked if I could send him the name and address of the child's parents "so that I could write to them how deeply I feel for them." Contrary to what many musicians thought, the Maestro had a heart.

Stokowski gave great thought to raising his sons, often telling me, as we ate together, about his concerns. When they were little, he said, he'd give them a dollar and send them to Lamston's variety store around the corner. "With their mother's situation, and mine, I wanted them to understand the value of money," he told me. He'd made them hold hands because he was fearful of kidnapping, a reasonable concern for someone whose young daughters, Luba and Sadja, had been threatened around the time of the Lindbergh kidnapping in 1932. One afternoon, I noticed an open copy of Hawthorne's *The Scarlet Letter* on a table in his study. I looked at him questioningly. One of the boys, he said, had been assigned the book in school and he wanted to be familiar with what his son was reading. Even minor issues related to the boys seemed important to him. To avoid conflict, he'd have one boy divide a piece of food and give the other right of first choice. "Those pieces are always divided evenly!" he told me, laughing. But even with his beloved boys his temper flared. "It didn't happen often," one of them recently told me, "but it happened. And that can be even more frightening than if it happens all the time: You just never know."

※

Stokowski didn't need me in New York on April 20, 1967, so I was working in the Philadelphia Orchestra library that morning when Jesse stopped by on his way to a recording session. He told me that following the session, the Russian cellist Mstislav Rostropovich was going to rehearse the Dvořák Concerto for a concert with the orchestra at the Ann Arbor May Festival a few days later. Because of their crowded schedules, Jesse said, this was the only opportunity they'd have to work together before meeting in Michigan. I knew about Rostropovich but had never heard him play.

"This man is a phenomenal musician!" the usually reserved Jesse raved. "I don't think any other cellist can do what he can do." He told me about Rostropovich's spectacular performances of the Shostakovich Cello Concerto with the orchestra eight years earlier; Shostakovich, a close friend and mentor of Rostropovich's, had written the work for him. "I think you should hear him play," Jesse said. "Come an hour early and bring the score and parts for the rehearsal with you."

A few hours later, I arrived at the old hotel on North Broad Street where the orchestra rehearsed and recorded in the dilapidated ballroom. As I entered the lobby, a tall, portly man carrying a cello case raced playfully to my side and grinned at me. Despite his balding head and metal-rimmed glasses, there was an appealing boyishness about him and I assumed he was the great cellist's assistant.

"Give to me!" he joyously commanded, grabbing the thick stack of parts I was carrying. He pressed the music between his left arm and his body, still gripping the cello case in his right hand. There were no boundaries of personal space: He stood too close and didn't break the direct eye contact he'd immediately established. We continued to smile at each other until Bill Smith, who had witnessed the exchange, rushed over. "Mr. Rostropovich, this is Nancy Shear, who works in our library."

Surrounded by musicians and instrument cases, Rostropovich and I stood together in the crowded elevator. I felt compelled to make conversation. "What kind of cello is this?" I asked, pointing to the scratched and dented case, expecting to hear the name Stradivari or Guarneri.

"Is Russian cello!" he roared happily, and everyone laughed. It was the equivalent of putting a "Made in Japan" sticker on the instrument.[2] "You call me Slava!" he insisted, using the Russian diminutive of his name. As we stepped off the elevator, he thrust the pile of music at my startled boss then led me by the hand to the other side of the room, where he gingerly extracted the cello from its case. After tuning the instrument, he again reached for my hand. Wordlessly, he led me to a space in front of the orchestra where a chair and a music stand sat atop a low wooden platform. He leaned the cello on its side against the chair and pushed down on my shoulders until I sank to the floor just in front of where he would play. I sat on the bare wood as the musicians tuned. Then, led by conductor Thor Johnson, the orchestra intoned the hymn-like opening of the concerto. Rostropovich settled the cello into a

---

[2] Russia has never had a reputation for producing great instruments. Rostropovich's cello had been made in Cremona, Italy, by the renowned late-eighteenth century luthier Lorenzo Storioni. Rostropovich would play this instrument until he acquired the famed "Duport" Strad in 1975.

kind of embrace, his knees tight against its sides, his arms reaching around to its front. The long introduction built in volume and intensity to the point where the cello enters—a declaration of the main theme so ardent and powerful that my breath caught in my throat.

Rostropovich's head was turned slightly to his right, his face lowered, eyes closed and lips pursed. Drawing the length of the bow across the strings, the full width of the horsehair pressed flat against them, he pulled tones from his cello that were richer and fuller than anything I'd ever heard. Then, with a slight turn of his wrist, using only a few hairs at the edge of the bow, he reduced the instrument's voice to a whisper. There was rawness and refinement, strength and subtlety. Tonal colors, as if passing through a sonic prism, shifted within a single phrase. At its most intense Rostropovich's sound filled the huge hall and vibrated inside my lungs. When the orchestra took over the melody he had launched, I saw his body shudder in response. I didn't try to study what he was doing. I didn't observe how he projected his sound or how he varied his tone. I didn't look at the way his fingers pressed the strings or the way he gripped and moved the bow. I just listened. By the beginning of the third and final, movement, I felt a strange familiarity, as if I'd known him a long time. When he reached the slow, soulful section near the end of the concerto, he raised his head and looked at me. Wordlessly, we commiserated with each other as the music poured from his cello. The directness of our gaze was no longer uncomfortable.

At the jubilant, fanfare-like close of the work, orchestra members shuffled their feet against the floor and tapped the wood of their bows against the metal of the music stands, murmuring astonished "bravos." I was left in a state of stunned silence. But Slava-the-child now re-emerged. He shifted his cello from left shoulder to right, the bow from right hand to left, and played it in reverse position. Along with the orchestra parts, I had brought my camera to the rehearsal, and he mugged like a clown as I snapped away.

I was amazed by what I'd just heard. Needing time to think, I decided to walk back to the Academy, but just as I reached the front door, Slava appeared. Without a word, he grasped my hand and led me to a waiting taxi. Settling into the back seat beside me, he slid the cello case across both our laps, our hands resting on its top. Again, he beamed his happy-kid smile.

"When will you come back to Philadelphia?" I asked as we drove off. He didn't understand. I repeated the question in varying degrees of volume and tempo, then acted it out as mime. The process seemed to amuse—not frustrate—him, and he kept smiling. Finally, a gleeful sign of comprehension! He felt around inside his jacket pocket, then extracted a fistful of paper that looked as if it had gone through a shredder. He straightened and scrutinized one strand after another, stretching each one between his long, almost double-jointed thumbs and index fingers. He held one piece out for me to see. The typing showed a date in May, apparently noting when he would return to give a recital. "Vat you vant I play?" he demanded. Could he really be asking for requests in the back seat of a taxi? I asked for a Bach solo suite—any one of the six.

We drove to the Bellevue-Stratford Hotel, where he was staying, and I made my way to the Academy of Music a block away. When he returned in May to play the recital, a Bach Suite—the Third—was on the program. Now, hearing him play chamber music repertoire, alone or with only piano accompaniment, I was able to hear the astounding range of his expressiveness: from operatic grandeur to whimpers, painful in intensity one moment, luminescent the next. Even in the highest register his tone was focused and steady, never shrill, and he was able to project the most delicate phrases to the back of the highest balcony.

I knew that there were other great cellists—Pablo Casals, Pierre Fournier, Gregor Piatigorsky, and Leonard Rose among them—who had something profound to say and the technique with which to say it. But at that concert in the Academy, I experienced Rostropovich's uniquely intense and expressive style of playing. He engaged the audience as soon as he stepped onstage, smiling and making eye contact, almost jogging to his place on the platform. Rather than sitting down quickly, he placed his right hand over his heart and bowed deeply several times. Even his posture was different from other cellists I had seen: Instead of the straight metal endpin that protrudes from the bottoms of most cellos, Rostropovich's "spike" extended straight out for an inch or two then bent downward at a slight angle, placing his cello higher off the floor, in a more horizontal position. I watched as he negotiated the upper reaches of the fingerboard, his shoulders hunched over the instrument, amazed that he didn't crush it into splinters.

His big, rich program—the Bach suite, sonatas by Brahms (the Second), Debussy and Britten (the work was dedicated to him), and four encores—lasted almost two hours. One encore—Stravinsky's "Russian Maiden's Song"—seemed like a miniature drama. Beginning the piece in a plaintive, vibrato-free style, he portrayed a simple peasant who, as the piece progressed, became increasingly intense and passionate. Then, as the maiden regained control of her emotions, Slava returned to the simple folk-like style and ended the piece. The audience cheered and rose to their feet after the first half of the concert, the end of the main program, and the final encore.

Accompanied by my piano-student friend Russell, I made my way backstage. Dozens of people, many chattering excitedly in Russian, jammed the hallway and Slava's dressing room. When he spotted me, he bellowed a long, joyous "Aaacchhh!" and opened his arms wide, pressed me against his soaking wet shirt, and covered my face with kisses. Finally releasing me, he scrawled autographs on every program, record album, and photograph thrust his way and threw his arms around almost everyone he saw, bestowing three kisses, Russian-style, on the cheeks of startled men and women alike. Russell and I stood off to the side, watching him. We had never seen a great artist greet admirers with effusive gratitude and humility. It was the opposite of Stokowski's backstage demeanor.

All that night and the next morning, the sound of Slava's concert played inside my head. It was like being possessed. Russell called; he'd had the same reaction, so we decided to go to the Bellevue-Stratford. After standing across the street for almost an hour, we saw him—a plodding figure in shirtsleeves descending the front steps of the hotel, a large suitcase in each hand. He was following a red-haired middle-aged man and relinquished the luggage when they reached a car waiting at the curb. Slava, we'd learn a few minutes later, was carrying his manager's luggage. We ran to him, he yelled "Aaacchhh!" then hugged and kissed us both. "Go like dees," he ordered in his version of English, cupping his hands together, and we complied. Digging into his pockets, he extracted little pyramids of shiny, wrapped Russian chocolates. "All the good best in life and love!" he wished us as he filled our hands. More than half a century later, those chocolates sit on a shelf in my living room bookcase, uneaten. I can look at them and still hear the profound expressiveness of the Dvořák concerto, and see him standing in the sunlight on Broad Street.

I didn't see Slava often—he'd come to Philadelphia only a few times a year to perform with the Philadelphia Orchestra or to play solo recitals, and I'd go to New York when he performed there—but each time we were together, our friendship deepened. However, even though Slava's musicianship was extraordinary—his *molto espressivo* interpretations came from the same roots as Stokowski's—and his effusive personality was irresistible, Stokowski's supremacy in my life remained unchallenged. I continued to work with Stokowski in New York and attend as many of his concerts as I could.

Luckily Slava's concerts never took place when Stokowski wanted me to be with him, so I was able to attend most of his performances and, if I was able to contact him in advance, his rehearsals as well.

Slava began calling me "Nanchinka" and expected me to be waiting for him before rehearsals and concerts. I'd sit alone with him in his dressing room while he warmed up, listening as he played passages he wanted to perfect over and over. Every so often, knowing that I was studying with Elsa Hilger, he'd thrust his cello toward me: "Now you!" I'd hand it right back to him. One evening, after I had yet again declined to play, he sweetly said, "I teach you."

"No, Slava," I answered, whining a bit, "it's too late for me to learn to play on that level."

"I say I teach," he said. "I not say you learn!"

Although his thick accent coated the English words he knew and I couldn't speak any Russian, we managed to communicate. But about a year after we'd met, he tired of struggling with English. "You learn Russian!" he ordered, and I nodded. "You promise!" I nodded again. The next day, I borrowed a beginner's Russian language textbook from the library. Cyrillic letters, the book informed me, were little symbols of sounds: Russian was basically a phonetic language. I memorized the alphabet in about three hours then started piecing together simple words and short sentences. Soon I could say hi to someone named Nina and ask how things were going at the factory.

By the time Slava returned to Philadelphia some six months later, I spoke Russian like a toddler. He patiently corrected words I mispronounced and provided additions to my vocabulary. Backstage after one concert, I decided to try my new language skills on a few expat Russian musicians. One looked puzzled. "You sound like Rostropovich," he said. "You don't speak English with a lisp but you do Russian, just like him." I replayed Slava's voice in my head and there it was: the little "s" sound that often replaced his "th." An American violinist who was listening to the conversation pointed at me. "Be careful," he warned. "I was going on a concert tour of the USSR and asked Slava to teach me how to introduce myself, to say that I'm an American violinist. I went throughout the Soviet Union, extending my hand to strangers then telling them, in polished Russian, that I was 'the worst violinist in America.'"

Slava had a lot of free time when he wasn't rehearsing or performing, so we'd wander, hand in hand, around Center City Philadelphia, people-watching and window shopping. It would be years before his image would appear on the covers of *Time* and the *New York Times Magazine* and he was interviewed on shows like *60 Minutes* and *Live from Lincoln Center*. There were no smiles of recognition and requests for autographs from strangers. All that would come in the 1970s, after he gained extra-musical fame as a dissident, openly defending the writer Aleksandr Solzhenitsyn and championing human rights and artistic freedom.

I never told Stokowski that I had become friendly with Rostropovich. It was a strange situation; even though Stokowski and I weren't romantically involved, I wasn't comfortable mentioning other men in my life except for Allen, whom he knew only as my fellow music student. And knowing Stokowski's suspicious nature, I didn't want him to question my loyalty musically or personally.

I did, however, discuss Stokowski with Slava. I can still hear him saying the name, slowly and reverently, "Maestro Stokowski," never using just the last name when he spoke about his admiration for his older colleague. "He such great conductor!" I thought of the two of them as artistic twins—fraternal, not identical. Both were rooted in the grand Slavic, romantic tradition and both seemed to invest themselves completely in their performances, holding nothing back. Both were also devoted to the music of their time, eager to expand the repertoire and advance the evolution of their art by premiering and commissioning new works. But while they both gave intense, dramatic performances, Stokowski was unpredictable, not wild. There could be a sense of danger in the power of his expressiveness but never of his losing control. When Rostropovich played, I felt that the entire performance might veer out of control. He took astounding chances: leaps up the fingerboard to high tones that sang, frenzied passages that elicited gasps from the audience. I felt as if he was holding my hand as we raced along a precipice—an exhilarating, breathless binge. I imagined, in the heat of his performances, his cello igniting like dry timber.

As men, Stokowski and Rostropovich were polar opposites. Rostropovich bestowed bear hugs and copious kisses on anyone he met more than once. Even onstage after performances, he'd feverishly embrace the person who conducted him as soloist or the soloist who played under his direction when he conducted (he was developing a career on the podium). He would also hug and kiss the composer of the work performed, the concertmaster, and a variety of section soloists. He insisted that everyone call him by his nickname, which as I got to know him better, became "Slavichka." He eagerly relinquished the status most conductors coveted; they insisted on being addressed as Maestro or, at least, by their last names. Most great musicians wanted to maintain their status onstage and off.[3]

Stokowski, the epitome of dignity, greeted his admirers—even people he knew well—with icy formality. He'd applaud members of the orchestra who had played solos, his hands high above his head, and would occasionally walk into the orchestra to pull a player out of his seat to receive an ovation. But he was never effusive. And everyone—even people who worked closely with him or with whom he was on friendly terms—invariably addressed him as "Maestro" or "Mr. Stokowski."

Rostropovich spoke openly about his struggles, be they with the Soviet government, members of his family, or with his own emotions. Stokowski, on the other hand, kept interviewers and colleagues at bay with the stock reply, "I never speak of personal things." He rarely engaged in relaxed conversation and often left receptions, even those held in his honor, prematurely. It was yet another way of distancing himself from people. Slava, I'd eventually see, couldn't bear to be alone. Stokowski preferred loneliness to being with people who might ask personal questions or expect to be treated as equals. Despite the similarities of their musical expressiveness, the two men's verbal styles were radically different. Slava's language, one could say, was down-to-earth. (Shortly after he and I met, I picked him up at the Philadelphia International Airport, located near a refinery. In the car heading to his hotel, he inhaled deeply. "Aaacchhh," he exclaimed, "eez like ar-ti-feeshul

---

[3] I once went with him to a church dinner in Washington. At the end of the evening, after he'd disappeared, I found him in the kitchen, wearing an apron, washing dishes.

sheeet!") Only once, after I had known Stokowski for many years, did I hear him curse, and that was quite mild. (More surprisingly, he was expressing anger at himself.) When I got to know Slava well, he'd come to me after a performance he didn't feel was up to his standards and quietly lay his head on my shoulder. Stokowski would look at me with dignified tenderness and open his arms for a loving embrace, but I cannot imagine him putting his head on *anyone's* shoulder to elicit sympathy.

Stokowski's ego was enormous; Rostropovich didn't seem to have one. He admitted to being a great musician but gave complete credit to God. "I *born* with talent for cello," he protested when I praised him for his artistry after a performance.

"But look what you do!" I exclaimed, trying to convince him to take his share of the credit. "You've developed that talent; you've worked hard!"

"Housewife work hard," he calmly responded.

Unlike Stokowski, Slava often talked about his parents. Sitting in a Center City restaurant one afternoon, Slava told me that his mother had been pregnant with him for ten months. When he was grown, he asked her why, in all that time, she hadn't made his face more attractive. "I was too busy with your hands," he quoted her as saying. He wasn't boasting; he was only acknowledging that his talent was a gift. The highest form of veneration, he felt, should be accorded to the composer. Proof of this could be seen at the beginning of the concerts he conducted, when he didn't allow the librarian to put his scores and baton on the stand in advance; instead, he humbly carried them onstage himself. After a performance, particularly of a work by Prokofiev or Shostakovich, as the audience cheered, he'd hold the score aloft like a priest holding The Book of the Gospels then kiss its cover, often with tears in his eyes. He took the art, not himself, with profound seriousness. Stokowski took both the art and himself with utmost gravitas.

While both musicians were known to be highly libidinous, *everything* Rostropovich did was in excess. He ate too much, drank far too much, awakened early and often socialized all night after performances. He loaded his schedule with as many engagements as possible, often commuting between continents. After one long flight, Slava complained to me, "Nanchinka, I become alcoholic."

"Why?" I asked.

"Because I drink cello's drinks!" (He had to pay full fare to airlines for his cello, which couldn't travel safely as baggage.) From his expanding waistline, I suspected that he also ate cello's meals. One afternoon, when I was spending the day with him in Washington, he took me to lunch at the rooftop cafeteria at The Kennedy Center. It was Russian Orthodox Lent and he had given up drinking, but after filling his tray with meat and vegetables and starches and desserts he reached for an entrée-sized salad. I couldn't keep silent.

"What are you doing?" I asked accusingly.

"Doctor tell me I eat salad, I lose weight," he innocently explained.

Stokowski did little in excess, possessing a strong instinct for self-preservation. He ate and drank in moderation, was conscious of good nutrition, meditated, and took siestas. Even his reticence about flying worked in his favor: He'd rest and study scores on ocean liner crossings. No jet lag for him. Unlike Stokowski, Rostropovich had a highly developed sense of guilt and could be persuaded to do something by my look of disappointment. Stokowski gave in to no such manipulations; he did only what he wanted to do. He'd often say that he never felt guilty because it was "the one thing that feels bad when everything else feels good."

Although Slava's artistry was on the highest level, I didn't think of him as a god, as I did Stokowski, nor did he want to be regarded as one. At that time, his attitude was highly unusual. In the US and Europe, classical musicians were exalted beings placed on pedestals. They were even more highly regarded in Russia—considered citizens of the first rank, accorded the highest honors and esteem. Russians always told me that great artists should be given license to do as they wished, regardless of the consequences to others. Although Slava never demanded the adulation that Stokowski expected and received, he needed a different kind of devotion: constant attention, like a puppy always wanting to be petted.

During the 1960s and '70s, most Americans regarded Russia—the USSR—as a mortal enemy, but not many of us fully understood to what extent the Soviet regime was also an enemy of its own people. They suffered constant shortages of food, good health care (Slava would visit dentists in New York and Boston whenever he came to the States), material goods, and personal freedom. Unless an American knew someone from the USSR or had traveled there, it was difficult for him or her to imagine a modern nation where the terror of arrest and incarceration—in gulags, prisons, and mental institutions—was widespread among innocent people. By knowing Slava, I came to understand that his country was a massive police state. And Soviet Jews suffered from additional threats: denied education, property ownership, and career advancement. Prominent Soviet citizens—such as musicians, dancers, and athletes—were forced to leave collateral like children, spouses, and material valuables at home when they toured abroad, yet while traveling, these "ambassadors of Soviet culture" were often guarded like state-owned treasures. But the safeguards didn't always work. Several Soviets slipped away from monitored groups or made spectacular, daring escapes. In addition to risking physical danger, they knew if they failed they'd pay dearly for their actions. And whether they failed or succeeded, family members and close friends would be considered guilty by association, suffering official ostracism that could involve unemployment and other severe punishment. The Soviet authorities probably allowed Rostropovich a degree of freedom abroad because his family, which stayed at home, included a famous wife, the prominent Bolshoi soprano Galina Vishnevskaya. (When he and his wife traveled together, their two daughters often remained in the USSR.)

I wondered if Slava could get into trouble for befriending a Westerner, but he didn't seem concerned. On a beautiful sunny day, when he was in Philadelphia for a recital, he and I walked up Walnut Street past the Bellevue then over to Chestnut Street, stopping for lunch in a coffee shop. Slava ordered tea, which was served with a tea bag. After the meal he picked up the cold, soggy bag by its string and dangled it between his thumb and forefinger, watching it swing back and forth like a pendulum. "In Soviet Union," he quietly told me, "people are like tea in bag: prisoners." Terrified that someone might have overheard, I froze. "I just kidding," he said quickly, his face innocent, eyebrows raised like a fibbing child's. But his eyes revealed deep sadness.

I was increasingly attracted to Rostropovich, and he to me. Of course I knew he was married and I had met his daughters, but I also knew that his marriage had been turbulent, so I didn't feel guilty. The couple, friends had told me, had separated more than once and both were known to have had other romantic partners. There had even been an announcement in the *New York Times* in December 1964 that he would sue her for divorce. (That never happened.) Slava's extramarital involvements, which included well-known musicians, were open secrets in the music business. A girl named Barbara, who frequently came backstage after Slava's concerts, quoted him as saying that his marriage had been "like a button missing from my shirt all these years."

Although Slava and I would eventually become romantically involved, I did not want a serious relationship with him, or with anyone. Several of my friends were getting married, but it wasn't something I wanted. I didn't like the way women constantly deferred to men at that time, or the demeaning way many men treated women. I might also have been put off by my parents' explosive marriage, but I've known other people, growing up under similar circumstances, who got married to right the wrongs of the past. Instead, I continued to dream of an independent, adventurous life. I wanted only to be with Stokowski and Slava—and hear their music—as much as possible.

Chapter Sixteen

BY DECEMBER 1968, I HAD been working for the orchestra for almost five years, and I could see that Jesse was aging. His strength and stamina had diminished but I didn't think it was serious. He and Bill and the orchestra's assistant manager talked about hiring a co-librarian and I silently wondered where we'd all sit. When I came into the library one morning, Jesse stared at me for a moment then spoke. "I have to do something that I hate to do more than anything in the world," he said quietly. "I have to give you notice." At twenty-two, I didn't have enough technical knowledge to become his co-librarian—nor would a woman have been considered for the job. I'd have to leave in two weeks.

I was stunned. The music and the musicians had been at the center of my life for almost a quarter of my existence. Most of the orchestra members, visibly upset, hugged and kissed and consoled me. A few others, including Bill Smith, who was never emotionally demonstrative, said they were too distressed to talk about it.

Stokowski's reaction, when I phoned to tell him the news, was subdued. "I thought you would be there for many years," he said thoughtfully. Then his tone became defiant. "Don't think about it! You should thank them!" he said. "It's like my divorces! They set me free!" (I didn't remind him of the regrets he had expressed in his apartment a few years earlier: "I failed in my marriages," he had surprised me by saying, shaking his head vehemently when I disagreed. He always ended, however, saying that by divorcing him, his wives had given him freedom and he "should have thanked them!") He didn't have enough work to employ me full time, he said, and later wrote that he'd call the New York Philharmonic on my behalf. (I never heard anything more about that.) From then on, whenever I mentioned the orchestra, he'd yell, "I told you not to think about it!"

I asked him for a letter of recommendation. "Nancy Shear," he wrote, "has worked with me as librarian for orchestral parts and scores for about seven years.[1] Because of her intense love and understanding of music she is unusually gifted and experienced in this kind of work. I can recommend her with confidence."

In 1969, I was accepted at Temple University's School of Music as a music history major, cello performance minor. Although I, not my parents, would now pay for my education, I was in no hurry to graduate—I was hesitant about finding my way in the world and school would provide a delay. Stokowski, pleased with my plans, told me to bring him the college catalog. Sitting with me at his desk as sunlight poured in and the smell of broccoli filled the room, he advised me on the courses I should take. "No counterpoint," he said. For some reason, he didn't approve of studying counterpoint.[2] It was, however, a required course, so I had no choice. I still have the 1968–1969 Temple University catalog containing his notations, in red ink and crayon, just as he marked his scores. At the top of the page titled "Bachelor of Music, Concentration in History of Music," he wrote "French" and "German," emphasizing the languages he thought I should study, and drew a line pointing to "Solfeggio" (sight-singing), which he felt was essential.

---

1   He had added two years. I'd eventually work with him for more than twelve.
2   I have a copy of a letter written by James Felton, music critic of the *Philadelphia Bulletin*, detailing Stokowski's early years. It says that the boy Leopold "spent 3 years at the RCM 1896–1899 without graduating, but re-entered briefly to improve his counterpoint grade." Stokowski might also have felt that studying that subject wasn't valuable. He occasionally spoke about contemporary music, which, he felt, redefined the nature of counterpoint.

"How long will it take you to get the degree?" he asked. Four years, I replied. Since I was no longer a cello major, few credits from the Philadelphia Musical Academy had been transferrable. "Can you go during the summers and shorten the time?" he asked. I didn't like where this was going, but as often happened when I was dealing with Stokowski, I had no control. "You tell them that you will do this in three years! You tell them today!" he ordered. He followed this by saying something I didn't understand: "Then," he told me, "when you graduate, you will live here."

I now made the trip to Stokowski's home as a college freshman. When I had difficulty doing assignments in harmony or composition (not counterpoint), I'd ask his advice, but my teachers never knew who had helped me with my homework. If I expressed discouragement about school, he'd insist that I look at his Oxford diploma, framed on a wall in one of the back rooms. "Go look at the diploma!" he'd order, and I'd dutifully go down the hallway to stare at the document. "If I could do it, you can do it!" he'd tell me when I returned.

Because I was a full-time student, I attended his concerts but went to 1067 only if he needed help with special projects. To earn money, I cataloged books in the campus library between classes. The boredom was so painful that while working one day, I was startled to see drops of liquid on the catalog cards and realized I was crying. At that moment, the head of the department came to my desk. "Your mother called," she said.

I dialed Mom. "Maestro just phoned," she said. "He wants you to call him immediately."

"Allo?" he answered in his distinctive voice, always dropping the H. "I have a project that I'd like you to work on with me. How soon can you come here?" I wondered if he had somehow sensed that I needed him. For a few happy months, I traveled to New York as often as my schedule allowed, helping him to redo the catalog of scores and parts in his library.

Stokowski's situation, however, began to change. Not long after I started school, the Maestro developed heart problems and, at the suggestion of his children, Faye Chabrow and Natalie Bender—the two women I had met at the Dell in 1964—moved into his apartment. Natalie, an amateur composer, began to do most of his library and secretarial work—a situation I regarded with both resentment and relief. As important as he was to me, I knew that living with or near him after graduation would have been difficult and demanding; the relationship might not have survived the stress of our constantly being together. But I also knew that Faye and Natalie's presence could be a barrier between us.

The two women had been among the kids who served on the Philadelphia Orchestra Children's Concert committees in the 1930s. They were the leaders of the group that serenaded the Maestro after his performances and went to his home for pie and conversation. The other children grew to have independent lives, but Faye and Natalie followed Stokowski to New York. He gave them nicknames to suggest that their origins, like those he claimed for himself, were exotic. I referred to them as Feodora and Natasha when speaking to him, but I used their real names when speaking to them.

Both women were in their mid-forties when I met them. Faye, a physicist, was short and plump and always a bit disheveled; her graying hair was rarely combed. Natalie, a clothing designer, was a bit taller than average. She was stout and matronly, had long, coarse blonde hair, and wore the exotic dresses and tribal jewelry she knew the Maestro favored. (Recently, however, one of Stokowski's daughters told me that Natalie, in her youth, had been "sensual and attractive.")

The Natalie I knew had the demeanor of a grande dame; I (and others) thought she fantasized that she was Mrs. Stokowski. Faye was sweet and winsome, a grandmotherly type. Many people laughed at "The Girls," as they were known, for their adolescent devotion, and some people called them "The Sisters," as in nuns, not siblings. Natalie tried to copy Stokowski's curving, distinctive handwriting and affected a manner of speaking that incorporated some of his unorthodox pronunciations.

The Girls had followed Stokowski to New York without his approval. I heard that he'd call them before he went out, warning them not to show up where he'd be. During his marriage to Gloria Vanderbilt, I don't believe they saw him except at his concerts. It was only when the marriage ended that they reentered his life, helping with domestic chores and the logistics of the shared custody of the two boys. From then on, they were there for whatever he needed or wanted. During the 1959 custody fight for the boys, leaks to the press claimed that Gloria had cited the presence of Faye and Natalie as proof that Stokowski was an unfit parent. The Girls, she claimed, were bad influences on the children.

The Girls ran errands, cooked meals, provided transportation, fielded questions from orchestra officials, and acted authoritatively on Stokowski's behalf, earning the resentment of those who should have had direct access to him. Both women had day jobs so they attended many—but not all—of his rehearsals and concerts. Faye, smiling sadly, once told me about the difficulty of trying to be with the Maestro while working full time. "We have to serve two masters," she said. I never saw him express warmth or affection to The Girls; his behavior toward them was tolerant and businesslike, often cold. One of his daughters was with him in a hotel elevator in Houston in the 1950s when Faye and Natalie appeared. They had made the trip from New York to hear him conduct a single concert. When they greeted him, saying that they were there "to hear the Tchaikovsky," he completely ignored them.

I chatted with The Girls at rehearsals and concerts but, because he wouldn't have liked our knowing each other, never spoke to them in Stokowski's presence. To maintain his mysterious aura, he kept most people at a distance and kept those he knew separate from one another; only then could the puzzle of his background remain disassembled. A few years after I met The Girls, my boyfriend Allen and I had an enjoyable dinner with them in New York, but when we were all together in Stokowski's dressing room the next day, we were curt and cordial, as if we had never before spoken to each other.

The Girls, who—before they moved in—had keys to his apartment, occasionally came for tea or to help with a chore while I was there, always tiptoeing in then whispering as they approached him. Even after he greeted them, they'd continue to tiptoe and speak softly. They showed up one evening with a new datebook for him. Natalie had hand-blocked and lettered every page in the distinctive style that mimicked his; no store-bought, printed calendar would have sufficed. I wasn't invited to join their teatimes, which I recall as short, but I was careful to greet them cordially when they arrived. I wanted them to think well of me in case they influenced his opinion. I stayed quietly in the background, usually in a room at the rear of the apartment, so they wouldn't feel threatened by my presence. It was a complicated situation that I would deal with for more than a dozen years.

Considering his history, The Girls must have assumed that I was sexually involved with Stokowski. They would have been amazed to learn the truth. They might also have been surprised that he was increasingly relaxed when we were alone together, smiling and laughing, even reminiscing a bit about people he had known and places he had visited.

I didn't know then, but would learn from one of his children fifty years later, that after The Girls moved in, he was frequently sleeping with Natalie, down the hall from Faye.

"So they had a romance," I commented to the daughter who had told me.

"Not a romance," she said, "sex."

By then Faye had serious health problems—a severely painful back condition among them—and in 1970, at age fifty, she died in a back room of Stokowski's apartment. A former violinist in the American Symphony recalled, in 2019, a rehearsal that had taken place either the day of, or the day following, Faye's death. The orchestra members had often seen Faye and were saddened, but Stokowski seemed untouched by the event, rehearsing as usual later that day, even bantering with the players. (He was, however, by his own admission, a good actor.) After Faye died, I never heard him mention her nor did I bring up her name.

Chapter Seventeen

BECAUSE I HAD BEEN WORKING professionally in music, putting into practice many of the concepts that would be taught in the bachelor of music program, I received permission to take graduate courses for undergraduate credit. One summer session, led by a well-known English author and journalist, would involve writing about music—a course made to order for me. Although I resented not having time off during the summer, I needed the credits to satisfy Stokowski's deadline, so I begrudgingly went to class. The entrance to the classroom was at the rear; I sat facing the blackboard at the front. As the professor entered, the formidable sound of a cultured English accent resonated throughout the room. "Good morning!" he said, and I felt my entire body react. I was in love with him before I saw him.

I spent almost two months studying his hands and forearms, and in spite of the gold wedding band on his finger, I kept imagining what it would be like to be held by him. Our eyes constantly met during his lectures; we'd hold the gaze then look away. As soon as class ended, I'd run to the campus library where he often did research.

"Hello!" I'd hear, and looking up, I'd act surprised to see him. Then we'd talk or take walks or go around the corner to Broad Street for something to eat. As an older student and a music professional, I was able to talk with him on a more sophisticated level than my classmates. On one of our walks, he began to tell me about

Sir Arthur Sullivan of Gilbert and Sullivan fame, a composer not known primarily for his classical works. "Yes," I remarked, "his 'Irish' Symphony is very Mendelssohnian." He abruptly stopped walking. "Fancy your knowing that obscure work!" he laughed. He also seemed impressed that I personally knew many of the musicians, composers, and critics we were discussing in class.

I was troubled by the thought of his leaving for England at the end of the session. He and I were having lunch with a few other students when someone asked what I was planning to do when summer school ended. He answered before I could: "She's going to New York."

"I don't have any plans to go to New York," I answered. He smiled.

"Yes," he said, "she's going to New York." I didn't know what he was talking about.

He had been staying at the home of a faculty member who was away for the summer. "Why don't you come for dinner?" he asked after our final class. All dressed up, I arrived with a bottle of wine and a pounding heart. He broiled steaks, baked potatoes, and poured the wine. We moved to the sofa after dinner.

"I wouldn't touch you while you were my student," he said, as he took me in his arms and kissed me. We did not, however, move to the bed. A week later, he made arrangements for me to meet him at the Paramount Hotel, near Times Square. This is what he'd had in mind when he said I'd be coming to New York.

"It's my first time," I confessed.

"I had no idea," he said, shaking his head. We spent two intense nights and days together before I returned to Philadelphia and he went back to London. The following winter, while his family was out of town, he and I spent almost a month in a small flat he sublet in the Kilburn district of London. Arranged through contacts in the music business, I did freelance assignments for the editorial department of The Macmillan Press and for conductor Charles Mackerras, preparing his set of parts for Janáček's *Sinfonietta*. My professor returned to Philadelphia the following two summers and we spent additional time together in England and Austria. This continued, sporadically, for eight years.

My lover was twice my age—forty-eight to my twenty-four. He had wiry gray hair and wasn't much taller than I—compact and intense. I rarely saw him relax and began to think of him in musical terms: *presto* and *moto perpetuo*. Oxford-educated and opinionated, he seemed to know everything, especially concerning philosophy, literature, and history. Even in Philadelphia, my hometown, he'd teach me about the significance of historical sites. We went to concerts, museums, and the theater; discovered brunch (then a new fad); and even went to the horse races, which neither of us had ever done before. But I most loved the quiet times with him, reading, talking, and spending hours in bed. I saw nothing immoral or unethical about our relationship. His wife was thousands of miles away, so she couldn't be hurt; I thought I was the vulnerable one. Although I didn't want to marry him, I became upset when he spoke about his family. I told him about my closeness to Stokowski and Rostropovich, but my relationships with them had nothing to do with my connection to him. Each had its separate place in my life.

On November 16, 1970, my pianist friend Russell called. "Get a copy of the *New York Times*," he said. Slava was in trouble. The paper had published a letter he had written defending Aleksandr Solzhenitsyn, the Russian author who was being ostracized by the Soviet authorities. The letter dealt with the broad issue of artistic freedom by focusing on Solzhenitsyn's right, as an artist and a human being, to express his thoughts and feelings, and it also addressed Rostropovich's own right to defend Solzhenitsyn and his work. Slava had sent the letter, dated October 31, to the editors of the four major Soviet publications. Not surprisingly, this powerful indictment of Soviet repression had appeared only in the West.

Rostropovich had written, "Explain to me, please, why in our literature and art so often people who are absolutely incompetent in this field have the final word? Why are they given the right to discredit our art in the eyes of our people?" He recalled "with pride" his refusal to join other cultural figures to condemn the writer Boris Pasternak. Slava wrote that he had been expected to deliver a speech criticizing *Doctor Zhivago*, which he had not yet read. "Every man," he said, "must have the right fearlessly to think independently and express his opinion about what he knows…" He referred to the official campaigns decades earlier against Prokofiev and Shostakovich, composers who, by 1970, had regained honor in their homeland. "Has time really not taught us to approach cautiously the crushing of talented people?" One line was particularly prophetic: "I recall the past not to grumble but in order that in the future, let's say in twenty years, we will not have to hide today's newspapers in shame." (Nineteen years after Slava wrote this, the Berlin Wall fell; twenty-one years later, the Soviet Union was dissolved.) "I know," he wrote in the final paragraph, "that after my letter there will undoubtedly be an '*opinion*' about me, but I am not afraid of it. I openly say what I think. Talent, of which we are proud, must not be submitted to the assaults of the past."

Defending human rights at personal risk wasn't new to him. He had also refused to discredit Andrei Sakharov—scientist, dissident, and human rights activist—and when he was just out of his teens, he had maintained his closeness to Prokofiev and Shostakovich after they'd become targets of Soviet campaigns. He had left the Moscow Conservatory in protest when Shostakovich was dismissed from its faculty and had lived at Prokofiev's dacha for three summers. He arranged for the Composers' Union to provide Prokofiev with much-needed financial assistance, knowing that these actions could jeopardize his own welfare. In an interview on CBS's *60 Minutes* years later, Slava explained to interviewer Mike Wallace why he took such risks: "I have a conscience," he said.

Soon after the publication of Slava's letter, I ran into the pianist Rudolf Serkin, a frequent soloist with the Philadelphia Orchestra and director of the Curtis Institute of Music. "Do you know how Slava is?" I asked.

"No one has heard anything from him in a long while," Serkin answered.

"I'm sure he's safe," I said. "He's too famous for them to hurt him."

Serkin looked at me as if I'd said something absurd. "In the scheme of things in the Soviet Union, he's nothing. They can send him to Siberia, even kill him, and no one could do anything about it."

After my conversation with Serkin, I constantly pictured Slava—free-spirited and ebullient when I'd been with him six months earlier, in May 1969—as despondent or, even worse, under threat. I became obsessed with the idea of going to Russia. I'd be able to see if he was all right and let him know I cared about him. I'd also be able to visit the country I'd felt connected to all my life. Perhaps, I thought, if I waited until spring, I could attend the Tchaikovsky Competition. But a lot might happen to him in six or seven months. And, if I went earlier, I'd be able to experience a real Russian winter, replacing the ones I had fantasized about as a child in my snow-filled schoolyard.

It would be the ultimate adventure: at the height of the Cold War, in the middle of winter, only a few months after the Leningrad Trials,[1] I—a twenty-four-year-old American Jew—was going to search for one of Russia's most prominent dissidents. I didn't mention the trip to Stokowski. Now that I was a full-time student and Natalie was doing most of his orchestra library work, I wasn't in touch with him as often. I decided I'd tell him about it when I returned.

By doing freelance orchestra library projects in Philadelphia, I scraped together six hundred dollars and found a fellow music student who had the interest, money, and courage to make the trip. I announced to my parents that I'd leave during Christmas

---

[1] The trials involved eleven Russian Jews who were accused of trying to hijack a plane to flee the country.

break from school. My father thought I was a double traitor to my people: the Americans and the Jews. My mother, I'd learn later, was terrified that she'd never see me again. We had all heard stories of Americans being thrown into gulags for doing something seemingly innocent. But I had no fear—only a sense of purpose and adventure. So, one month and two days after Slava's letter was published, I left for Moscow.

I barely knew my traveling companion, a bassoon student named Carol, but that wasn't important. I didn't feel safe going alone, nor could I consider joining a tour group because I'd have to maintain secrecy about my search for Slava. I was lucky to have found someone—anyone—to go with me.

At that time, international travel was mostly for the wealthy, and even those tourists rarely ventured "behind the Iron Curtain." To most Americans, Eastern Bloc countries were perceived as dangerous as well as bleak, having few amenities or comforts.

A Pan American flight took us first to Copenhagen, where we refueled. On that leg of the journey, I happily helped to pour drinks and serve snacks in the back of the plane, feeling like the host of a party. But when we re-boarded, the cabin was mostly empty, the atmosphere was subdued, and I could sense tension just beneath the quiet.

When only half an hour remained until the scheduled landing time, I waited for the changes in speed and altitude we had experienced before arriving in Copenhagen, but nothing happened. Then, only minutes before we were to land, the plane lurched downward, beginning a nosedive descent through snowflakes tinted red by the airport's neon sign, into Sheremetyevo Airport.[2]

---

2 Years later, a pilot informed me that for security reasons, foreign aircraft landing in the USSR had to maintain high altitude until they were close to the airport. The Soviets wanted to avoid espionage.

When we arrived at the Hotel Berlin on Zhdanova Street, a ferocious-looking taxidermized bear, standing on its hind legs, loomed over us just inside the doorway. Heavy upholstered furniture filled the lobby and long brass rods creased worn Oriental carpeting on a stairway across the room. The place looked like a tsarist-era museum but its faint mustiness smelled safe and familiar.

The hotel staff stared at us like children, openly intrigued by their American guests. I spoke my infantile Russian, and we eagerly passed my Russian–English English–Russian dictionary back and forth, trying to link words into sentences.

When Carol and I entered our room, I found a brochure listing local events and discovered, to my huge relief, that Slava was scheduled to play a concert near the end of the month. Finding him had been easier than I'd expected. Early the next morning, I rushed to the concert hall box office to buy tickets, but when the attendant heard the name Rostropovich, he waved his hand dismissively. The concert had been canceled.

"*Pochemu?*" I demanded: "Why?" He shrugged. I repeated the question and he shrugged again. I ran back to the hotel. Being careful not to reveal more than casual interest in Rostropovich, I asked the concierge about the concert. Another shrug. Asking questions was obviously not encouraged in the USSR. I could only hope that Slava wasn't ill and that the concert would be rescheduled. From that moment, in every restaurant and shop I entered, on every street I walked, I searched for Slava's face.

Because of the hostility between the US and the USSR, my interactions with the Russians took on deep poignancy. To meet as many people as possible, I'd have each of my meals in two or three different restaurants. The status of each place was reflected in the quality of the holder for my glass of tea: heavy and ornate in fine restaurants, tinny and plain in less-expensive ones. Russian tea, always served in a glass, was weak but fragrant, almost floral. Its light amber hue triggered memories of when I had first made American tea for Slava and he had gagged. "Is too strong! Put more water!" he implored. Now, in Moscow, I understood the Russians' need to stretch expensive tea leaves as far as possible, diluting the brew to increasingly light shades.

※

I walked miles each day in the cold, exploring historic sites and residential neighborhoods, examining the mosaic walls and crystal chandeliers of subway stations, periodically stopping for a glass of weak but comforting tea. In parks and on the streets, the sky and the ground and the trees were often the same stark shade of white. I sometimes felt dizzy, as if I'd turned upside down.

Every afternoon, as early darkness settled on slushy streets, dim yellow light began to seep through windows opaque with patterns of frost. I'd stand outside apartment building windows, watching silhouettes moving around inside, listening as the low chatter of small groups of people drifted into quiet singing, joined by the soft strains of an accordion. I longed to be on the other side of that window, singing with them.

I was the only member of my family who felt a connection to our ancestral home. Everyone, even members of my generation, referred to Europe—particularly Eastern Europe—as "the old country," and their tone always expressed resentment if not contempt. One of my uncles, hearing about my trip, had pointedly teased, "Our ancestors risked their lives to get out of there and now you're paying to go back!" I, however, felt at home in Moscow, even with the constant violation of the American zone of personal space. I also "got" Russian jokes; they were subtler than American humor and more revealing about human nature. I studied the postures of old men as they walked, recognizing the bend of my grandfathers' and great-uncles' backs and the hunch of their shoulders. *This is who they really are*, I thought, suddenly grasping the connection between my grandfathers' and my great-uncles' demonstrative, loving personalities and Russian culture. This country had shaped my family, and me. It was the land of Tchaikovsky and Pushkin, *and* the land of the Shears and the Goldsteins, whether my family liked it or not.

✣

I was startled one day to realize how quickly I had adjusted to my loss of personal freedom. Instead of just asking if Rostropovich would be performing in a concert, I now found it natural to bury his name in a list of others.

"Excuse me," I'd say in Russian to the hotel concierge. "Will there be any concerts by Emil Gilels? Or David Oistrakh? Or Leonid Kogan, Mstislav Rostropovich, or Sviatoslav Richter?"

"*Nyet, nichevo*," he'd reply: No, nothing. I learned that Slava's concert had been reinstated then, once again, canceled.

Every morning I'd ask the hotel concierge about concerts but nothing by Slava had been rescheduled. Our time was running out; only a few days remained in our visit. Upset and sad on the morning of the canceled concert, I decided, for the first time, to have breakfast in the hotel restaurant. As I was leaving, a couple from Texas arrived; I could hear their accents. I didn't want to break the total immersion of the trip by speaking to Americans but, for some reason, was drawn to them.

"Where are you from?" I asked, and we exchanged the kind of small talk that people from the same country often do while traveling. They asked why I was in Russia and I mentioned Rostropovich, which I hadn't done with anyone else, and the fact that his concerts had been canceled.

"No," they said authoritatively, "he's playing at the Conservatory this afternoon. It was just announced. We're going." I have no memory of saying goodbye to them. I searched in vain for a taxi then started to run in the direction of the Conservatory but my boots kept slipping on the icy sidewalk. Desperate, I raised a handful of dollars and a pack of Marlboros—both currency in Russia at that time—above my head. Instantly, a taxi appeared. Minutes later, I was in line at the box office. Minutes after that, the person in front of me bought the last ticket. Again, I held up a fistful of cash. A man in black pants and a white shirt came through a doorway and spotted me. He was a member of the orchestra and had one ticket to sell.

Rostropovich was scheduled to play after intermission so I decided to take a walk and have a glass of tea to calm down, then return for the second half. But just before the concert began, I changed my mind and entered the hall. To the wild cheers of a capacity crowd, I saw a familiar figure walk onstage, a cello held aloft in his left hand, a bow in his right, his large figure buoyant as he made his way to the front of the stage. At the last minute, the order of the program had been switched: The Beethoven "Triple" Concerto would be performed first, by the Moscow State Symphony under the direction of Evgeny Svetlanov. The soloists were David Oistrakh, Sviatoslav Richter, and Mstislav Rostropovich.

This was more than "just" a concert. Planned as a celebration of the bicentennial of Beethoven's birth, the event evolved into a show of support for Slava, whose struggles with the Soviet authorities had become well known. The soloists formed an intense, cohesive trio, and the conductor and the orchestra provided seamless accompaniment. Because of the circumstances, the unity of the performers seemed to go beyond music, expressing personal and political solidarity, and the audience screamed when the concerto ended. For almost ten minutes I watched Slava, his hand on his heart, bow deeply as the audience continued to applaud, cheer, and toss bunches of flowers from the balconies. His two colleagues stayed slightly in the background.

I was desperate to see him but I certainly couldn't ask for him; familiarity with a Westerner wouldn't help his situation, nor did I want to be associated with a dissident while I was on Russian soil. I knew not to ask for Richter, who suffered from phobias.[3] At a door leading backstage, I asked for David Oistrakh and was directed to a flight of wooden stairs. At the top stood Oistrakh, and next to him was Slava. "Nancy Shear, Philadelphia Orchestra," I announced as our eyes met. He nodded, we shook hands, and I left. He hadn't uttered a word. I had no way of knowing what he had been through physically or psychologically, or if the authorities had permanently damaged his career. I stood off to the side, watching him greet other people. He seemed well, and I was grateful not to see any evidence that he had been ill or mistreated. Although we were separated only by yards, I couldn't hug him or kiss him or, in a loud mix of English and broken Russian, tell him how much I missed and cared about him.

On January 2, 1971, I boarded the plane to New York feeling a double sense of loss: for the people I had come to love and identify with, and for the proximity to Rostropovich, whose future was in question. As the plane raced down the runway and lifted off, I sobbed. I wish I could have known then that I'd be back at that airport two decades later when Slava, after sixteen years in exile, would return to his country as a hero.

Carol's parents treated us to a night at the New York Hilton and to a concert the next day at Carnegie Hall conducted by Maxim Shostakovich, the composer's son. At intermission, I looked up to see Stokowski in the first-balcony box. He was surprised to see me, and even more surprised when I told him that I was just back from Russia. "What were you doing there?" he asked, and I told him about the concerts and the sightseeing, but not about my attempt to find Rostropovich.

---

3 During concerts and rehearsals at the Academy of Music, I loved to peer through a crack between the edge of the door and the frame of the entrance onstage. I was warned to stay away from that crack only when Richter was there: "If his eyes meet anyone else's, he'll run off the stage, even in the middle of a performance," the stagehands said. To prevent this, they'd place duct tape over the length of the gap.

Chapter Eighteen

AS SOON AS I RETURNED from Russia, my mother began to make arrangements to leave my father. For thirty years, regardless of how ghastly the situation at home had been, she had never considered doing this. Because of her illness she wasn't able to work, and as a full-time student, I wasn't earning enough money from part-time jobs to move out or to help her financially. But just before I'd left on the trip, the situation had suddenly become intolerable. Mom had sat with me in my bedroom as I packed. My father, in the living room downstairs, had probably resented our laughter and excitement. We didn't know the context for his outburst, but as Mom and I talked, we'd heard Leonard yell, "I hope her plane crashes."

We were stunned. "That's it," Mom had said, shaking her head. "We've got to get away from here."

The tension at home had been building. A few weeks before I'd left for Russia, Leonard had had one of his tantrums, and I had calmly told him that I'd never speak with him again. After that, my parents and I continued to live together for more than a year—a tension-filled, frightening time—while Mom made arrangements for us to move. To keep the goal—graduation—in sight and to gain strength from inspiration, I converted a double-sided picture frame into a college credit countdown: The left frame displayed the number of remaining credits I needed to graduate, and the right a small black and white portrait of Stokowski. Because of school, I no longer saw him often, but I somehow felt safe knowing that he existed. I also thought there still might be a possibility of working with him after I graduated.

My father's support payments wouldn't be enough to provide Mom—and me—with decent housing so, to be able to make the move, my mother asked my grandmother, who was in an assisted living facility, to buy a home in a nearby Philadelphia suburb with her. She, my mother, and I would live there together. I had concerns about this arrangement. My grandmother had not been a loving parent to my mother and I knew this had contributed to Mom's condition. I also knew that if my mother became ill I'd be fully responsible for her, but there didn't seem to be another option. Whatever happened would be better than what we had endured while living with Leonard.

On the morning of our departure, I called a cab to pick us up. A moving van had already taken Mom's share of the furniture and the rest of our belongings. I saw my father peering out at us from behind the shade of the front door window as we drove away, and unexpectedly felt a twinge of sympathy for him. He'd now be alone in the house without anyone to torment. A few days later, when Mom and I unpacked in our new house, I found that my father had taken my Jewish prayer book (a gift from my parents years earlier), two books I had won in a citywide writing competition, and a globe of the world I had cherished.

※

In January 1972, I received my bachelor of music degree, and a few weeks later, I went to see Stokowski. He was studying a score when I arrived but I put my diploma on the desk in front of him. "It's as much yours as it is mine," I said, sitting down opposite him. "But I'd like to know why you wanted me to graduate in three years."

He looked at me intently. "Because I know you better than you know yourself, and I knew you would become bored with school in four years." He also said that he wanted me to have the security of a college degree if or when I tired of orchestra library work. He was correct on both counts, but I also wondered if his desire to have me live and work with him had played a part in his advocating for the earlier graduation. I didn't see Natalie, who was then living at 1067, that day, but—from our conversation—I understood that she was still doing whatever library work he needed. I wasn't terribly disappointed. Although I would have loved moving to New York, I knew that living in close proximity to him would have been isolating and restrictive. It was not the life I wanted.

I needed time to think, to plan. I was well connected in Philadelphia's music circles but knew almost no one in New York. I decided to go to England for a few weeks to see my lover–professor and consider my options. His family was away, so he had time to spend with me in London and on trips to Buckinghamshire and Oxford. The day I arrived back home, I called the president of the Theodore Presser Company in Bryn Mawr, Pennsylvania, near Philadelphia, looking for work. Luckily for me, Presser's, a prominent music publishing company, needed a part-time person in the rental music library as well as someone to do freelance editorial work under the direction of composer Vincent Persichetti. The library position involved keeping the materials in good condition, sending scores and sets of parts to orchestras throughout the US, and making sure that the sets were complete when they were returned. The editorial work was more interesting: preparing orchestral and chamber music scores and parts for publication, correcting errors in the master copies by hand—an exacting job. The company was using a photographic, not an engraving, printing process, so my work had to look as perfect as machine-set type. I'd cut out sections of printed notes or individual notes with clean-cutting scissors then, using sharp-pointed tweezers, a see-through lined ruler, and fast-drying glue, I'd move them into their correct positions. I also had to work with dynamic markings,[1] rehearsal numbers and letters, bowings, slurs, and other interpretative notations. Even a

---

1   Dynamic markings include letters that indicate degrees of loudness or softness, and the symbols for crescendos and decrescendos.

single note or dot had to be perfectly placed on the staff. There couldn't be any perceptible flaws or irregularities in the note itself or in the lines it intersected; the horizontal staff lines and vertical bar lines had to be straight and seamless.

I enjoyed working at Presser's but needed the security of a full-time job. Through the music business grapevine, I learned that there was an opening for a librarian at a major orchestra in the Midwest, and that an orchestra official would soon interview qualified candidates in New York. I contacted him, and we met in the elegant restaurant of the Mayflower Hotel, near Columbus Circle. It was early—breakfast time—but because I was nervous, I had only tea and toast. I remember him talking a lot—about his business experience, where he had gone to school—before the questioning began.

Leaning forward to stress the importance of the subject, he asked, "What will you do if you take the job, then at some point your husband won't want you to work?" At first, I didn't understand. Did he think I was married? Was he confusing me with someone else?

"I don't plan on getting married," I answered. "It's not something I've ever wanted." He shrugged, looking skeptical; it was, after all, the 1970s, and he probably thought all women eventually would want to get married. I didn't even want to marry Allen.

He moved on to the next question. "How will you carry the heavy music—all the parts plus the folders? And the scores." I suddenly experienced a wave of nausea, caused either by the gist of his questions or by the sight of him shoveling scrambled eggs, covered with ketchup, into his mouth. (I suspect it was both.)

"I'll do what I did for five years with the Philadelphia Orchestra," I answered. "I'll make two trips instead of one, or use a cart on wheels, which even Jesse uses. It's not a problem." It was obvious that he had no intention of hiring a woman, regardless of her capability. Sadly, his behavior was acceptable, and legal, at that time.

The experience was frightening. I realized that my future might be limited because of my gender. But part of me was relieved that I hadn't gotten the job. It would have been difficult to leave my mother, especially now that she had separated from my father. It would be better for me to look for work in Philadelphia.

I phoned Rudolf Serkin, the concert pianist who was director of the Curtis Institute of Music. He was in a position to know about other opportunities in the city. Curtis, located on Rittenhouse Square three blocks up from the Academy, was (and still is) one of the world's great conservatories. It is perhaps the most elite of all, having an enrollment of only about 140 students, with every student on full scholarship (even millionaires don't pay). Serkin told me that there was an opening (which I hadn't known about) for an orchestra librarian who could also manage the orchestra's rehearsals and out-of-town concerts, and I immediately joined the staff. I would now be able to move into an apartment of my own, even if it wasn't in the best neighborhood, and I would have a substantial part of the summer free.

On May 15, 1972, Stokowski was sailing to Europe on the *Queen Elizabeth 2*. At that time, there were no security restrictions, so passengers could receive guests in their staterooms before the ship departed. Chris, Stokowski's younger son, poured Champagne—which his father often referred to as "Champagneski"—for everyone: Natalie, who was sailing with him; her sister and nephew; two assistant conductors from the American Symphony; and Urania Giordano, a copywriter for Bloomingdale's who attended Stokowski's concerts and cooked Italian dinners for him. We talked and laughed and ate macadamia nuts from a bowl on the bed until it was time to go ashore. I drove Chris uptown in my newly acquired dream car, a used beige Volkswagen Beetle. But instead of heading home, I was drawn back to the pier. A few other cars were parked by the river, their owners standing quietly outside, watching the ship sail away. The vessel's deep horn sounded, and suddenly I was back on Fifth Avenue watching Stokowski impishly blow across the top of an empty wine bottle. The memory of that sound now merged in unison with the boat whistle. I stood there until the ship disappeared.

Stokowski never returned to America. Later that year, he tore a ligament in his leg while traveling by train from Paris to Prague and decided to stay permanently in England. He'd guest conduct and record there and elsewhere in Europe, but would give up the American Symphony. His final appearance with the Philadelphia Orchestra had been the February 13, 1969, Pension Foundation Concert. He didn't move to London or to another major city but to Nether Wallop, a village in Hampshire (the name sounded like a punch line) where Natalie would continue to live with him. He had chosen his new house from a picture in a real estate catalog. He liked its character and its location, about an hour and a half from London.

I helped dismantle the New York apartment and pack his belongings, making arrangements for the shipment of the huge, moving van-sized container and, separately to ensure security, the key to its lock. Jack Baumgarten—a personal assistant to Stokowski—Urania, and I sorted, according to the Maestro's (and Natalie's) wishes, what was to be sent to England, thrown away, or given to people he knew. He requested that the bottles of his favorite sweet Novitiate wine be given to friends and colleagues. Rather than seeing them discarded, I took a toaster, some kitchen equipment, one of his pin-striped suits with the French Legion of Honor ribbon in the lapel, a dress shirt with his initials, and the black lacquer bar, its single shallow drawer filled with corks he had saved. Seeing them, I thought of the morning, years earlier, when I had arrived at 1067 to find Jean Leslie, Stokowski's secretary, frantically searching through the filing cabinet.

"Have you seen the folders containing Maestro's correspondence with Stravinsky and Rachmaninoff?" she asked. I never opened the files; I worked only with the music. She called to

Stokowski in the next room. "Maestro, do you know what happened to the Stravinsky and Rachmaninoff folders?" He had gone through them the night before, he told us, and thrown them away. Jean and I dashed downstairs, in vain, to rescue them. He said they were full of old letters he no longer wanted. But he had saved dozens of corks.[2]

We corresponded—he signed his first letter from England "That! Maestro!" and drew a line pointing to his new address—and we spoke on the phone. In September 1973, before Curtis resumed classes, I was finally able to make the trip to see him. I wasn't sure how Natalie would react to my being there, so I planned to go for only a day. It was the longest period of time—more than a year—that Stokowski and I had gone without seeing each other in at least eight years.

Herman E. "Skip" Muller Jr., Stokowski's trusted accountant whose father had also worked for him, was in England too; we met at Waterloo Station to make the trip to Nether Wallop together. As the train sped out of London into the countryside, we discussed Natalie's often-irritating personality. I was careful not to overly criticize her, but agreed that she could be annoying. But what options did Stokowski have? Skip asked. Natalie ran the house, coordinated his conducting appearances, and took care of his music materials. She managed his doctors' visits and acted as a go-between with family and friends (although often more as a barrier than a facilitator). To emphasize the lack of an alternative—Stokowski was no longer married, his sons were still young, and his daughters all had

---

[2] I have given great thought to why Stokowski discarded the files. Rachmaninoff had loved Stokowski's Philadelphia Orchestra, saying that its sound was in his head when he composed. But he and Stokowski had feuded over tempos in 1926 and 1930, and there might have been evidence of that in the files. The Stravinsky correspondence might have included critical remarks from the composer, particularly about the cuts and re-juxtapositions in the *Fantasia* version of *Le Sacre*. It's also possible that the files contained proof that Stokowski was the source of $6,000 given to Stravinsky anonymously in the 1920s. (If he made such a gift, he might have had motives other than generosity: to be considered for Stravinsky's world premiere performances, and to have support for being given the French Legion of Honor.) But it's also possible that Stokowski really did consider the files full of old letters he no longer wanted.

families and professional responsibilities of their own—Skip asked, "Are *you* prepared to move here? Will *you* come here and stay with him?" I kept silent, not wanting to articulate the "no" that had to be my answer. Despite Stokowski's importance to me, I didn't want my future to focus on him in a house in a small English village.

Natalie met us at Andover station in Stokowski's dark-blue Volvo. As we drove, she spoke about the two of them in the first-person plural, as if they were a couple. Skip and I exchanged knowing glances but said nothing. For about ten minutes, we drove along narrow, curving roads past farms, ancient buildings, and thatched cottages, finally pulling into a dirt and gravel driveway. A large three-story brick house stood to our left, a small fenced-in field bordered the driveway to our right, and a tree- and flower-filled garden was visible in the back of the property. The front of the house, close to the road, resembled an antique postcard: Vines of red roses clung to white-washed brick walls, Wedgwood-blue trimming framed the windows, and baskets of pink flowers hung above the doorway. Three large hedges, sheared into the shapes of sheep, stood close to the house, and the curved roofs of two thatched buildings could be seen just beyond it.

We entered directly into the living room through a side door. There were the floral and Oriental-patterned wing chairs, the Venetian carved-wood candlesticks on the mantle, and the famous Leopold Gould Seyffert portrait of Stokowski in profile painted when he had first arrived in Philadelphia. It was unsettling to see them here. "This," I told myself, "is Maestro's home." Ten-sixty-seven was gone.

The house, cool and quiet, was redolent with the aroma of cooked fish, herbs, and fresh vegetables. I stopped to peer through the partially open doorway of Stokowski's bedroom, just off the first-floor hallway, and saw his tall, blue-blanketed figure lying in bed. Speaking softly so they wouldn't awaken him, Skip and Natalie showed me the rest of the house, the cottages, and the lively, clear trout stream that burbled through the garden. The house had an impressive history. As a native Philadelphian, I considered the late eighteenth century to be old. This six-bedroom property, called Place Farm House, was basically a fifteenth- and sixteenth-century structure but Natalie said it contained elements dating back to the twelfth century. I found one room particularly charming: Its ceiling rose to a point, and a single cathedral-shaped window, filled with panes of old glass, offered a wavy, impressionistic view of the garden. Originally separate from the house, this room had served as a little chapel at a time when traveling to the village church had been difficult. Even the house's walls bore evidence of its history: In the dining room, just behind the table, a long plank of wood was embedded diagonally in the ancient brick wall. The wood, Natalie said, had been salvaged from a ship that got stuck as the River Test had shrunk to what was now the stream in back of the house. She also told us that King John was rumored to have stayed there.

Skip and I were in the kitchen chatting with Mrs. Bolton, the housekeeper, when Natalie announced, "Here he is!" I walked into the hallway to face Stokowski for the first time in more than a year. At ninety-one, his skin was slightly more lined, his face leaner, his hair just a bit thinner than when I had last seen him. But his posture was still regal, his gaze intense and direct. I stood still until he was only a few feet away then walked toward him. He reached for my hand and kissed it, never taking his eyes from mine. We walked into the dining room, and he motioned for me to sit across from him at the table. Skip and Natalie soon joined us and Mrs. Bolton brought us drinks. I watched Stokowski sip his ginger beer and listened to the sound of his voice and his deep, throaty laugh, dreading the thought of leaving him at the end of the day. He smiled at me while Mrs. Bolton delivered dishes of sole, with beans and parsnips from the garden, to the table. "I like the way you are wearing your hair," he said quietly. I had gathered it into a knot at the top of my head.

"It's very long now," I told him.

"Is it?" he asked, sounding intrigued.

"Yes," I answered, "several years ago you told me not to cut my hair, so I haven't. See how I listen to you?"

"That can be very dangerous!" he replied. "Let's see.... What else can I tell you to do?" He quickly found something. "Can you play that?" he challenged, pointing to a straight brass hunting horn several feet long that hung on the wall behind the table. A leather ring encircling the horn's mouthpiece looped onto a nail protruding from the brick.

My God, I thought, *I can't play that in front of him!* I knew I'd probably produce some very ugly sounds. But fearful of disappointing him, I moved quickly toward the horn and gently removed it from the wall. I turned to Stokowski, who was watching me from the other side of the table. "I've never played one of these," I said, gesturing to the instrument, its bell resting on the floor at my feet.

"Try to," he said encouragingly.

"Will you teach me?" I asked.

"Yes, of course," he said sweetly, rising from his chair. "Tighten your lips and blow through that." He pointed to the mouthpiece, then, like a teacher, told me about lip tension and breath control.

My hands, at least two feet apart, supported the slender but heavy instrument extending straight out in front of me. I took a long, deep breath, filling my lungs with air, and could see Stokowski practically holding his breath in anticipation. I forced air into the horn, producing an almost-obscene sound that bounced off the bricks then steadied into a low, even tone.

"Good!" he shouted. But not good enough. "Blow higher!" he ordered, and I tightened my lips against the mouthpiece. The tone skipped up a fifth.

"I got the fifth, Maestro!" He was smiling.

"Now," he said, "go for the octave!"

I braced myself to blow more powerfully, but then lowered the horn from my lips. Feigning annoyance, I turned to face him. "Aren't you going to give me a cue? I can't play this thing without a cue!" He stood bolt upright, moving his feet apart for stability, then raised his arms dramatically. His body tensed and blue eyes blazing, Stokowski threw me an over-the-top, exaggerated cue worthy of the brass choirs of Gabrieli, the Berlioz and Verdi Requiems, and all the Bruckner and Mahler symphonies combined.

There was the octave! Stokowski beamed and everyone applauded. Mimicking his famous bow, I kept my arms at my sides, bending formally from the waist in all directions to my audience around the table. He looked at me when the applause ended. "And," he said, looking impish, "you came in right on the beat!" He and I exploded in laughter. It was an inside joke, referring to Eugene Ormandy's practice of having the Philadelphia Orchestra play just after the beat.

Natalie asked Stokowski if he wanted vegetables or fish first. "Whatever Nancy wants," he replied. I quickly glanced past him to her. "Fish," she mouthed.

"Let's start with the fish," I said. She later explained that it was better for him nutritionally to have protein and not fill up on vegetables. As he had often done during our meals at 1067, Stokowski asked, "Do you have enough?"

"Yes, I do," I responded.

"Show me your plate!" he demanded.

Between mouthfuls, I told him about the Philadelphia Orchestra's tour of China, then in progress, and read letters I had brought from Ferdinand Del Negro, Carl Torello, and Sol Schoenbach— veteran Philadelphia Orchestra members. These distinguished men sounded almost childlike in their devotion to their former music director. Stokowski listened intently, nodding in response to what the letters expressed; he seemed deeply touched. The conversation then wandered happily. When it was time for Skip and me to go, Stokowski looked sad. "When can you come here again?" he asked. So I returned the following morning.

I was staying in a hotel in central London for a few nights during that trip. Sitting in the lobby one afternoon, I heard an announcement over the loudspeaker: "Will members of the International Festival of Youth Orchestras please come to room twelve?" Sensing an opportunity, I got up and went to room twelve, a large space that might have been a ballroom, where about a hundred young people were talking and tuning their instruments. "Who's in charge?" I shouted over the din, and a few of the kids pointed to an official across the room. "Do you need an orchestra librarian?" I asked her, and told her about my background.

"When you get back to the States, send me your résumé," she said. I did just that, and for the following three summers, I worked with the festival in England, Scotland, and Wales. I was paid only a modest fee but also received travel expenses, meals, and accommodations. I adored traveling and was able to see places I'd never been. But most importantly, I was able to see my professor and spend substantial time with Stokowski.

Chapter Nineteen

I STILL DIDN'T MENTION ROSTROPOVICH or his situation to Stokowski, but I thought about him constantly while I was in Britain, staying with Stokowski, working at the festival, and seeing my professor. As Slava had predicted in his letter to the Soviet editors in 1970, the Soviet government had indeed developed "an opinion" about him. Early in 1971, they had announced that he wouldn't be permitted to tour for at least six months. They finally allowed him to conduct the Bolshoi Opera in Vienna in October 1971, and play the Dutilleux Concerto in Paris in November. He had also been allowed to return to the US late that year, playing a major recital program of Bach, Richard Strauss, and Prokofiev in Philadelphia on December 13 and, a few weeks later on January 5, performing three works—by Nicolas Nabokov, Haydn, and Tchaikovsky—with the Philadelphia Orchestra. We hadn't been able to spend much time together during those visits, and he hadn't told me what he was enduring back home. After those performances, I wouldn't see him for more than three years—until 1975.

I later learned that after early 1972, when he was back in the USSR, he played mainly on makeshift stages in villages, often to half-empty houses, sometimes with only accordion accompaniment. He had to promote the concerts himself, having flyers printed, then nailing them to telephone poles. His wife, Galina, was allowed to sing only minor roles, and neither of them was permitted to record. Their names were removed from books and re-released recordings and not mentioned after broadcasts. According to an official history of the Bolshoi published around this time, Rostropovich and Vishnevskaya had never existed.

The situation changed in 1974, when Senator Edward M. Kennedy, prodded by Leonard Bernstein, used a meeting with Leonid Brezhnev to ask about releasing the Rostropoviches to the West. Brezhnev agreed to issue two-year travel visas ("for artistic purposes") to the entire family, and on May 26, 1974, Slava left the USSR to stay with friends in England. He had brought with him only his dog, two cellos, a suitcase of clothing, and the fear of not being able to earn a living. (He should not have worried. He was soon booked solid as both cellist and conductor.)

Around that time, I called Stokowski to tell him that I'd soon be back in England. I tried to find out where Slava was staying, but my efforts failed. I was, however, just a bit relieved not to know. Almost two and a half years had elapsed since I'd seen him and I wasn't sure if we'd still be close. I'd visit Stokowski and work with the festival.

"How long can you stay here?" Stokowski asked when I called. Both he and I (and to my surprise, Natalie) now assumed I'd stay there and not at a hotel.

"For eight days," I answered, and he seemed delighted.

He and Natalie met me at the train station in Andover. I quickly settled into the slow rhythms of the English countryside—the syncopated cooing of the wood doves in the garden, the banter of the men who hunted hare in the field across the road, the soothing monotony of the bell ringer's practicing at a nearby church, the occasional whoosh of cars passing the house at night. Stokowski, who had always been running to rehearsals, concerts, or meetings in New York, now surprised me by contentedly relaxing in the shade of an old tree in the garden, having afternoon tea or sipping a cool drink from a big silver goblet. I had never enjoyed being a guest in someone else's house, feeling pressured to make conversation and to fit into my host's schedule, but I felt at home there.

I loved the relaxed intimacy of talking with him for hours, doing mundane errands together, looking up to see him entering a room.

Natalie frequently disappeared into her bedroom for long periods of time or went into the village to shop. I didn't know if she sensed that he and I wanted to be alone or if she needed time for herself. As soon as she would leave, he'd become more animated and cheerful, even reminiscing about his youth.

"How was Maestro?" Natalie always asked when she returned.

"Fine," I'd say, not mentioning the change in his mood. I also didn't tell her that he had repeatedly asked about my staying there permanently. "Why must you leave?" he kept asking. "Why can't you live here?" I told him about my job at Curtis, that I was helping to prepare the next generation of musicians, so he'd understand that there were important reasons for my not staying on. I was careful not to make the issue financial, knowing that he could offer to support me or pay me to work on his music. He'd accept my explanations then, a few hours later, ask me again; he was accustomed to getting what he wanted. I was deeply touched that he wanted me to stay, and there was a part of me that wanted to say yes.

Like a good conductor dealing with an orchestra, I had to balance my relationships with Stokowski and Natalie carefully. She and I had strong bonds: We were both middle-class Jews from Philadelphia, and we were both devoted to him. Because he had accepted me as a close friend—and because I knew the cast of characters in his life and was personally acquainted with many of them—she could talk intimately to me about him, which she seemed to need. But, like relatives who don't always get along, there was also tension between us—an understandable rivalry. When the three of us were together, I had to be friendly to her without alienating him, and warm to him without having her feel threatened. During my first trip to Nether Wallop, I'd been startled and concerned when she had said, "Maestro loves you."

Natalie, always chattering, never seemed to think about the ramifications of divulging secrets. She had been telling me personal things about Stokowski since the early 1960s, when we had first met at a rehearsal at the Dell. She had provided details then about his doing yoga each morning and washing his own laundry. She had also told me that the previous spring, Stokowski and his ex-wife Gloria Vanderbilt, had disagreed about their sons' plans for the coming summer. I'd been shocked when she told me all this. Even back then, before I knew him well, I realized that he would have considered it a violation of his code of secrecy. Now, when we sat at the dinner table, Stokowski freely discussed family, health, and financial issues. She probably understood that he had taken me into his confidence years earlier. And she probably assumed that we had been lovers.

He never seemed as concerned as I was about inciting Natalie's jealousy. The three of us were relaxing in the living room after dinner one evening when Stokowski got up and stood in front of me. "My nails need trimming," he said.

"Would you like me to do it for you?" I asked.

"Yes," he said, looking pleased. He retrieved a metal nail file then sat down on the sofa to my left, not in the chair across from me. I held my hand out for his but he pressed the full length of his right arm against my left arm, the palm of his hand flat against mine. I elevated each of his fingers and filed each nail carefully, once coming a bit too close to the skin. He drew back slightly and pouted. "I'm sorry," I said, as one would to a child. He smiled and we switched arms. Holding his hands in mine, I thought of how they moved when he conducted. But I was also aware of the sensuousness of his arm against mine, the warmth of his skin, the pressure of the palm of his hand. I finished the remaining nails, squeezing his hand gently. "Thank you," he said softly, got up, and left the room. I wished he had a hundred fingers. Apparently, he did too. A few minutes later, he was back. "There are a few nails that need a bit more," he said, sitting down beside me.

One day, he chose lunch to make an announcement: "No more concerts," he said. "Now I will do only recordings."

I was stunned. "Why?" I asked him, wondering if his decision could be reversed.

"When I give a concert, how many people are in the hall?"

"A few thousand," I answered.

He nodded his head. "Exactly. When I make a record, millions of people can hear it. It can go to every corner of the world." (Almost fifty years earlier, it had been his recording of the Bach Toccata and Fugue in D minor, in addition to his performances of the Mahler Eighth, that had propelled the Philadelphia Orchestra, and him, to global prominence.) He had made his decision and I knew it was final.

Making records, and improving the recording process, had been a priority of his for decades. The author Helene Hanff, in an essay about Stokowski's Philadelphia Orchestra Children's Concerts, wrote about the night the kids learned that he was leaving Philadelphia for Hollywood—"of all places," she had commented. But his reasons were understandable: "We want to take music out of the concert hall and give it to everybody," she quoted him as saying. He'd record, conduct radio broadcasts, and make movies. More than any other musician, he had used, and improved, the technology of his time.

That night in Nether Wallop, I remembered a discussion at dinner a year or so earlier when Natalie had raised a sensitive subject. Noting a trend in the record business, she had asked Stokowski, "What if record companies would no longer have you record for them?"

"What would be the options?" he had responded.

"You'd have to pay for it yourself," she had told him.

"Then I would pay," he had quickly answered. He knew that recordings not only gave some degree of permanence to a musical interpretation; they could also sustain an artist's legacy.

Most days, after lunch, Natalie did chores or errands while Stokowski went to his desk just off the living room to study scores. I'd follow the road that ran in front of the house, passing thatched cottages, cows grazing on hillsides, and riders on horseback cantering through open fields. I inspected St. Andrew's Church, the local eleventh-century Saxon church, hiked across roads that formed bridges over streams where boys clung to fishing rods, and visited the thickly thatched post office and wine shop. I got to know people in the village and enjoyed greeting them as if I were a neighbor. Retracing my path, I'd sneak around the back of the house to peer through the window-paned double doors to see if Stokowski was still engrossed in a score. If so, I'd stay in the garden, watching him slowly turn the pages. I'd take pictures of him through the glass, not fearful of distracting him; I knew he was focused on the music.

Early in the afternoon, Stokowski or Natalie would ask what I'd like for dinner. I was given a choice of entrées and vegetables, including dishes made by the proprietor of a nearby restaurant. They'd give her fresh duck or chicken and she'd prepare frozen, ready-to-eat meals (a service I was told she also performed for Fortnum & Mason). One afternoon, I chose potatoes as a side dish. "Go to the shed," Stokowski instructed, gesturing toward the thatched cottage used to store garden tools and the food freezer, "put on the boots, and go into the garden with Mrs. Bolton." I watched as she plunged a pitchfork into the earth, lifting it to reveal dirt-encrusted, soil-scented orbs—a procedure I, a city kid, had never seen. I raced into the house, a filthy potato in each hand.

"Look what Mrs. Bolton got out of the ground!" I yelled, as if they were truffles.

"Where did you think they came from?" Stokowski asked disdainfully. He was also unamused when I raved about the thick-leaved, exotic green vegetable served in the hollowed-out raw-wood bowl that matched the table.

"This is fantastic!" I repeatedly exclaimed, savoring its earthy, raw-pea flavor.

"It is called lettuce," he drolly informed me.

Still, he continued to reveal the childlike part of his personality. While he got ready to nap, I'd start to work at the desk near his bed. As we talked, he'd sit on the edge of the mattress, vigorously bounce up and down like a kid, then throw himself backward onto the pillow.

One evening I bounded down the stairs before dinner—not knowing that he was walking through the hallway to my right—and we almost collided. Startled at first, we rushed into each other's arms and held each other tightly. Later that afternoon, sitting on his bed before he fell asleep, I began to tell him about the concept of "the music of the spheres." I went on to talk about the physical nature of music and vibrations. "Do you realize that all of your concerts are still playing, vibrating their way through the universe?" I asked as he looked up at me, entranced. "They're out there, every one of them, still sounding!" He was as thrilled as a kid. It was something he had never considered.

As he began to relinquish some of the control—the Stokowskian rules—he had always imposed on people, I was able to joke with him in ways that would have been risky even for me years before. And, after being famous for not wanting to be photographed—even with Greta Garbo or his high-profile wives[1]—he began to ask if I had my camera. "Let's take a picture!" he'd say. During one outdoor teatime, I mentioned that members of the Philadelphia Orchestra had been asking about him. It had been years since they'd seen him. "Let's take a picture for them," he suggested, and smiled sweetly into the camera. A few weeks later, I thumbtacked the photo onto the bulletin board backstage at the Academy of Music for the orchestra to see.

Despite his reluctance to acknowledge his English, not Slavic or European, origins, he'd have fun with me by using words like "ha'penny" (halfpenny) when challenging me to a bet, and "duffer" (a stupid, incompetent person), both common in the England of his youth. During one animated meal in Nether Wallop, I responded to something he said by asking, "How come?"

"That sounds like a Philadelphia expression," he commented. "Only in Philadelphia would they ask a question that way."

"I don't speak like a Philadelphian," I answered defensively. He had hit a nerve. "I've don't even have a Philadelphia accent."

---

[1] At Carnegie Hall in the 1930s, the paparazzi had to hide behind garbage cans near the stage door to take his photo.

"Yes, you do," he replied, nodding.

I was annoyed. It was time to get even. "How about *you*?" I said, pointing. "What about *your* accent?" He stared at me.

"What about my accent?" he challenged. People in the music business and the media had long cited his mysterious, exotic accent as the chief evidence of his fabricated personal history.

"Someday," I said, drawing out the word, "they're going to discover an island where everybody speaks just like you! Everyone is going to have an accent exactly like yours!" To my relief, he started laughing.

"Am I a limey?" he asked during another meal. He had a way of asking me questions, without warning, that raised subjects he usually wanted to avoid. I thought he was acknowledging or testing the closeness of our relationship, and how much I knew about his background.

"If that means you were born and raised in England, I suppose you are," I answered.

He thought for a moment. "What kind of accent do I have?"

"People have been trying to figure that out for decades!" I answered, unable to resist. He grinned, openly amused.

I knew him well enough to be able to break down his resistance. He had medication to take at mealtimes—four or five pills that Natalie placed in a small dish just above his plate. One evening, he suddenly refused. "No more pills!" he declared like a rebellious child, then sat sulking.

"Tchaikovsky took pills!" I blurted out, my voice as strong as his.

Stokowski turned toward me. "He did?" he asked, his tone still defiant.

"Of course he did!" I answered. "Didn't you read his letters to Madame von Meck? The pills are mentioned throughout the book. They're on every other page!"[2]

---

2   Nadezhda von Meck, a Russian businesswoman, had been Tchaikovsky's patron.

Stokowski pondered this for a few moments, his demeanor softening. "All right, I'll take them," he finally said, reaching for a glass of water. I had no idea if Tchaikovsky had ever taken pills.

Despite our closeness, halfway into my second visit I was still calling my host "Maestro." When I rose from the table after dinner one evening, he quietly said, "You may call me anything you wish." I hadn't anticipated that. Everyone addressed Stokowski as Maestro, even people who, in parallel relationships with other conductors, would have used their first names.[3] (The only person I ever heard call Stokowski by his first name was the music administrator, and eventual Stokowski biographer, Oliver Daniel.) I couldn't imagine calling him anything but Maestro, just as I couldn't use that title for any other conductor; I regarded it almost as his proper name. Ironically, years earlier, he had begun to use the title as a way of moving away from formality, signing his letters "Maestro" rather than writing his full signature, which he used even with long-term friends and business associates.

From then on, when we were alone, I used endearments. Had I thought of it, I would have called him by his middle name, Anthony. (I would have changed it to Antoni, which he often claimed was his given name.) The name Leopold remained too intimidating, even though he used it to sign some of his letters to me.

I can trace the evolution of our relationship by the way he signed his letters. Shortly after we met, he began to handwrite comments on the letters his secretary typed, sometimes signing a small "Stoki" in the corner. Over the years, he signed "Maestro me," or just "M!" and, eventually, "Leopold." When he wrote from France, his name became Léopold (and mine Nanci). In a letter thanking me for a list of his orchestrations performed by the Philadelphia Orchestra, he signed his name large—then picked up the end of his signature and ran it up, around and off the page, with a little exclamation mark at the top. My favorite "signature" was a portrait

---

[3] The title "Maestro" was, and still is, used to address anyone who mounts a podium, but only the great conductors—like Stokowski and Toscanini—were referred to as "Maestro" even when they weren't present.

he sketched of himself on the podium—arms out, hair sprouting in all directions from the top of his head.

Near the end of my eight-day stay that summer, he gently took my hand in his. "I know that you are busy and have things you must do, but if you could come back soon, that would be wonderful."

"I don't think you understand," I began, and explained the strength of my feelings for him. I had never told him that the fantasy of my youth had been to shake his hand. His mouth opened in amazement. The famous ego vanished. The next time he asked about my returning, Natalie was listening nearby. "I have an idea," I told him. "What if I came back at Christmas?" There was nothing she could say.

"Yes!" he said. "Yes! That would be perfect! Come back at Christmas!" A few weeks later, I sent the dates for my return and received a telegram in response: "Renting house South of France come Christmas and New Year." At ninety-two, Stokowski had decided to build a house in Vence. He—and Natalie—would escape the damp chill of England for several weeks each year.

A few days before Christmas 1974, he and Natalie were waiting when my plane made its way over palm trees, sun-bleached sand, and the opalescent Mediterranean to touch down in Nice. The villa he was renting, in nearby La Colle-sur-Loup, was a sprawling, two-level structure: a main house and a separate apartment one floor beneath it. Because of the steep, hilly terrain in Provence, both entrances were accessible from the same road. We entered through the main doorway. The rich scents of the housekeeper's cooking—roasted meats and gravies, vegetables in savory sauces, fruit pies and cakes that helped satisfy the Maestro's sweet tooth—permeated the house.

Marcos Klorman, president of Desmar Records, had come to France to talk with Stokowski about conducting a series of recordings, and had invited Stokowski and Natalie to dinner. When he heard I was coming, he included me. Dressed and ready, I answered the door when he arrived to pick us up. He stared at me in amazement. I learned months later, when I saw him in New York, that he had assumed any close friend of the Maestro's would be in her seventies or eighties (I was twenty-eight). Marcos also told me that he had offered to pick me up at the airport. "Oh, no," Stokowski had told him. "I must be at the airport myself when Nancy arrives."

We all went to dinner at La Colombe d'Or, in nearby Saint-Paul-de-Vence, where artists including Picasso, Miró, Bonnard, and Braque had been fed for the "price" of a painting. Stokowski, in a buoyant, flirtatious mood, walked into the restaurant with his hand on my shoulder. We dined near a massive stone fireplace, Stokowski just to my right at the head of the table. Shortly after we sat down, he complained that somebody was whistling. No one else could hear it. After he mentioned it a few times, and was obviously annoyed, Marcos got up from the table and walked through the restaurant. Only when he got close to the kitchen could he hear that one of the chefs was indeed whistling.

In the middle of our meal, I was talking to Marcos when Stokowski overheard me use the word "minded."

"What minded are you?" he whispered in my ear.

I remember thinking that it wasn't any of his business; I was having a conversation with Marcos. "I'm Stokowski minded," I whispered back.

He looked surprised, then grasped my hand and kissed it. Soon, he was ready to make a deal: "I'll sign a contract with you," he suggested, leaning toward me conspiratorially. I listened intently; he didn't like contracts, always saying that they restricted one's personal and artistic freedom. But dessert was important enough to warrant an exception.

"I'll give you a corner of mine if you'll give me a corner of yours," he said, and I agreed. He ordered tarte aux poires and I had Grand Marnier soufflé. When the dishes arrived, he looked at me. "There aren't any corners," he said, gesturing helplessly. We traded spoonfuls.

We brought the happy mood home with us that evening. Marcos had given Stokowski a dressing gown and me a bracelet (I don't remember what he gave to Natalie). "Why don't you try on the robe Marcos gave you?" I suggested. "Let's see what it looks like." He slipped it on over his clothing then sat up straight in his chair. The robe was voluminous and flowing, embellished with the reds, blues, and golds favored by ancient emperors. "You look like the sultan in *Scheherazade*," I said, unable to take my eyes off him.

Each day at dawn, the house would be surrounded by mist that slowly floated away. I'd stand on the wrought iron balcony, surrounded by lemons as big as oranges, and look up at the rising haze, then down to the curving roads and red-tiled roofs of houses below ours. The village of Saint-Paul-de-Vence rose mystically in the distance, and the Alpes Maritimes, like stage scenery, formed a spectacular backdrop.

I opened my bedroom door each morning to see Stokowski from the back, seated at the breakfast table in his terrycloth robe, looking through the picture window at the exploding sunrise as if it were a performance. The colors had a clarity I'd never experienced in a sunrise—pure, vibrant yellow like the lemons growing on the balcony, rich gold and orange like transparent autumn leaves, bright red like the roses and gladiolus we'd brought home from the flower market. Those colors, I realized, could be described relative to what most people have seen. But sounds, particularly the tonal colors created by my host, were more difficult—perhaps impossible—to describe.

As I slumped into the seat beside him, the questioning began.
"Did you dream?"
"Yes, dear."
"Did it have music?"
"Yes."
"What kind of music?"
"I don't remember."
"Was it in color?"
"Yes. And you?" I asked.
Yes, he said, he always had dreams—"too many to sleep well." I asked if all his dreams had music. He thought for a while, then said

yes. My mind reeled. What could the soundtracks of his dreams possibly be like?

One evening, I saw how his imagination translated from one sensual context into another. After dinner, we sat next to each other at the table in front of the window, watching a blazing sunset burn itself out. He stared for a long while then, without looking away, finally spoke. "You can do *that*," he said quietly, "through *sound*." Goose bumps erupted all over my body. He was both seeing and hearing the sunset. How would he represent this phenomenon musically? The conventional way would be with brass. "*With strings*," he said, not taking his eyes from the window. I began to wonder about my robe, a thin, lightweight fabric that had vivid pinks, purples, greens, and blues splashed all over it. He loved that robe, and always commented on the colors. Now I wondered if he was hearing it as well as seeing it.

The more time I spent with him, the more insight I gained into his music. He was a complete sensualist. Any sound, musical or not, fascinated him; he'd often stop to listen to the mundane street noise—car horns honking, people talking, children playing—that most people ignore. He seemed hyperaware of smells, pleasant and unpleasant, and tastes, favoring unusual combinations of flavors. The visual seemed almost as important to him as the aural. When we parked the car, if he and I were to remain inside, he'd shout, "View!" wanting the most beautiful or interesting sights possible. Over the years, I had heard stories about his fascination with color. When he was music director of the Philadelphia Orchestra, he had a dressing room complete with a bath. A member of the stage crew was Theodore H. Hauptle, whose son, Theodore E. Hauptle, served as a stagehand when I worked with the orchestra. "Young" Teddy told me that Stokowski had called "old" Teddy to his dressing room where he was sitting naked in the bathtub, holding a peach. He pointed to a small section of the fruit. "Paint the bathroom this color," he directed. When it was time for new décor, Teddy Senior was called back. "Start at the floor with dark gray, almost black," Stokowski ordered, "and as you go up, on all the walls, have the gray become lighter and lighter until it's white at the ceiling." Teddy did as he was told.

I also saw the role that Stokowski's intense powers of concentration played in his musicianship. A good conductor can't let his attention lapse for even a second; a lot can happen during that time. He must not only focus on what's happening as it happens (accuracy of pitch, length of notes, phrasing, balance, tone quality, emotional expressiveness) but must also *influence* what will happen a fraction of a second later. On the rare occasions when we watched TV, Stokowski would stare at the screen with unbroken concentration. He seemed to have entered into the action. I suspected that what he was seeing had become his reality, and I never knew where his reality ended and his imagination began. Late one evening, when profound darkness had obliterated everything outside, he pointed to the reflection of a lighting fixture in the dining room window. "Look!" he yelled. "There's a lamp in the sky!" I didn't know if he was being lighthearted or if his imagination had transformed the reflection into a light hanging from the heavens. The trance-like state he often entered while conducting seemed connected to his vivid imagination and to his ability to concentrate (both probably strengthened by his yoga and meditation practice). I suspect that his imagination was also fully engaged when he gave accounts of his fabricated childhood. He probably would have passed a lie detector test when he talked about his Slavic or aristocratic birth.

A few days after I arrived at the French villa, one of Stokowski's daughters, Luba Rhodes (the elder of the two girls from his marriage to Evangeline Johnson), was due to visit with her two teenage daughters. Stokowski became increasingly excited as the time of their arrival approached. He asked me to bring him his electric shaver and, sitting with him on his bed, I watched the white stubble disappear from his face. He and I went to the door to greet them.

Luba was an attractive forty-seven-year-old, tall like most of his children, with shoulder-length reddish-brown hair. She and her family stayed in a hotel for a few days, then moved to the apartment below the house. The kids busied themselves by washing the car and reading while Luba prepared fragrant dishes of baked fennel in creamy cheese sauce and demonstrated Chinese brush painting for the rest of us. She sat with me as I dressed, telling me stories about her childhood, and I loved hearing about "Daddy" rather than "Maestro." I was, however, troubled to hear accounts of her father yelling at her when she had practiced the piano.

After dinner one evening, Luba suggested that we all listen to one of her father's recordings. I pushed the dishes aside as she set up the cassette player at the center of the table. Natalie brought a stack of tapes.

"How about *Scheherazade*?" Luba suggested. I dreaded listening to this music with Stokowski sitting close beside me. To avoid distracting him, I'd have to be still and quiet, not react outwardly, and not look at him while the music played. But this wasn't Mozart or Bach; it was one of the most romantic works in orchestral literature: the symphonic suite by Nikolai Rimsky-Korsakov based on the story of *One Thousand and One Nights*.

I lowered my head as the music began but I could still see his hands resting in his lap. Every so often, he'd make a small, characteristic conducting gesture. The first two sections—fiery and dramatic—give way to the third, "The Young Prince and the Young Princess," and a simple nine-note phrase unfolds in the violins. It's sweet and innocent, even a bit shy. The line immediately repeats, slightly embellished. Most conductors take this at the same steady tempo and degree of loudness as the first, as it's written in the score, but Stokowski made the repeat softer, hushed, more hesitant. The slight drop in loudness intensified the music's sense of yearning, and I felt like we were eavesdropping on a lover's whispers. As he had carefully shaped these lines, Stokowski had made gentle *rubatos*; teasing the tempo, he had slowed it to a sweet seductiveness then pushed ahead with ecstatic impulsiveness. All this detail had occurred in just over one minute.

I was astonished at what I was hearing; he had invested great thought in a work that many conductors consider trite. I particularly loved that, to give the repeated phrase more dramatic power, he had made it softer, not louder.

Suddenly I sensed something stirring and glanced up. The children, struggling to suppress giggles, were playfully pushing against each other. I saw Stokowski stare at them and turn away, then saw their mother do the same. The kids sat still. Finally, when the piece ended—softly, tenderly—Stokowski rose. "Goodnight, everyone," he said, gesturing with both hands, palms up, to the group around the table. He bowed slightly and left the room.

About twenty minutes later, Luba, Natalie, and I went to his bedroom. He talked about the new house and getting ready to sleep, then said goodnight. No one mentioned the music. I went into the kitchen with Luba and Natalie, desperate to share my feelings about the intensity of the recording—but I didn't want to interrupt their conversation about the color scheme of the new house. I knew there was someone lying in bed down the hall who would understand. Stokowski's face filled with childlike delight when I went back to his room. "Wasn't it wonderful!" he said in an excited whisper as I knelt beside his bed. "Such great music!"

"That was incredible!" I whispered back. "No other conductor can do what you do!"

Coyly, mischievously, he grinned at me. "I think I'm a pretty good conductor!" he said.

The next morning, Luba was upset. She hadn't slept, she said, worrying about the children's behavior the night before. "It's a long work, Luba," I replied, "as long as a symphony. Young people can't be expected to sit quietly for such a lengthy recording." But Daddy, she said, had given them "a look" which she knew well. I didn't want to criticize him so I didn't share my feelings with her—that it would have been nice if the kids' grandfather had engaged them in conversation, asked about their lives, gotten to know them. I wished he had spent time with them, just as he had engaged with young people in his home after concerts in Philadelphia years earlier.

During dinner the next evening, we were all chatting when Stokowski, without any pretext, said "Garbo!" Everyone froze. I looked at Luba, whose parents' marriage had ended because of her father's affair with the actress, then at Natalie. Stokowski was deep in thought. "I went somewhere with her years ago, where they had reindeer.... Where was that?"

"Lapland," Natalie said. He nodded and the discussion ended. I remembered him rushing me out of the New York apartment years before, earlier than I usually left, suggesting that I share a taxi with his secretary. The next time I saw her, she whispered, "Remember when Maestro was in such a hurry last week? Garbo was here that night!" A mutual friend of theirs who lived in his building had arranged a reunion. (Biographies of Stokowski and Garbo, as well as newspaper and magazine articles, say that the two never saw each other after their affair ended in the late 1930s. However, Luba's sister, Sadja, told me that she had visited Garbo in New York many times with her father.)

After dinner one evening I looked at Stokowski. "You've taught me everything about music, but you missed one thing," I said accusingly, "and it's put me at a great disadvantage."

"What is it?" he asked, looking concerned.

"You never taught me how to play poker."

"Do we have cards?" he asked, echoing the seriousness of my tone.

"Yes, we do," Natalie answered, and extracted a pack from a drawer. Stokowski, Natalie, Luba, the children, and I, sitting around the table, began to play while I wrote down his instructions. We were using wooden matchsticks instead of money and soon I was losing badly. To keep me in the game, Natalie suggested that they each give me a few of their matchsticks. Only Stokowski balked; I was losing and that shouldn't be his problem. But soon, in the face of everyone else's generosity, he reluctantly handed me a few of his matches. He was a strong player and was obviously having fun, at one point uncharacteristically commenting, "This is like the good old days." On board a ship years before, when their wives retired early, Stokowski and Rachmaninoff had played poker.

During one of our talks, Luba surprised me by asking if I'd consider moving there to replace Jack Baumgarten, a New Yorker who often came to England to handle Stokowski's concert and recording contracts, and to help Natalie with whatever was needed. I think Jack was more Natalie's friend than Stokowski's, sharing her interest in decorating, and together they were furnishing the new house in France. Despite Jack's dedication to Stokowski personally and artistically, Stokowski had spoken critically about him to Natalie in my presence and didn't seem to want him at Nether Wallop. I told Luba I wouldn't—couldn't—consider making the move (I wondered how she would have approached Natalie about this). Even more surprisingly, Luba asked if I'd collaborate with her on a book about her father. At that time, I had no intention of writing about any aspect of his life other than the music, so I turned her down. She wrote to me a few years later, repeating the request. Again, I declined, but it was something that happened during our time together in France that decades later would encourage me to write about him.

We all had finished dinner one evening when he excused himself and left the room. For a moment, we were all silent. Luba looked at her children, then at me. "Please tell my children what you know about their grandfather, what he's done," she implored. For about twenty minutes, I explained his history, his accomplishments, and his controversy. I wanted members of future generations, related to him or not, to be aware of him and his art.

After a quiet dinner on Christmas Eve, Stokowski went to bed early. Close to midnight, the tolling of bells began to cascade down the Riviera hillsides. Natalie and I threw open the floor-to-ceiling windows to let the sound pour in, but he was sleeping through it.

"Should we awaken him?" she asked warily, and I nodded. We crept into his room. "Wake up! Wake up! Listen to the bells!" we implored. He blinked and smiled as the sound flooded the room.

We listened together for about ten minutes before the pealing dissipated and the Riviera went silent. It was time to sleep, but he was energized. Natalie left and we began talking about pure sound as opposed to music, and the differences between concert music and music that served a purpose. Were the bells "pure sound," to be experienced without added associations? Were they music? Were they part of a religious ritual? We then talked about religious music, in church and synagogue.

During this trip, I realized that any "overindulgences" in his conducting and transcribing were the products of his personal taste—or lack of, as some would say—and not by a desire to impose gratuitous theatricality on the music. One afternoon, Mr. and Mrs. Giselbach (he was the builder of Stokowski's new home) had come for tea. After they left, Luba and the children went out for dinner and the house was quiet. I had teasingly requested his permission to put my hair up and was wearing long Indian earrings. Stokowski, sitting at the dining room table, stared at me as I stood up and walked in front of him.

"I'd like to dress you in Oriental clothes," he said.

"I have a dress that's sort of Oriental," I told him.

"Where is it?" he asked, and I said, "Here."

"Can you get it?" he inquired.

"In about ten seconds," I said, and he began to count.

I ran to the bedroom and retrieved a floor-length white linen Moroccan dress. I knew he'd love the exotic gold embroidery that wound its way around the neck and cascaded down the sides. I'd brought it in case there was anything that required a bit of "dressing up."

"This is magnificent!" he said when I draped it across his lap. "Can you put it on?"

"Go over there," he instructed when I returned, motioning for me to move across the room from where he sat. I turned to face him.

"Oh," he said, in a way that expressed great appreciation, "that is beautiful! Turn around," he ordered softly, his right hand making a circular motion, and I obeyed. He looked intently at me for several seconds. "That's a wonderful dress," he said. Then he paused, obviously considering some important thought. "Do you know what that needs?" he finally asked, his voice rising with excitement. "A rose sash! That would make it perfect!"

I thought immediately of the little bells that chime at the end of some of his transcriptions—the intense, poignant Étude in C sharp minor by Scriabin, the sorrowful *Solitude* by Tchaikovsky—the little splashes of color that are superfluous and out of place. The rose-colored sash and the bells came from the same aesthetic.

※

Throughout this trip, my relationship with Stokowski had been shifting. I don't remember what we were discussing but Luba, Natalie, and I stood talking to him one afternoon as he sat at the dining room table. I looked down at him and for the first time saw him as a man—not a god, not "the Great Maestro." I suddenly wanted a different type of relationship with him and he must have sensed this. The next afternoon, missing him while he napped, I went to his bedroom.

"Where are the others?" he asked.

"Luba and Natasha went into the village to exchange the dress Luba bought yesterday, because it's too small."

He grinned. "Why do women always say a dress is too small, not that they have to reduce?"

His remark caught me off guard and I burst out laughing. "I don't like women who are too thin…" I began, when I noticed that he had extended his hand toward me. At first, I thought he was pointing at something, then realized he was holding his hand out for mine. I stopped talking and placed my hand in his. Gently, wordlessly, he drew me onto the bed beside him. He took my face in both his hands and slowly caressed every part of it with his fingertips. "Kiss me gently," he whispered. "A light kiss, a gentle kiss, where lips barely touch, is the most intense." A pianissimo kiss, I remember thinking, as our mouths met for the first time.

As I'd learn a year later, Luba had noticed the change in my relationship with her father, but Natalie had not. Natalie wasn't intuitive, rarely able to sense what others were thinking or feeling. I was always amazed at her inability to "read" Stokowski, to be able to gauge his mood and act accordingly. I saw this again one evening when Luba and her children had gone out to eat. Stokowski, Natalie, and I had dinner then she went to her room. He and I decided to have dessert in front of the fireplace. After talking for about an hour, he said it was time for him to sleep. I cleared the dishes from the table and went into his bedroom, where Natalie was puttering around while he got ready for bed. She had an idea for the new house, she announced. He groaned and grimaced and shook his head, but she began to talk. He started to interrupt and tease her, grinning and winking at me, but the chattering continued. I was worried that she'd change his mood and end the good time we were having, but he put his head back on the pillow and began to laugh. It was contagious and soon Natalie and I were laughing too. Then, still not picking up signals that he wasn't in the mood to talk about the house, she resumed her monologue. Suddenly, he looked over at me, his face registering alarm. "Call the policemen!" he shouted, pointing to the phone across the room. "Get three of them to take Natasha to the insane asylum!"

Playing along, I ran to the phone and picked up the receiver. "What should I tell them?" I yelled. Loudly, urgently, he began to dictate in French what I should say to the police as I repeated the order into the dead receiver. He started to laugh so hard that he wasn't able to speak. Natalie went silent, looking defeated; he looked victorious. He reached over to the night table for his eye drops, putting his head back on the pillow, still laughing. I felt bad for Natalie but also realized we were lucky. He could just as well have exploded in anger. Legions of musicians could have attested to that.

The next afternoon, while the others were out, he came into the kitchen as I was washing the lunch dishes. I decided not to stop—everyone altered their activities to accommodate him and I wanted there to be some normalcy at home. Out of the corner of my eye, I saw him look for a chair, then, with effort, begin to push it toward me. I pretended I didn't see what he was doing; I didn't want to diminish his dignity by offering help. He slowly moved the chair near the sink, sat down, and, to the accompaniment of running water, began to talk.

The normalcy didn't last long; his voice soon rose with annoyance. "Stop washing the dishes! Come here and sit down!" My mother had sent a holiday cake, and I cut a slice for each of us, then moved another chair close beside him. As I walked past him, he caught my hand and pulled me to him. I tasted the sugar that coated his lips. We started talking again but, agitated, he soon interrupted me. "I want to ask you something. You must do something for me!"

I was startled by the abrupt change in his mood. "Of course," I answered. "What is it?"

"You must tell me how much your education cost! I want to pay for your education!" A few nights earlier, relaxing by the fire, we had talked about the high cost of college and I mentioned that I had gone into debt to pay my tuition. He offered then to pay off the debt for me. I was deeply touched by his concern but refused. I knew that there were people in his life who tried to take financial advantage of him—some successfully—and I never wanted him to question my devotion. But now he was insisting.

"I have never asked to pay for your clothing or your food or anything else. I want to be the one to pay for your education. You must tell me what it cost!"

"No, dear," I said firmly. "It means everything to me that you want to do this, but it's not necessary. I don't want you to be concerned." Looking distressed, he insisted again that I tell him the amount. I had seen him this upset only once before, back in New York, when he told me why he had left the Philadelphia Orchestra.

I was especially moved by his offer because it was out of character for him. He had a reputation for being frugal in spite of his wealth. (In New York, he rarely offered visitors, even distinguished ones, anything to eat or drink; the most they usually received were Turkish or Bulgarian cigarettes.)

I have never regretted my decision.

A few days later, standing near the door in his bedroom, he stared at me. "Did we…ever…make love years ago?" he asked, obviously searching back in his memory.

"No," I answered, shaking my head and smiling.

"Why didn't we?" he asked incredulously. Now it was my turn to give a classic Stokowski response. Still smiling, I left the room. I didn't want to emphasize our age difference, which neither of us seemed to think about, by telling him that I had been too young and innocent years before, and that being intimate with a deity had been unthinkable. But now we were like naughty adolescents, sneaking time together until we heard Natalie's car in the driveway.

Our relationship was complicated. A few years earlier, while helping to pack his belongings for shipment to England, I had realized that there had always been a romantic undercurrent flowing between us. I had known instinctively not to mention other men in my life. And I was uncomfortable with the intimacy of a suitcase, in a back bedroom, bearing the initials "GV," obviously belonging to ex-wife Gloria Vanderbilt and probably brought to 1067 by one of their sons.

Recalling the way he looked at me in the early days of our relationship, when I was a teenager in Philadelphia—his eyes always a bit narrowed, a little smile playing around his mouth—I think he was at first intrigued and amused, then a bit infatuated.

I had come along at a good time. He had returned to the Philadelphia Orchestra in 1960, only a year or two before I met him, after what had to have been one of the most difficult periods in his life: the end of his third and final marriage; not getting full custody of his sons; and breaking his hip playing with his boys.

I must have been a strange creature for him to encounter: a young girl who didn't want anything from him except his attention; who didn't want a sexual relationship; who, on a highly sophisticated level, understood and admired what he was doing musically; who intuitively knew what he wanted and needed (which included not letting him know that I consciously knew); who idolized him but was comfortable in his presence; and who was from Philadelphia and was close to its orchestra—an added connection to the city and the ensemble that represented the pinnacle of his career, perhaps of his life.

In all the years we had known each other, he had never articulated his feelings about me, about death, or about life after death. It was not his way. As we sat and talked one afternoon during that Christmas of 1974, he quietly said, "I love you." I stared at him as he paused, then continued. "I will love you forever. And when I die, I will love you in the other country, if there is an other country."

Whenever I arrived at any of Stokowski's homes, I always asked about music that needed work. This trip, two of his transcriptions, the "Dead March" from Handel's *Saul* and Palestrina's *Adoramus te*, had to be prepared for publication. This involved identifying errors or unclear elements in the scores and telling the publisher what needed to be corrected. Early one morning, when Stokowski and I were alone, I was working a few yards away from where he still lay in bed. He called to me, asking what I was doing. When I told him I was working on the Handel, he began to whistle then conduct it, flat on his back, as if a full symphony orchestra was spread out on the ceiling. "Bring the score here," he said, and side-by-side, the two of us examined the proof.

Counting his stylistic additions and changes and my discovery of printing and notation inaccuracies, there were twenty-nine changes to be made in the four-page, sixteen-measure "Dead March" score. (These included adding Stokowski's instruction, "bells up," for the horns in the loud and louder-still fortissimo/fortississimo section, to push the sound forward for a brasher, brassier effect.) He also indicated that the beginning of every important string phrase was to be played upbow rather than the more common downbow. An upbow would produce a more delicate, fragile sound than a downbow, where more pressure is applied. After the upbow start, the musicians were to bow freely—as they wished and felt.

There were also twenty-nine corrections and changes to the four-page, thirty-two-measure transcription of Palestrina's *Adoramus te*, including the directive for other conductors: "Individual bowings except where otherwise indicated," an order he did not include in the "Dead March" score. He also provided set, uniform bowings for a few measures in the second violins, violas, and cellos to achieve specific articulations and effects.

Unique in musical notation, many of the scores of his transcriptions show only measures that contain notes; measures without notes (that have only rests) simply drop off the page, leaving blank spaces. The measures that have notes seem suspended in midair. Many conductors find this disorienting, and have difficulty knowing which instruments are playing.

If one of his scores or a set of orchestra parts needed to be marked or repaired, I'd work at the desk in his bedroom as he took his siestas. "Would it be all right if I came over and watched what you're doing?" he cautiously asked one afternoon. "Would you mind?" We sat together at the desk as I showed him how to reinforce the corners of the *Scheherazade* score by using clear tape. To keep him involved, I repeatedly asked his opinion about the best way to fix the music, and we discussed the options. He worked with me for about fifteen minutes, then decided to continue his nap. But soon he was out of bed again, happily serving as my assistant.

I often had to write out lines of music for inserts, then cut them to fit—like pieces of a puzzle—precisely over the notes they were to replace. Stokowski kept a pair of long metal scissors on his desk that cut cleanly and evenly and I repeatedly commented on their quality. When I was packing to leave, he appeared in the doorway holding the scissors, their sharp points embedded in a Harvey's Bristol Cream cork. "I want you to take these with you," he said.

"I'll use them when I'm here," I answered, not wanting to take them away from him.

"No," he said decisively, "I want you to have them." The scissors, which appear on the cover photo of Glenn Gould's recorded interview with Stokowski, now sit on my living room desk.[4]

---

[4] Having a bit more knowledge of psychology now, I suspect that he was uneasy about my departure and wanted me to have a physical object to associate with him.

Chapter Twenty

ON THURSDAY, FEBRUARY 27, 1975, two months after my trip to England, I left for New York to attend Slava's recital in Carnegie Hall. I drove my VW as fast as I legally could up the New Jersey Turnpike, but had to pull in at every rest stop along the way to quell my nervous stomach. As I drove, I not only thought about my reunion with Slava after more than three years, but about no longer having Stokowski's live concerts. I was grateful that Slava, at forty-eight, was still comparatively young and had years of concertizing ahead of him. But I had no idea if his troubles with the Soviet authorities had affected his playing, or if we'd be as close.

I didn't try to see him before the concert but pushed my way through crowds jamming the sidewalk in front of the entrance on 57th Street, waving away people who were begging to buy tickets. Slava's fame now extended far beyond music; he was a heroic humanitarian celebrated by the media. And because he was a dissident, he was a Russian Americans could love.

When Slava came onstage, almost running, the audience rose en masse. I was seated on the orchestra level and I looked all around me, high up into the balconies, where I saw that many people, like me, were crying. Did they know him and care about him as I did, or were they just fans? His hand over his heart, Slava kept bowing, attempting many times to sit down to play. Finally, all went quiet. He settled into his chair, anchored the endpin in the floor, touched the bow lightly to the strings to be sure that his cello was in tune, and nodded to pianist Samuel Sanders to begin. I closed my eyes, absorbing the distinctive "voice" of his playing. Rich, throaty, delicate, soaring—unmistakably his—that sound was even more expressive and profound than I had remembered. Utterly silent while he played, the audience shouted and applauded after each piece and leapt to its feet the moment the concert ended.

Backstage, I heard more Russian than English, all of it loud and excited. Impatient fans clogged the corridor outside Slava's dressing room, rushing in when his manager opened the door. Standing in line, my heart pounding, I watched Slava boisterously embrace dozens of people. When I finally moved in front of him, he didn't yell or grab me in a bear hug. He simply opened his arms and held me tightly, repeatedly whispering, "Nanchinka, I love you, I miss you," until the person behind me pushed himself into Slava's view. "Take my number at hotel," he said, and told me to call him at the Blackstone, a few blocks from Carnegie Hall. Over the next two weeks, I left several messages and sent a note through the mail, but didn't hear from him until he returned to Philadelphia on March 15, the day before his recital. Knowing Slava and I were friends, the director of the concert series asked if I'd pick him up at the airport. On the way back to his hotel, Slava recited the list of places he'd been since I had seen him at Carnegie Hall, and I realized that I couldn't expect to hear from him as often as I'd have liked. Although he was still a Soviet citizen, his travel permit allowed him to live and perform wherever he wished, and he was playing as many concerts as he could, all over the world. His life now consisted of constant traveling, performing, and recording.

I saw Slava briefly for breakfast at his hotel the morning after the concert. I told him a bit about my trip to Russia—how I had searched for him, my fear about his well-being, and made some observations about life in the Soviet Union—but I was far more interested in hearing what he had been through. In vivid detail, he described the process of writing and sending the letters defending Solzhenitsyn: In Sheremetyevo Airport in 1970, before he left for performances abroad, he had held the envelopes just inside the opening of the mail box, hesitating to release them from his grasp.

"I know if I let go, my life and my family's life change instantly… but I let go," he said, nodding his head.

"Then what did you do?" I eagerly asked.

"I go to bar and drink lots of vodka!"

The following month, April 1975, I attended his rehearsals and all three concerts of the Schumann Concerto with Leonard Bernstein and the New York Philharmonic, but I didn't have much time alone with him. At least, I thought, we'd be together in Philadelphia when he'd play the Saint-Saëns Concerto and the Tchaikovsky *Rococo Variations* at the Dell in late July. But shortly after his arrival in the city, I knew that things would never be the same. From then on, instead of having blocks of free time, he'd have a heavy schedule of press interviews and business meetings added to his musical responsibilities.

I attended his rehearsals and concerts and sat in on the master classes he led at Curtis and Juilliard. During those sessions, he'd articulate his ideas and concepts about interpretation and cello technique. In colorful English, he'd detail what he felt the students needed to alter: bowings, fingerings, tonal coloration, shaping of phrases. He'd also talk about style and historical context, revealing what he was thinking and feeling when he played. I remember one particularly poignant session. After a highly accomplished young musician had played for several minutes, Slava interrupted her. He didn't feel that she was ending phrases with an adequate sense of completion, of resolution. Instead of demonstrating what he wanted by playing it, which would have encouraged the student to imitate him, he dramatized the concept. Singing the phrase at full volume, he began to wander around the stage like someone lost. Then, as if searching for something, he walked into each of its corners, continuing to sing. Hesitating, he turned, looked around and, as if making an important discovery, focused on a chair near the piano. Still singing—he never stopped—he walked toward the chair and sank into it. "Ah, home," he said, his eyes closed, then sang the end of the phrase with a feeling of finality. Because of his troubles with the Soviets, he wasn't able to go home. The student got the point, even if she didn't connect his dramatization to his personal situation.

But just as Slava would have never openly bemoaned his situation, his playing never became *too* emotional; it was dramatic, not melodramatic. He knew that artistic expressiveness, to communicate most powerfully, required restraint. "Not too much suffer!" I remember him telling a particularly effusive young cellist. And commenting on another student's superficial performance of one of the Brahms sonatas, he admonished: "You not yet suffer enough to play this music!"[1]

Slava's English was improving but it remained, at best, a child's version with expletives. His television interviews—in English—needed English subtitles and his radio interviews had to be heavily edited to be understandable. He once left a message on my home answering machine: "Nanchinka, vairyoobeeIvaitchoo." To me, it was as clear as the Queen's English, but a friend standing nearby didn't understand a word. "Nanchinka, where you be, I wait you," he had tried to say.

In a quiet moment, Slava, in his version of English, said he loved me and I reciprocated in my version of Russian. He exploded in laughter. "You sound like nineteenth century!" he teased. I had learned the phrase from Tchaikovsky's opera, *Eugene Onegin*. Slava usually said yes or no five times, in English or Russian—"*da da da da da*" or "*nyet nyet nyet nyet nyet*." One of his favorite words was "FAHN-TAHS-TEEK," every syllable stressed. How was a concert he'd just attended? "Fantastic boring!" he'd bellow. I wondered how he expressed himself in his native language. "What is Slava's Russian like?" I asked a Russian mutual friend of ours. "Like Tolstoy," he answered.

Slava loved my dented little VW. "You take cello, I go vis her," he'd tell his chauffeur. (This was before he acquired the renowned

---

[1] Slava regarded suffering as essential to an artist's—and to a person's—understanding of the world. Expressiveness, he felt, had to grow out of the authenticity of a musician's personal experience. He defended Solzhenitsyn by saying that the author "sought the right, through his suffering, to set down on paper the truth as he saw it."

"Duport" Strad, which he wouldn't leave in anyone else's care.) His body crammed into the brown bucket passenger seat, he'd shift the four-on-the-floor gear into neutral whenever we stopped. When I stepped on the accelerator, we'd go nowhere. Ignoring my pleas not to push and pull the car's buttons and levers, he'd have the heater blasting away during the steamy Philadelphia summers.

In those days, Philadelphia didn't have many restaurants to choose from but there were a few fine ones. Slava's favorite, however, was Happy Paradise, a slightly seedy place in Chinatown that I had introduced him to. We first went there with two or three carloads of friends, Slava wedged between two people in the back of the VW. Our evening progressed like a Sergei Eisenstein film that starred the Marx Brothers. Slava told us what he wanted, then we translated his Russified English into English understood by the Chinese staff, ordering too many dishes for even our hungry crowd. A parade of waiters delivered metal-domed plates of delicacies not represented on the printed menu—VIP fare specially prepared for the hungry guest who simply said, "You bring food!"

After our first meal there, Slava made the gesture of writing on his palm with an imaginary pen, and the waiters, nodding, filled a little piece of paper with Chinese characters that listed what they'd served us. Hours later, when we finished eating, David Finckel, a superb cellist who had studied with Slava,[2] extracted a wad of cash from Slava's shirt pocket to pay the check.

A year later, back at Happy Paradise, Slava produced the paper and our original marathon meal was duplicated. (I was amazed he still had it. Except for his cello, he was constantly losing things.) Before we began to eat, Slava said that a friend of his would join us, and soon a stout, bespectacled man dressed like a banker appeared at our table. Slava greeted him with a huge hug and a roar of welcome, now in his own language. He took the man's right hand and mine and joined them, saying, with sweet sincerity, "You two must love each other. You both have dear friend!"

---

[2] David would become cellist of the Emerson String Quartet and co-artistic director, with his pianist wife, Wu Han, of the Chamber Music Society of Lincoln Center.

"Do you know Stokowski?" I immediately, instinctively asked.

"Yes," answered the man, whose name was Juri Jelagin, in a deep, Russian-accented monotone. "I haven't been in touch with him in years, since I was a violinist in the Houston Symphony. We were close friends." I doubted that; Stokowski had few friends, let alone close ones. But years later, after Juri and his daughter, Carolyn, and I got to know each other, he showed me letters Stokowski had written to him. They were among the most personal I had ever seen. Over time, Juri told me about Stokowski's accounts of his love affair with Greta Garbo in the 1930s, their tryst in Ravenna, Italy, and Stokowski's low estimation of Garbo as a lover.[3] He said that one of the reasons Stokowski had accepted the directorship of the Houston (which Stokowski pronounced "HOO-ston") Symphony in 1955 was his belief that he'd eventually have more substantial custody of his two sons. The three of them, Stokowski had thought, would share great adventures in the colorful, romantic American West. (This didn't turn out as he wished. He had to settle for a hotel suite instead of a ranch, and his custody of the boys was not increased.)

Juri and Carolyn, I'd soon learn, were like family to Slava. He frequently had meals with them and stayed overnight at their place in Chevy Chase, Maryland, near Washington. Juri had had three careers: as a violinist in Russia, then in the Houston Symphony after emigrating to the US; as the author of two books, *Taming of the Arts*, which detailed the Stalinist regime's treatment of Soviet artists, and *Dark Genius: A Biography of Vsevolod Meyerhold*, about the great theater director; and as an editor and translator for the United States Information Agency (now defunct).

On July 31, 1975, ten days after Slava's concert at the Dell, I arrived in London. I'd spend a week at Stokowski's, see my professor, then

---

3   Years ago, someone told me that Stokowski, in a rare moment of candor, said that having sex with Garbo was "all rehearsal and no performance."

work with the youth orchestra festival in Cardiff, London, and Guildford. I called Stokowski and Natalie as soon as I landed at Heathrow. It would take about four hours for me to get the bus to Woking then the train to Andover, where they'd pick me up. Natalie answered. "I don't know if you can come here now," she said.

"What's happening?" I asked, my heart racing. Was he all right? Had I done something to anger them? Would I not be able to see him?

"I don't think we have enough clean sheets," she said. There was a hint of craziness about it.

"I'll bring some with me, Nat," I offered, feeling overwhelmed at having to find a place to buy them. I also felt anger at myself for tolerating that kind of treatment. I reminded her that I had made the trip to see them "both."

"Oh, come," she finally said. "We'll manage." I never heard another word about the linen shortage and there seemed to be a good supply of sheets when I arrived.

Stokowski was now ninety-three and I was concerned about what I might find. As promised, he and Natalie were waiting in the parking lot when I arrived. I scanned his face through the car window. *Please let him be well; don't let him have aged.* But he was smiling broadly at me through the window, looking healthier and stronger than when we had been together in France six months earlier. As I slid into the back seat, Natalie began to chatter. "We're going to stop in the village and do some errands, then we'll go home and have lunch," she said as he reached back with his left hand, out of Natalie's line of vision, for mine. I found his strong grasp reassuring.

As we pulled into the driveway next to the fenced-in field, I could smell the familiar, earthy sweetness of hay, grass, and thatching. A horse looked suspiciously at us as we got out of the car. "Watch this," Stokowski said, walking over to the fence. "Here, Blackie! Here, Blackie!" he ordered, clapping his gloved hands. The horse looked lazily up at him but didn't move. "Here, Blackie! Here, Blackie!" he repeated, a note of authority strengthening his voice. The horse looked away. "I'm happy your musicians pay better attention to you than he does," I called over my shoulder as we walked into the house. I felt as though I had come home.

Mrs. Bolton still came most mornings to tend to the housekeeping and prepare lunch. She and Mr. Gallop, the gardener, had to have known each other for years but, when I overheard them greet each other, they always spoke formally: "How are you today, Mrs. Bolton?" "I am well, Mr. Gallop, and you?" At the end of each of my visits, Mr. Gallop presented me with a small potted rosemary plant. He knew I loved the herb but didn't know it was against the law for me to take the plants back to the States. I gratefully accepted them, then gave them to a London friend whose windowsill eventually resembled a little garden.

We continued the tradition, started at 1067, of Stokowski's choosing anything he wanted from my orchestra librarian's kit—a soft-lead pencil; a small, rectangular white eraser; a red or a blue crayon. Then it was my turn: I got to choose tea from his kitchen cupboard. The Royal Rose tea with rosebuds, in a little gray box with a pink blossom in the middle, still sits on my kitchen shelf.

After lunch, he'd ask if there was a site I wanted to visit and we'd make trips to local landmarks like Winchester Cathedral. Natalie stayed in the car while Stokowski and I entered the soaring Gothic structure. He asked me to bring him a chair, and I knelt on the ancient stone floor beside him. Surveying its magnificence, his hands raised toward the ceiling, he spoke of the shared characteristics of the towering architecture and the formal structure of the organ works of Bach. (In the preface to the printed score of his transcription of the Passacaglia and Fugue in C minor, Stokowski wrote, in part: "Bach's passacaglia is in music, what a great Gothic cathedral is in architecture—the same vast conception—the same soaring mysticism given eternal form.")

We also did errands. Natalie had been talking incessantly about buying a chest of drawers for the house so after lunch one afternoon, we three set out for an antique store in the village. Stokowski wanted to wait in the car, and I moved from the back seat next to him in the front. He watched as Natalie walked in front of the car and into the store. "Look at her," he said contemptuously. "She loves this." We sat and talked, but he grew restless. "Let's go in," he said, but he didn't look happy.

It was a typical English village antique store crowded with furniture, the polished wood shining in the afternoon sunlight. We stayed back near the entrance as Natalie conferred with the proprietor, but neither of them looked our way. He guided her to a chest at the front of the shop, opening one of the upper drawers. "Notice the bottom, the rounded shape, and fine manner of construction," the antiques dealer said. I suddenly felt a large hand on my derrière.

"It's perfectly smooth, perfectly fitted," the dealer remarked.

"Oh, yes," Stokowski said appreciatively, his hand moving in a wide arc. "It is perfect!"

Hearing Stokowski's enthusiasm, the dealer quickened his pitch. "Note the shape on the side, the way it curves," he said.

"You are right," Stokowski said, moving his hand a few inches sideways.

"And the section underneath," the dealer said, pulling the drawer further out.

"That, too," the Maestro agreed, moving his hand downward.

I was staring at the floor, struggling not to laugh, but stole a sideways glance. Stokowski's expression, intent and serious, betrayed an interest only in high-quality furniture. This went on until he'd had enough, and I followed him out the door. "You are outrageous!" I whispered loudly.

"Do you think so?" he asked, a self-satisfied smile covering his face.

A visit to another antique shop a few days later wasn't as amusing. As we emerged from the car, he said, "I am an antique." This frightened me—he never referred to his age—and I thought if he were in denial, he'd live forever. But before I could respond to what he had said, Natalie spoke up, as usual not tuned in to his psychology. She didn't understand the need to avoid mentioning his chronological age. "An antique has to be one hundred," she chirped. "You're not a hundred yet."

I came up beside him. "You are anything but," I said, too softly for her to hear. He looked at me, I think a bit gratefully.

He was increasingly bringing me into his confidence, at one point even revealing the pressure he'd felt from maintaining a super-human image. We were sitting alone in the car when he said, with great sadness, "Because I did one thing well, people expected me to do everything well." But there were still times, in the midst of having fun or relaxing, when he'd suddenly withdraw into himself, not making eye contact or interacting with me or anyone else. These episodes weren't frequent nor did they last long, but I could never find out what brought them on. And although I never took them personally, I found them troubling.

During my trip, the summer of 1975, Stokowski had seemed happy and relaxed, and Natalie and I were getting along beautifully. I hoped this lovely atmosphere would last but he seemed to have other ideas. One afternoon, I was with him in his bedroom while she did errands. When she returned, I went into the dining room to read and she stayed with him. A few minutes later, I overheard him ask her where I was.

"She's in the dining room," Natalie responded. Then she called down the hallway: "Nancy, Maestro wants you." I walked into his room and stood near the door. He was lying in bed; she was standing at the far end of the room.

"Come here where I can see you," he said, without making any effort to get up. I walked around the bed and bent down. He held his arms out and I moved closer. In one motion, he took my face in his hands and kissed me passionately. I pulled away. Natalie looked horrified.

"What's going on?" I demanded, looking first at him, then at her. "Will someone tell me what's happening?"

There was explosive silence. Natalie looked at Stokowski.

"Would you like me to go now?" she asked, her voice quavering.

"Yes," he said, "go away!" Then, after pausing, he shouted, "Where is your room?"

"Across the hall," she answered meekly.

As one might scold a child, he screamed, "Go to your room!" I hoped his outburst had ended, but there was more. "Whose house is this?" he yelled at her.

"Yours," she quietly replied.

"Yes," he said, "this is my house. Mine! This is my room, and my garden!"

Natalie looked at him. "I thought it was ours, but I was wrong. I know now that it's yours."

"Who are you?" he asked, his voice filled with disgust.

"That's a good question," she replied sadly.

"Yes, it is!" he said.

Then, timidly, she answered, "Natasha?" and walked slowly out of the room. I began to follow her.

"You stay!" he ordered.

"I'm going until things quiet down," I said, and went upstairs. I waited a few minutes, then returned downstairs to see him almost running through the hallway toward the kitchen. Natalie was still in her bedroom. I followed him.

"You and I care about each other but that has to be kept between us," I told him.

"No," he answered calmly, shaking his head.

"Please help me with this," I begged.

"No," he said coolly. "Help yourself! She must help herself and so must I." He bent down to kiss me and I hesitated. "Oh," he said indignantly, "you don't want to? All right!" This was hardly the time for a kiss, I thought, but I did as he wished.

He walked quickly back to his bedroom, then passed between the billowing white curtains of the doorway to the garden. I followed and found him sitting on the low wooden bench, looking straight ahead, his jaw set.

"Why did you do that? Why did you kiss me in front of Natasha?" I asked, exasperated.

He looked up at me. "Why not?" he challenged. "She can't tell me what to do. It's my house and I will do as I wish! She is jealous!"

"Yes," I said. "I would be too, if you kissed someone like that in front of me. If someone came into this garden now and kissed me, how would you feel?"

"No one will come," he said confidently.

"What if I were to call someone and he came?" I was trying to engage his empathy for Natalie.

"Go ahead and call! No one is going to come here!" I wasn't reaching him.

Distressed, I walked a few yards away then, returning to where he sat, put my hand on his arm. I told him how much I loved him. With great intensity, he said he felt the same way about me. But we cannot hurt anyone out of love, I said firmly. "All right," he agreed, then defiantly repeated, "But I will do as I wish!"

Natalie appeared in the doorway, looking distraught. "I'm sorry," she said. "I was hurt and I acted badly."

I fumed; she was not the one who should have been apologizing. "It wasn't your fault," I said. Then, not wanting to criticize him, I added, "It's not anyone's fault." He continued to stare straight ahead.

No one spoke. Finally, I felt I had to break the silence. "It might be best for me to leave," I said.

He looked shocked. "Do you want to go?" he shouted. "I don't want you to!"

Just as loudly, I answered, "No!"

"Then don't!" he yelled.

Suddenly, as if nothing unusual was happening, Natalie asked Stokowski if he wanted tea. "Yes," he answered calmly, and she headed toward the kitchen.

"If Natasha is angry with me or jealous, she could stand in the way of my coming here," I calmly explained.

A plane buzzed high overhead. "What's that noise?" he asked suddenly, looking up. "A plane? It's up in the clouds."

"Yes," I said, "but we're down here, and we have a problem."

"This is my house and I want you to come here whenever you wish!" he shouted.

I stood over him, looking at the top of his head, and began to yell. "When I call, who answers the phone? When I write to you, who opens the mail? When I come here, who do I make the arrangements with? I have to go to Natasha! Without her, I might not be able to contact you! Without her on my side, you and I will not be able to be together! Why do you think, for all these years, I've written to her, spent time with her, sat and talked with her?" I looked at him, stone still on the bench, pouting like a child, and realized who was sitting in front of me.

"Yes," he said after thinking a moment, nodding his head. He was finally beginning to understand what was at stake. "Go talk with her and make everything all right. Say it straight out!" I was left to pick up the pieces.

My outburst had been upsetting yet cathartic. I had deferred to Natalie for years, and now the built-up resentment toward her—and him—had finally been released. But he had put everything at risk. I didn't know what he had been thinking. He may have thought that Natalie would leave and I would stay, but he might also have known that Natalie wouldn't leave under any circumstances. More likely, he probably hadn't given any thought to the consequences of his actions. He had always been fiercely independent and impulsive, personally and professionally. I often heard him proudly describe himself as "obstinate" and "egocentric," and brag that he would never compromise.

I walked down the hall to the kitchen. A kettle steamed on the stove as Natalie quietly sobbed. "I've seen this coming for three days," she told me. At fifty-four, she lamented she was no longer good looking and said I was "young and beautiful."

Stokowski entered the kitchen and the three of us sat silently at the table sipping cups of tea. I was desperate to make things right. "You know what our problem is? We're human," I said. She looked away; he blinked. After ten tense minutes, he returned to his room. I stayed with Natalie.

"I shouldn't have been surprised," she said, dabbing her eyes with a tissue. "Last Christmas in France, Luba told me, 'Something's going to explode between Nancy and Daddy.' He's never done anything like that before. He never kisses *anyone*," she cried, and I suddenly realized that, in all the years I had known him, I had seen him kiss women only on the hand, never on the face. I now knew that there was only hand-kissing between him and Natalie.

And then it all poured out. She was a prisoner, didn't have a life, was close to having a nervous breakdown. She wanted to leave but she didn't want him to be alone. The French house was too much responsibility, and she wasn't even able to take a holiday. She'd never have a boyfriend or marry, never have that type of relationship. "I thought I had this one settled," she sobbed. We talked and I lied, softening the strength of my relationship with him. But I welcomed the opportunity to let her know that I didn't want to replace her, that there was no need for her to feel threatened by me. Then he called—"Allo?"—and she raced down the hall. She later told me that she had kissed his hand and, for the first time, annoyed, he had asked, "What was that for?" She had been hurt again.

Late that evening, after Stokowski had gone to bed, Natalie came to me and kissed my cheek. For her, the situation seemed to have created a bond between us, not a barrier. She didn't want me to leave. I wondered if she didn't want to lose the socializing and the freedom my visits provided, or if she would have agreed to anything to continue their relationship—including the presence of another woman. She also might have feared building an independent life of her own. I also knew that there was an element of masochism in her relationship with him. Why else would she have tolerated the cool, often dismissive, treatment I had witnessed for years—not to mention this latest insult?

For the next two days, the three of us acted as if nothing had happened. We talked and listened to music and took drives through the countryside. But he was still more openly affectionate with me than I felt was safe.

I needed him to know that I wouldn't stay in Nether Wallop but I wanted to express it gently. Alone in the car with him, I said we needed to talk. "I'm upset about what's been happening." I mentioned Natalie and the need to be discreet. "It *is* nice to live with someone, isn't it?" I asked, implying that if she left, he'd be alone.

"Oh, yes," he answered.

"Then we must keep to ourselves how we feel about each other," I said. "We must behave with good taste and discretion."

After silent consideration, he looked at me. "I think you are right," he said, and lovingly, we agreed.

The next day in his bedroom, while Natalie was out doing errands, he talked about her. "Perhaps," he said, "Natasha is jealous of you. She would like to be in here as you are." He pressed the tip of his nose against mine, looked deeply into my eyes, and kissed me. "What you and I have certain people are jealous of. They want it too, but it cannot be," he said with great emotion. "I wish it could be so, but it cannot."

His harsh treatment of Natalie disappointed me but didn't surprise me. I had detected undercurrents of resentment—blatant and subtle—flowing between them for years. When Natalie looked at him, there was both adoration and fear in her eyes; she was always cautious and deferential. He was usually distant and formal. "Yes, please," he'd say, when she asked if he wanted her to do something for him. I rarely saw him look directly at her or use her name. "Allo!" he'd yell down the hall when he wanted something, and she would run to him. Only rarely did I hear him call her "Natasha" or "Natash." He probably resented what she represented—that he was no longer independent and that he had failed to form close, supportive relationships. But there might have been warm, loving moments between them that I didn't witness.

Natalie expressed her resentment toward him more subtly, often by denying him small things. He loved eating outdoors and, during one of my visits, he asked about having dinner in the garden. "It's so difficult," she complained, "to carry the dishes and the food outside." I had to be careful not to challenge her in front of him but wanted him to be happy. "I'll help carry everything," I said, and we had a lovely dinner under the evening sky.

I endured Natalie's inconsideration, always careful to camouflage my resentment with good humor: "I really wish you would use my new address and write…" "I hope you received my letter sent last week. It is necessary for me to set my travel arrangements now…" "I wrote to you quite a while ago but have heard nothing. Knowing your impeccable manners, I can only blame Her Majesty's letter carriers!"

All of us in his personal and professional lives were, in effect, held hostage by Natalie. Urania Giordano, who had cooked Italian dinners for Stokowski and accompanied him on trips to New York farmers markets, had written to me in 1974: "Have no news from the other side of the pond. Not from LS or any of my onon [sic] friends. It's as if that chapter in my life never took place." Then, in early 1977, Urania wrote: "I've had no word or news from that sector since I last saw them in Nether Wallop in '73," and referred to Natalie's "insecurity syndrome." Natalie even intimidated members of his family. One of Stokowski's daughters, two and a half years after her father's death, wrote to me, "How are your relations w. Natasha? (Please don't tell her you're writing to me if she's at all strained with you, because she gets so easily upset over nothing.)"

I signed my letters to him, which I knew Natalie would open, "With my best regards." Only rarely would I write, "With all my love" or "With loving thoughts." I was afraid that if she felt threatened, she wouldn't give him my letters. But there was a flip side: Knowing how close I was to Stokowski, she might have feared *not* giving him my letters. If the periods of silence became extended, I'd make expensive transatlantic calls. One of my letters to Natalie, in April 1977, reveals my difficult position: "I was shocked when Maestro hung up the phone on Wednesday!" I didn't want her to think I hadn't wanted to say goodbye after I had spoken with him. And when I wrote about visiting "them," I was sure to mention that he had asked me to return and that I had promised to do so. An entry from my diary reveals the complexity of my predicament: During one of my visits, Stokowski asked me to extend my stay. I should have said yes immediately but, to remain on Natalie's good side—and not knowing what plans might have existed—I responded, "I'll see what Natasha says."

"I'm in the picture, too," he said resentfully.

It would have been easier for me to feel sympathy, or at least compassion, for Natalie had she not affected the authoritative arrogance she thought befitted a Mrs. Stokowski. Her use of first-person plural to refer to herself and Stokowski rankled those of us who knew they weren't a couple. Orchestra and record company executives frequently had to deal with her rather than communicate directly with him, and people who had enjoyed friendly relationships with him in New York eventually lost contact as their letters and phone messages went unanswered. (To maintain his Great Maestro image, he wouldn't have contacted them or asked Natalie about them.) They suspected that their correspondence hadn't gone beyond Natalie. She was, and still is, referred to by Stokowski's surviving music business associates as "The Dragon Lady." (More harshly, when Faye passed away, one American Symphony official bitterly told me, "The wrong one died.") Stokowski used her—and Faye when she was alive—as a buffer between himself and the mundane world. He didn't have to be bothered with anything less exalted than Great Art.

The great ambition of Natalie's life would seem to have been satisfied by the move with him to England—except that he didn't marry her. They never became partners; he never recognized or treated her as an equal. But Natalie provided him with more than the services of running the house, organizing his rehearsal and recording schedules, keeping his scores in order, preparing meals, and overseeing his medication and doctors' visits. She provided familiarity, knowing his personal and professional history—musical milestones, and the identity of colleagues, family members, and old friends. And she was part of his Philadelphia past. She knew who he was and treated him accordingly. She gave him the adulation and control he required.

In addition to the proximity to Stokowski, Natalie enjoyed other perks: living in an English manor house and in a custom-built home in the south of France; the expensive AGA cooker she had insisted on for the Nether Wallop kitchen; the costly thatching of the two structures on the property (which Stokowski referred to as "Natasha's folly"); a rented white Mercedes-Benz in France; and valuable antiques in both houses. She also must have known that she was in his will. But I don't think the material things were of primary importance to her. She wanted his attention, his affection. No one could understand that desire more than me.

At this point in his life, Stokowski's options were limited. He was no longer married; his sons, now in their twenties, were building their lives; his daughters all had families and professional responsibilities of their own; and he didn't have close friends he could depend on. But he would have been reluctant to show weakness and accept help in any case. Even when he softened a bit toward the end of his life, his personality was so dominant, and his need to control so great, that people still had to suppress their own personalities for him to accept them.

Like many celebrities, Stokowski was spoiled—always getting his way, given the best of everything. Standing beside him after concerts, I'd noticed that every face he saw was smiling at him. I remembered the eager fans who always showed up at the stage door bearing gifts, invitations, and offers of assistance with anything he might need. Most had been coolly rejected. He had been—and had remained—highly selective about who was given the honor of serving him.

His second wife, Evangeline Johnson, in an interview with Stokowski biographer Abram Chasins,[4] said, "There is nothing Stoki liked so much as service for free." (She was commenting on his willingness to have a relationship with Faye and Natalie—"those unattractive girls" as she referred to them.) I thought it went

---

4   Abram Chasins, *Leopold Stokowski: A Profile*, Hawthorn Books, 1979.

far beyond that—he needed *reverential* service. I think he needed adulation more than love.

The former Mrs. Stokowski also spoke of his strong feelings of inferiority, which she called "indescribable." It is, however, difficult to imagine how anyone harboring feelings of inferiority could have mounted the podium with such dominating confidence. After reading her comment, I wondered if that confidence was genuine until he referred to it one day when we were alone. "I was so damned conceited, so sure of myself," he said, using the only curse word I'd ever hear him use. That conceit, however, might have been limited to music. Feelings of personal inadequacy could have figured in his failed marriages, his need to have constant affairs, and particularly his fabrication of an impressive family history.

I shared a trait with Stokowski's wives, but it wasn't wealth or glamour. We all desperately wanted to please him. Gloria Vanderbilt, in her book *It Seemed Important at the Time*, wrote that from the moment she met him, all she wanted was "to please him and make him happy." Olga Samaroff had written similarly in a letter to John Erskine, president of The Juilliard School, eight years after her divorce from Stokowski: "When one has worshiped a man and done everything humanly possible to make him happy…" And there were Faye and Natalie and, to a large extent, me. The best way to get his attention was to serve him.

I don't think, however, that it was possible for anyone to keep him happy, so great was his need for total devotion. And if it had been possible to give him that, he might have become bored and moved on. I've often wondered if a Stokowski–Garbo marriage, which he very much wanted, would have lasted. He might have tired even of someone with her extraordinary beauty, talent, and worldwide fame. I see a pattern in his many liaisons with prominent, beautiful women: He eventually rejected or alienated all of them.

No one had forced Natalie to stay in Nether Wallop. The rewards were apparently adequate enough to keep her there, so it seems unfair to cast Stokowski in the role of exploiter. Considering her psychology, the ultimate cruelty might have been for Stokowski to have deprived her of serving him. And no one forced me to be part of this complicated trio. My relationship with him obviously satisfied my own psychological needs. Regardless of his youthfulness and vitality, Stokowski had to have been a father figure; my non-musical attraction to him was probably rooted in my troubled relationship with my father. But a childhood like mine could have led to other needs—a desire for a family of my own to supply the closeness I hadn't known, or to provide an opportunity to "fix" the past. But I never did marry or have children; neither was something I wanted. As demanding and controlling a person as Stokowski had been—I would not tolerate that kind of behavior today—I have no regrets.

I returned to Nether Wallop for only a few days the following summer, 1976. Neither Stokowski nor Natalie mentioned the tension we'd had the year before; there was, in fact, a familial feeling now—the kind of intimacy shared by people who have gone through a trauma together.

However, despite our closeness, he remained unpredictable. On the way home during one of our afternoon drives, we passed a charming building with leaded windows glinting in the waning light.

"That house," Stokowski said, pointing, "is where Lady Godiva is said to have been born."

I noticed a sign outside. "What is it now?"

"It's connected to a restaurant next door," he answered. "Would you like to have dinner there?" I said I would. "When we get home, call and make a reservation," he said.

His elder son, Stan, now twenty-six, had just arrived, and a few hours later, he, Stokowski, Natalie, and I drove off to dinner. The dimly lit restaurant was even more charming than it looked from the outside. Stokowski ordered sweetbreads and enthusiastically allowed the chef to refill his plate from a cart he wheeled to our table. It was a happy evening, and eventually we began to discuss desserts, Natalie, Stan, and I excitedly arguing the strengths of our preferences. Stokowski, more than any of us, was usually a dessert devotee but, without provocation, he suddenly bellowed, "I want to leave!" Natalie jumped up, waving her hands at the waiter as if there was an emergency. Stan ran to get our coats, and I held the door. One person didn't want dessert so three others did without. I began to question this balance of power.

On my final day of that visit, he, Natalie, and I drove to an acupuncturist in London where he'd be treated for his sore leg. He was quiet in the car, and silent and stoic in the waiting room, looking straight ahead, not engaging with Natalie or me. I had experienced a similar situation just before one of his recording sessions (of the Mahler Second Symphony) in London two summers earlier. Five or six of us, including one of his daughters and members of the recording production team, sat with him in an anteroom, not talking or even looking at each other because he wanted to concentrate. Those silences were uncomfortable, and I was beginning to find his demands difficult to accept. But on the drive home after the acupuncture, his mood brightened when we stopped for lunch at a quaint French inn on the banks of the Thames in Old Windsor, and, at my request, drove to Runnymede, where the Magna Carta had been signed. Because it was my last day, rather than saying goodbye in London, I prolonged my visit by driving with them to Andover, near Nether Wallop, where I got the train back to London. As always, he seemed upset when it was time for me to leave, and asked if I could stay on. I explained that I had to go to Scotland for my third summer at the festival, but promised that I'd come to his London recording sessions of the Bizet *Carmen* Suite after Aberdeen. Although I too hated to say goodbye, I was excited, anticipating the fun I knew I'd soon have with my friends and colleagues.

My visit with Stokowski a year later, in August 1977, was one of the shortest. I planned to stay for only a few days then return at Christmas. He was now ninety-five. I watched as he walked down the hallway of his home, no less regal than when he had walked onstage at Carnegie Hall. But his knees were beginning to weaken and bend slightly, and he'd move his right hand along the brick wall as he slowly made his way into the dining room. There he'd stop to reverently touch the carved wooden cabinet from Poland that connected him to his heritage and to the grandfather whose name he carried.

We listened to his recordings of Tchaikovsky and Bach in the evening; he could no longer bear the raw emotions of Mahler or the power of Wagner—music he had conducted so magnificently. Witnessing the depth and strength of his reactions to the music, I thought again of those who accused him of superficiality.

He was spending more time resting than he had during my last visit, and I became concerned. One afternoon, when he'd been napping longer than usual, I wondered if I should let him rest or push him a bit in the hopes of cheering him up and energizing him.

"Is there a man in the house?" I shouted down the hall from the kitchen where Natalie and I were preparing dinner. "We need a man in here!" I knew if he wished he could ignore me, but soon I heard footsteps shuffling down the hallway. He stood in the doorway, his hand on the jamb. "Here is your man!" he said, smiling sweetly.

There were other signs of aging I couldn't ignore. We were sitting next to each other at the dinner table when I looked down. His hands were in his lap. The smooth, celebrated flesh had grown gaunt; dark-spotted translucent skin had shrunk tight against long thin bones and dark-blue veins that stretched from his wrists to his fingertips. A long reddened gash ran horizontally across the back of his right hand. He had cut himself but seemed not to have noticed. I looked away, tears filling my eyes.

His memory wasn't as sharp as it had been, but I saw no change in his ability to carry on complex conversations. Natalie, however, had begun to speak to him in increasingly simplistic language. As soon as she left to do errands one afternoon, he turned to me, anguish covering his face.

"Why does she speak to me that way? Why does she treat me like a child? And she doesn't let me do anything for myself!" His head was lowered slightly, his hands rested in his lap.

I sat down close beside him. "It has nothing to do with you," I said softly. He looked at me questioningly. "She needs to feel needed, and she needs to feel important, and that's why she treats you that way. It has only to do with her and nothing to do with you or your ability."

He digested the comment, then smiled, looking a bit embarrassed. "So when are you going to write a book on psychology?" he asked, reclaiming his confident demeanor. I realized that our roles had shifted: I was now in a position of authority.

He began to speak more freely about his past and his family, including the recent reunion with his brother Jim after some five decades, arranged by Stokowski's eldest child, Sonya.

"It's so nice to have a brother," I sighed. "I'm an only child." He looked at me intently. "No!" he said with great emotion. "No, you are not! My brother is also your brother." He had said something similar in the south of France. He, Natalie, and I were in the living room of the villa, chatting and wrapping Christmas gifts for the housekeeper, Jeanette, and her little son, Jean-Michel. There was a roaring fire, and the air was suffused with the burnt-wood and floral perfumes of the Riviera winter. I was deeply moved by the intimacy. "This is like a family," I said. Stokowski became indignant, his eyebrows raised. "This *is* a family," he said, "you and Natasha and me," pointing first to me, then to Natalie, then to himself. He spoke passionately about "friendship always." Then he turned to face me. "My father and my grandfather," he said, "they are your relatives, too."

He seemed concerned about honesty in our relationship. Alone in the car together, we talked about sex and I told him that, for me, it had always been an expression of love, not just a physical act. "I feel the same way," he said. About twenty minutes later, looking troubled, he put his hand on my arm. "I did not tell you the truth earlier," he said, pausing. "I was very wild!"

"That's what I've heard!" I teasingly replied.

After decades of constructing and perpetuating family legends that implied royalty and aristocracy, he now revealed the truth about his origins. "My parents were poor people, common people," he said. "But they were talented, and kings and queens are not necessarily talented." He had found a way to accept the truth. I wondered, however, if his parents had really been poor or if he had grown to regard them as such from the perspective of his own success. I already knew something about his parents. Years earlier in New York, he had spoken proudly about his father's work as a cabinetmaker. During a conversation about my job with the Philadelphia Orchestra, he asked what I was earning. "That's not enough!" he declared. He then led me into another room where we sat at a table next to a window looking out over Central Park. On a piece of paper, he wrote out the hourly amount he felt I should be receiving then multiplied it by the number of hours I was working each week. I told him I was hesitant about asking the orchestra for a raise, fearful that I'd lose my job. Smiling at his childhood memory, he began to tell me about his father's business methods. "A customer would come in, look at a piece of furniture, and when my father told him the price, would often say it was too high. My father would not lower the price. 'He will be back,' he would tell me as we watched the customer walk away, and he was always right!"[5] In virtually all of his business dealings as a conductor, Stokowski took the example of his father's independence as his own. He also had the need for wealth that many formerly poor or middle-class people possess.

When we were alone, he told me about his regrets. The man who'd stated, "I never feel guilty because it's the one thing that feels

---

[5] His father, however, had to support a family of three children, the eldest of whom was highly gifted and required a costly education. Young Leopold commuted to Oxford's Queen's College, not living in the dormitory. This might have been due to economic necessity. Stokowski's brother Jim is quoted in Oliver Daniel's biography, *Stokowski: A Counterpoint of View*, as saying, "My father did everything for Leo, and spent what little money he had on his music. I am afraid my sister Lydia and I had to suffer, as there was nothing left for us."

bad when everything else feels good!" had a conscience. I comforted and reassured him, but none of his admissions involved anything I regarded as serious; they were more about inconsideration than hurting others. I knew stories about him that were far more troubling: humiliating members of his orchestras in front of their colleagues; firing players without adequate notice or good reason; treating family members harshly.

What he didn't share were incidents of childhood trauma. There was no explanation for the sullen expression of the teenage choirboy in his robes, looking away from the camera, in a group photograph from around 1900. Perhaps something had happened in that boy's life that would have explained the often-narcissistic, temperamental behavior of the adult he became. Perhaps, by the time he allowed himself to open up to me, he had begun to make peace with whatever his childhood might have held.

"It's good for me when you're here," he told me one afternoon as I walked past him in the dining room. I knew he felt this way but I was surprised—and pleased—that he articulated it. He was becoming a person I could love as well as admire, but I still felt conflicted. Not wanting to fully relinquish my musical deity, I wasn't always as eager to see his human side as he was to reveal it. I was happy that he trusted me—rare for him—but I also knew that he wouldn't have confided in me if I had been famous, wealthy, glamorous, or from a distinguished family. This was ironic, since he was probably attracted to other women because of those attributes. I still wonder if he had ever felt truly loved, since most people in his life had known only the invented character he portrayed and not the person he authentically was.

The day before I was to leave, Natalie went out and Stokowski and I had lunch alone. After half an hour, he rose, placed the palms of both his hands on the table and bent down toward me.

"If you will excuse me," he asked with great formality.

"No, I will not!" I said, feigning annoyance. "I came all the way across the ocean to be with you and I don't want you to leave."

He tilted his head to the side and looked at me sweetly. "I must be with Rachmaninoff," he said. He was soon to record, for the first time in his career, the Second Symphony and he wanted to study the score. A few minutes earlier, I had noticed that he had become preoccupied. Now I understood that he had already been involved with the music.

The next day—the morning of my departure—I prepared his orange juice and took it to him. He was still in bed.

"This is very good!" he said, taking a sip.

"Are you impressed?" I teased.

"I *am* impressed!" he answered. We laughed and looked into each other's eyes. His gaze was strong and loving.

I knelt beside the bed. "I'm off to the airport," I told him, trying to add a note of cheerfulness to soften the pain of separation. I took a mental snapshot of the craggy, still-handsome profile.

He turned his face toward me. "Why must you leave?" he asked, as he had earlier that morning. Now there was a tone of anguish.

"I have to go back to Philadelphia, to my job at Curtis," I told him again, detailing the work I was doing with young musicians. He looked away, seeming to understand, then turned back toward me. We looked at each other in silence.

Suddenly, he reverted to the goodbyes of so many years ago at 1067. "Do you have your ticket?" he asked.

"I do," I told him.

"Do you have enough money?"

"Yes, dear, I do."

"But what if you see something that you want..." and he stopped, a look of confusion clouding his face. "Stand up!" he ordered, raising himself on one elbow. "I want to see how tall you are."

Watching him closely, I rose to my full height. Softly, almost to himself, he said, "You are tall. You are grown now." I kissed him gently and, my vision clouded by tears, walked out of the room and out of the house.

Seventeen days later, on the morning of September 13, he didn't awaken from his sleep. I was at Curtis when one of my colleagues called me into her office and told me the news. I remember my shock. "But I had so much to tell him," I said. It may sound sentimental, but I like to think that Stokowski did join Rachmaninoff in some celestial performance.[6]

---

[6] Two days after Stokowski's death, *The Philadelphia Inquirer* published a story about my relationship with him: that we had been close, that I had worked for him in New York, and that I had continued to see him after his move to Europe. Ormandy then knew that I had worked simultaneously for him and Stokowski. Ormandy and his wife, Gretel, stopped speaking to me for years.

Chapter Twenty-One

WHEN STOKOWSKI DIED, I ENDURED more than grief. I became fearful that at thirty-one I had heard the greatest performances I'd ever hear. Unlike some music professionals, I didn't attend concerts just to experience what the musicians would "do" with the music or to analyze the technicalities of the composition or its performance. Although I was fascinated by the interpretive choices musicians made, and by the technical construction of a work, I wanted—needed—to be moved emotionally, to be transported. I had, however, reason to be hopeful: Slava was developing a career as a conductor.

For years, Slava had expressed his frustrations about the limitations of the solo cello repertoire. Despite his efforts to commission and play new works, the list remained considerably smaller than those of the violin and the piano. "How many times can I play the Dvořák concerto?" he'd asked me, using that concerto symbolically. I knew he loved the Dvořák—and a great many other solo works—and I'd never heard him play any of them the same way twice. But, now almost fifty, he was eager to expand the scope of his musicianship. He needed more than a single instrument to express the breadth of his musical vision.[1]

"I become conductor! Then I have all of orchestra repertoire to conduct!" he exuberantly told me in his dressing room in 1975, holding his arms wide apart. He was considering a position with

---

1 Slava played the piano mainly to accompany his wife. He didn't perform as a soloist.

the National Symphony Orchestra in Washington, DC. He said it was Stokowski, backstage after one of Slava's cello recitals, who told him he should conduct; he'd said he knew it from the way Slava moved his body when he played. "He realized this before I did," Slava proudly told me.[2]

It's not unusual for great instrumentalists and singers to want to become conductors, but they often lack that talent; it's a separate gift that's rarely transferable. To be able to conduct from the keyboard, so that orchestra members could see him, Van Cliburn had a clear plastic lid installed on his Steinway grand. Despite having studied with the great Bruno Walter, and coached with Eugene Ormandy, Van was not a "natural" conductor and his conducting career never flourished. Others, like Daniel Barenboim, Vladimir Ashkenazy, and Christoph Eschenbach, have had highly successful double careers.

After years of conducting mostly opera in the USSR, with guest appearances in Europe and the US, Slava became music director of the National Symphony in 1977, the same year that Stokowski died. It was an ironic appointment: An exiled Soviet was now at the helm of an ensemble that represented not just a city or a state but a nation—one that remained the USSR's principal adversary. And the orchestra was based in the nation's capital.

Soon after Slava took over the NSO, cellist David Finckel and I drove from Philadelphia to hear him rehearse at The Kennedy Center. We arrived late, rushing down the center aisle while the orchestra played, and I stopped midway to listen. I heard what I'd hear in the months and years to come: Slava's phenomenal musicianship only sporadically transferred to the podium. His conducting technique was often awkward and choppy, and the players

---

[2] I was aware of Slava's high regard for Stokowski. "He such great conductor!" Slava always declared when we spoke about him. But I heard about that admiration also from Slava's—and Stokowski's—friend Juri Jelagin, who had played Stokowski's recording of the love music from the second and third acts of *Tristan und Isolde* for Slava. The work begins with an intense, ardent statement. "Is like instant hard-on!" Slava had commented appreciatively.

couldn't always tell what he wanted; he would never hold the baton with the same authority as he did the bow. Only rarely did I hear his orchestras produce the soaring lyricism and subtle nuances I heard in his playing.

At times, he drew beautifully shaped phrases and expressive eloquence from his players, but he rarely generated the qualities of pure sound—sonority—that he got from his cello or that Stokowski consistently elicited from his orchestras. I would come to realize that wasn't his objective; he had a different sensibility. If Slava paid attention at all to pure sound, it was more to achieve specific effects than for tonal coloration or "blend." This doesn't mean that his sound was inferior to Stokowski's, only that his concept was different.

Stokowski's sound, like in *Firebird* or *Carmina Burana*, could purposely be rough and raw, but when he felt that beautiful sound would serve the music best, his was characteristically lush and opulent. Ramon Scavelli, a violist who played in Stokowski's Houston Symphony and Rostropovich's National Symphony, compared the two conductors: In loud sections, Slava wanted *maximum* loudness—harsh, not blended; Stokowski did not. Slava had a more Russian sensibility, where instruments (and sections of the orchestra) don't blend but stay separate—sounding simultaneously but not merging. Lewis Lipnick, contrabassoonist of the National Symphony, played under both Stokowski (when he had guest conducted the orchestra) and Slava. Under Slava's direction, Lewis said, each section of the orchestra had its own distinct character even in "tutti" sections (where the entire orchestra played). But even two instruments wouldn't blend as they would under Stokowski's direction. Stokowski, Lewis said, ordered his players to listen to each other and blend their tones; Slava did not. These different concepts of sound can be thought of in terms of painting: Two or more adjacent, separate colors on a canvas can be perceived by a viewer to almost—but not quite—blend; they are not, however, actually mixed together to create a third, new color. The Stokowski technique would combine instrumental colors into a new hue. Lewis felt that Slava's approach worked best for him in Shostakovich, Prokofiev, and some Tchaikovsky. Prokofiev and Shostakovich didn't always require warm, blended sonorities; they needed big contrasts—sudden explosions, then quiet, and Slava loved those extremes. He wanted the players to dig in. "Make more noise!" Lewis—and I—remembered him shouting at rehearsals. Stokowski, he said, instructed his musicians not to play louder, particularly when they had the secondary voices. "Never force your playing," he remembered Stokowski saying. "Don't *make* your instrument play, *let* it play!"

Lewis also spoke about conductors who "get in the way" of the music. They over-conduct or micromanage every aspect of what the players do. Slava, he said, was often guilty of this, but Stokowski was not. I'd often see him step back and let the players do as they wished.

Because Slava's conducting technique was compromised, he'd often communicate by physically emulating the mood of the music. Friends of mine in the orchestra told me that they played according to the emotions he physically expressed. He'd grimace, scowl, frown, or look ecstatic. He also had to rely on metaphors and descriptions at rehearsals to convey what he wanted. One of the most vivid—which he used for single notes played as short and loud as possible—was "like fork in brain!" and the musicians would respond with explosive force. And for rapid, fast notes: "Like bugs on skin!" he'd yell, rapidly moving the fingers of one hand up and down his other arm, portraying scurrying insects. This was very different from Stokowski, who hardly spoke at his rehearsals.

I witnessed many occasions when the usually good-natured Slava would erupt in anger, castigating the musicians. I thought this was evidence of frustration caused by the limitations of his technique. He knew what he wanted; the sounds were in his head. But while he could make his cello do as he wished, he couldn't always transmit his concepts to his players.

In spite of Slava's limitations, however, all the elements of a performance would sometimes shift into place. A Tchaikovsky

Fourth he conducted at Carnegie Hall conveyed such torment and sadness that I was compelled to walk around the block to calm myself before going backstage to see him. And his performance of Shostakovich's Eighth Symphony was appropriately disturbing, powerfully reflecting the terror and brutality of World War II and Hitler, and undoubtedly the horror of the Stalin era, all of which Slava and Shostakovich had experienced firsthand. The shrieking dissonances, sinister snare rolls, and panicky tremolos did not, however, descend into the realm of superficial movie music. At its close, the symphony died away: quiet plucked notes in the cellos and basses against soft, sustained chords in the violins and violas. The performance left me stunned. In his dressing room backstage, our eyes welling with tears, he and I looked at each other and shook our heads sadly, not exchanging one word.

Slava was fortunate to have begun his conducting career in front of the best orchestras. And, since 1975, he'd had a cello to match: the famed "Duport" Strad. In addition to a resonant, multi-hued sound, the cello had an interesting history: The scratches on its side were said to have been made by Napoleon who, while attempting to play the instrument, had dug his spurs into its body. But after Slava got the Strad and stopped playing his old Storioni, I'd felt that a certain depth, richness, and muscularity were missing from his performances. After one rehearsal, he'd told me at length how privileged he was to own the Strad.

"I prefer your old cello," I'd told him flatly. His eyes and mouth had opened wide. It was as if I'd said that I no longer liked him or his playing.

"How can you say that?" he'd asked, disappointment covering his face.

"Well, perhaps I'm accustomed to that sound," I'd said, trying to soften my assault. I knew that other friends of his shared my opinion but apparently no one else had the courage—or the lack of good judgment—to confess it.

He was always interested in different types of cellos, particularly new ones. They were more affordable than distinguished older ones, although no one could know if they'd maintain their quality over the years. (I think he often had his students' needs in mind when he investigated new instruments.) Slava called me at home in Philadelphia early one morning. He was going to try out a newly made cello from the New Jersey violinmaker Sergio Peresson. "You come to Academy. I meet you there," he said. When I arrived Slava wasn't sitting onstage, but in an aisle of the auditorium ninety degrees left of the stage; a few other friends and I sat facing him at the opposite side of the hall. He played a virtuoso passage first on his Strad then on the new cello, and I had to listen intently to detect the differences in their voices. He held up the new instrument. "This cannot compare to the Stradivarius, of course, but it *can* compare!" He meant that while nothing could match a top-quality Strad, the new cello was able to hold its own. It was a great compliment to Mr. Peresson, but I wondered how the new cello would sound in the hands of a lesser musician.

At Curtis, I was not only preparing all the music the orchestra played, I was also organizing the rehearsals: welcoming whoever was conducting; taking attendance; making sure the stage was set properly; and fielding questions and complaints. Due to these responsibilities, I was only able to make the trip to Washington a few times each season. There, I'd attend Slava's rehearsals and concerts, and spend time with him at the Watergate. Our relationship, at first playfully flirtatious, became something more at his suite in the hotel, and in his apartment in New York.

On one of my visits that year—1978—Juri picked me up at Union Station. Visibly anxious, he grabbed my luggage and rushed me to his car, saying that Slava was waiting for us at Juri's place in Chevy Chase. Because of his defiance of the Soviet regime, his sister Veronika, a violinist in the Moscow Philharmonic, had been denied permission to tour the US with her orchestra. Her livelihood was threatened and her personal freedom—the Soviet version—violated. I was to help write a flyer exposing the situation; copies would be distributed at the upcoming Kennedy Center performance of another Russian orchestra. Slava would dictate the text in Russian, Juri would translate it into basic English, and I would polish it into a publishable version ("in your excellent Eeng-lesh," Slava later said).

Slava crushed me in his arms and covered my face and neck with kisses. "You sit!" he commanded, placing me next to him on the living room sofa. "You write!" All went well until he heard me mutter, as I was writing, that his sister was now "a pariah in her own country." He stopped, thought for a second, jumped to his feet and flapped his arms wildly, dancing around the living room like an enormous bird. "Murray Perahia!" he yelled gleefully, referencing the concert pianist whose name was pronounced the same as "pariah." I was amazed. Despite being concerned about his sister, he had maintained his sense of humor, and after shrieks of laughter, we got back to work. Although fearless about his own welfare, Slava continued to worry about his sister's wellbeing. Shortly after the brochure was distributed, he called from Europe asking me to write a letter on his behalf to Katharine Graham, publisher of the *Washington Post*. He wanted her newspaper to expose the fact that Veronika's orchestra, when it came to the States, "might not be sent intact." (He didn't want to specifically say that his sister would be left behind.) About a week later, I received a response from Graham saying that she had sent copies of my letter to the *Post*'s Style editor and to the Editorial page, but within the next few weeks, the story not only broke in *The Post* but was carried by the Associated Press. Ultimately, however, Veronika was denied permission to tour.

Although he desperately missed his country, Slava had remained defiant about human rights. Back in 1977 he'd stated publicly that he would not return to the USSR until there was full artistic freedom: "I will not utter one single lie in order to return, and once there, if I see new injustice, I will speak out four times more loudly than before." The following March, watching television in Paris, he and Galina learned that their citizenship had been revoked. Leonid Brezhnev, who had allowed them to leave but retain their citizenship, had just signed a decree making it impossible for them to return home. For four years, since leaving the USSR, they had traveled on extended Soviet visas. Now, having no country of their own, they traveled first on special Swiss papers then accepted an offer from Princess Grace, a friend of Slava's, to have Monégasque passports with the word "UNSPECIFIED" under "Nationality." They did not, however, accept her offer of citizenship. They didn't want to give allegiance to any country other than their own.

Free for the first time in his life, no longer required to give a substantial part of his income to the Soviet government, Slava bought homes in London, Paris, and around the corner from Lincoln Center in New York. This was the start of a more affluent life for him and his family. It was also the start of accusations by some people in the music business that Slava's criticism of Soviet policies was financially motivated. Those people could not have been aware of the harsh consequences he knew he would endure. His fate could have been disastrous.

Despite all he'd been through, Slava was still great fun to be with. "Now, cheeldren, you come vis me," he'd order mischievously as the last of the autograph seekers and adoring fans left his Carnegie Hall or Avery Fisher Hall dressing room. A few of us in the inner circle—a mix of music business veterans and friends he'd known for years—would follow him to his apartment. Too much food and drink and an endless supply of stories—some tragic, some hilarious—kept us around the dining room table far into the night. A typical evening began with Champagne, progressed to bottles of fine wine and whisky, then got to the serious stuff: Russian vodka drunk out of water glasses. We consumed pounds of smoked fish and meats and pickled vegetables—typical Russian fare. Around three in the morning, Slava liked to make kasha, a Russian peasant dish. Shoeless, the suspenders of his dress pants hanging from his waist, he'd stand at the stove measuring buckwheat groats and water into a pot using his vodka glass.

All of us around the table knew good stories and we told them well, but Slava's tales became high drama as he acted out each character's role.

He took special delight in telling us how he had outsmarted Soviet officials, particularly the powerful, much-feared Minister of Culture, Ekaterina Furtseva. While on tour in Europe, Slava had seen an antique sideboard he desperately wanted, but it was too large for his dacha. He contacted Furtseva. To continue to make music on the high level that brought such glory to the Soviet Union, he told her, he needed more expansive acoustics in his house and more space to practice. As we watched, he mimed the act of bowing in a tight space. He gave her measurements. The Minister arranged for his house to be enlarged and Slava had the sideboard shipped.

It was both hilarious and heartbreaking to hear Slava reenact his final goodbye to Shostakovich, who had died in August 1975, little more than a year after Slava's departure from Russia. Because of Shostakovich's declining health and the possibility that Slava's absence could be prolonged, both men knew they might not see each other again. "In whose arms now shall I die?" the composer had asked, as they had held each other and cried.

"I will conduct all your music," Slava had reassured him, "every one of your symphonies." Slava then mimicked the composer, speaking between sobs, "'Do the Fourth first!'"

During our post-concert socializing, Slava would talk about the performance he had just given. I knew that, like most professional musicians, he always listened from the perspective of an audience member: As he was playing or conducting, often intensely and passionately, he was listening critically. (During his master classes at Juilliard and Curtis, I often heard him tell students that it was essential for them to listen to themselves as they played, to know what worked or didn't work, not to become lost in the intensity of the moment.) Simultaneously, he had to anticipate what was coming. But he also listened with the composers' ears. "You know," he'd say thoughtfully, looking into the distance as we sat together, "sometimes during a concert I see the composer's face in front of me, especially when I conduct the music of Prokofiev or Shostakovich. The face is right here," he'd tell me, the palm of his hand only an inch from his nose. "Sometimes it looks happy, sometimes not so happy. If not so happy, I change what I'm doing—perhaps make the tempo faster or slower—and the face will become happy or it will disappear."

I loved hearing about his friendships with great composers, but one evening I wished that he hadn't been close to Prokofiev. He and I were to have dinner together in New York. I chose a dress I thought he'd like and remembered the perfume I'd brought back from Russia eight or nine years earlier—amber-colored liquid in a flat, clear-glass bottle that fit into the palm of my hand. The perfume was called "*Krasnaya Moskva*"—"Beautiful Moscow" or "Red Moscow"—the latter referring to communist ideology. The scent was sweet and floral and feminine and I thought he'd like it, but I also worried that it might remind him of home and make him sad. I decided to take the chance and dabbed some behind my ears, on my wrists, and between my breasts. When he opened the door of his apartment and bent down to embrace me, his eyes suddenly grew wide. He backed away, his hands in the air. "Aaaaacccchhhhhh!" he shouted, looking shocked. "*You smell like Prokofiev!*" (Prokofiev, I later learned, was fond not only of wearing perfume, but fine clothes as well. History now knows the scent he preferred.)

I often saw in Slava something that had surprised me when I first became aware of it years earlier: the sense of isolation that could engulf even the most celebrated musicians. Cheered by thousands after a performance, they could find themselves alone in a hotel room moments later. Many famous conductors and soloists seemed grateful when I offered to take them sightseeing or invited them to have a meal. Slava, who was almost always "on" when we were with other people, would wearily run his hands over his face, forehead to chin, after they'd left. It never took him long to recharge but I began to suspect that he maintained his frenetic schedule, and constantly had people around him, to keep sadness at bay. Not long after we met, he told me about the loneliness of constantly being on tour. He solved his problem by adopting a miniature longhaired dachshund he named Pooks. Her name was a Russian acronym, derived from an esteemed document in Soviet ideology.

"For just *dees*, I be in Soviet pree-zon!" Slava told me, laughing uproariously.

Pooks and Slava became inseparable. She'd lie on the first step of the podium during rehearsals and wait in his dressing room during concerts. She even played the piano. Slava would place the bench close to the instrument then quietly give a command—in Russian, of course—and Pooks would jump on the bench, throw her little paws onto the keyboard, and begin to concertize. On a second order, she'd scamper down the bench to the bass notes. As a practical joke, Slava would surreptitiously position the bench then sometime later secretly whisper the order. Henri Doll and his wife, friends of Slava's, had the unsettling experience of dining in their apartment alone with him (and Pooks) and suddenly hearing the piano being played several rooms away.[3]

Unlike the secretive Stokowski, Slava frequently shared too much information. Juri told me about having attended a National Symphony black-tie banquet where Slava was the guest speaker. Juri described him at the lectern: wearing a crimson velvet jacket, holding a bottle of vodka by its neck. Juri loved Slava dearly, but he kept shaking his head in amazement at the image. Slava began telling the dignified assemblage about a recent flight where, to avoid quarantine for Pooks, he had snuck the dog on board the plane. Slava was feeding her from his tray and something disagreed with her. Then, in detail, he described the poor animal's gastric distress. To calm her, Slava took Pooks out of the carrying bag and was quickly covered with excrement. He put the dog back in the bag, went into the lavatory, stripped to his underwear and, in the tiny sink, washed his shirt and pants. As he emerged dripping wet from

---

3   Mr. Doll, a wealthy former scientist and prominent arts benefactor, and his wife, Eugenia Delarova, a former ballerina with the Ballet Russe de Monte Carlo and the ex-wife of Russian dancer and choreographer Léonide Massine, were well-known patrons of the arts. They hosted a dinner in their Manhattan apartment, which I attended, to celebrate Slava's fiftieth birthday.

the bathroom, he told the distinguished diners, he could feel every passenger on the plane staring. I later asked Slava how he managed to get the dog on board. "Dog very quiet on plane," he whispered.

I often stayed at Juri and Carolyn's apartment and Slava—and Pooks—would come there, too. For one of our meals, I brought a special bottle of wine. Six years earlier, when Stokowski had moved to England, he had asked that the bottles of his favorite sweet Novitiate wine be given to friends and colleagues. I had waited for an appropriate occasion to drink my bottle. I pointed to it and said, "Someone is looking down who wants us to share this." Slava slowly filled each glass, then held his aloft.

"We have moment of silence for Maestro Stokowski," he said without hesitating.

During another long lunch at Juri and Carolyn's, Slava leaned across the table and looked into my eyes. "You need me, anytime, I come," he said. "I cancel concerts and I come." I walked around the table and hugged and kissed him. I knew he meant what he said, even though there had been stretches of time when I didn't hear from him. He had tried to prepare me for such disappointments. Shortly after we met, he had put his hands on my shoulders. "My love," he'd said, looking at me intently, "responsibility for this relationship will be on you." That seemed reasonable, acceptable: I was a young woman—only twenty—and he was a great musician. But now, almost a dozen years later, I was maturing. I needed to be treated with dignity and consideration, and I wanted relationships to be reciprocal.

One incident, which had occurred during the summer of 1975, seems small now, but it was painful then. While spending the day together in Philadelphia, Slava and I went into Brooks Brothers near the Academy. Slava was trying on a suit and a white tux when Fredric R. Mann, head of the Dell (which would be renamed the Mann Music Center in his honor in 1978), coincidentally walked into the store. Fred took over.

"Do you like those things?" he asked Slava, who said he did. "Put them on my bill," Fred told the salesman, and the three of us exited onto 15th Street. Fred took Slava by the arm and the two of them walked away, leaving me alone on the sidewalk.[4] Slava waved goodbye but said nothing.

In Slava's apartment one evening in the late 1970s, I mentioned that I was heading to London in a few weeks. He was ecstatic; he'd also be there and we could spend time together. He opened his schedule, which by now had been transferred from scraps of paper to a real date book. "Here is free day!" he exclaimed, and I gave him the number at the house where I'd be staying. On a sunny day in England, I waited eight hours for him to call, and then left.

Juri told me that he'd had his own disappointments with Slava, but Juri was old-school Russian. He felt that Slava, as one of the great artists of our time, was entitled to have or do anything he wished, regardless of the consequences to others. I, too, was a bit old-school. Great artists, I had always thought, were elevated beings who should be given license to do as they wished. Making them happy was a way of contributing to their art. But I soon learned that Slava was sincere about wanting to help me.

About two years after Slava became the music director of the National Symphony, I was asked to do interviews for Philadelphia's classical music station, WUHY-FM (now WHYY). Because of my work with the Philadelphia Orchestra and Curtis, I could have secured almost anyone, but I thought I'd start with Slava.

I drove to Avery Fisher Hall (as Philharmonic Hall was now called) in New York where he was rehearsing. Backstage afterward, I told him about my new venture. "Yes yes yes yes yes!" he roared. "You *must* do radio! You come home vis me." We walked around the corner to his apartment where his daughter, Olga, now staying in New York, was preparing lunch.

"Do an interview with me, Slava," I urged as we ate, "it would really help." He immediately agreed, saying that he'd have time in Washington a few weeks later. I'd stay at Juri and Carolyn's the

---

4   In Brooks Brothers years before, Eugene Ormandy had tried on suit jackets. The salesman watched as he made large circular motions with his arms, miming the act of conducting to test the jacket's comfort. "What do you do, juggle?" the salesman had asked.

night before—January 19, 1979—and he'd join us the following afternoon.

Despite a snowstorm on the morning of the interview, no one canceled. The recording crew drove down from Philadelphia and the engineer set up chairs and mikes in one of the bedrooms. Barefoot, I answered the door. There stood Slava in a three-piece suit, white shirt, and dark tie. "What are you all dressed up for?" I asked.

"We do radio interview," he explained, exasperated by so silly a question.

Slava's responses had to be edited because of his accent but the program was riveting. Using imaginative metaphors and analogies, he made connections between things musical and mundane, making the most complicated concepts understandable to less-knowledgeable listeners. Of all that he shared, I found his comments on tempo the most thought-provoking. Like Stokowski, he wasn't a slave to the markings on the page. Even when a composer—dead or alive—specified tempos, he, as cellist or conductor, felt free to change them. Otherwise, he said, it was difficult for him to maintain his involvement in the music; it caused him discomfort, "like shoes a little bigger than your feet or a little bit smaller." As he had frequently discussed with me when we were alone, Slava now talked about Prokofiev and Shostakovich, revealing the differences in their personalities and their music. Most interesting, he raised the subject of conductors' techniques, saying that some of the most beautiful, clear gestures generated boring results, while some conductors whose gestures were "difficult to understand" (he singled out Herbert von Karajan), drew marvelous results: The orchestra played with "great attention, understanding his feelings and his mind." (He might have been thinking of himself, as well, hoping that was true of his own conducting.)

Slava and I eventually did many interviews together, including one after his return to Russia in February 1990, after a sixteen-year absence; his citizenship had been reinstated a month before. I was present in the Moscow Conservatory's Bolshoi Hall when he conducted the National Symphony Orchestra and, with an associate on the podium, played the Dvořák Concerto thrillingly. But the strength of our relationship began to weaken. By 1990, we'd known each other for twenty-three years; I was in my early forties and had since moved to New York, and he was in his early sixties. Two years later, in 1992, the grandson of Sergei Rachmaninoff asked me to help produce and publicize a Carnegie Hall concert the following year that would observe the fiftieth anniversary of his grandfather's death. Alexandre Rachmaninoff, as he called himself (he was the son of Rachmaninoff's daughter Tatiana; his family birth name had been Conus), was unpleasant and unreliable and the project became fraught with problems. Shortly after I began to work with him, Rachmaninoff Junior—as people in the music business derisively called him—told me that Slava was a friend and asked me to contact him on his behalf. He wanted Slava to endorse the concert by being listed as an artistic advisor, but Alexandre didn't tell me that there had been tension between them. When I called, Slava was abrupt and turned me down, thinking that I was taking Rachmaninoff's side. I was hurt that after all those years, Slava would question my loyalty. I continued to go to his concerts and see him afterward, but I no longer felt as close to him. I was also going through a crisis. My mother, who had always dealt with emotional illness, was now suffering physical problems as well: diabetes, eye issues, and crippling arthritis. Then came hospital stays and the horrifying, heartbreaking moves into nursing homes.

I never told Slava why I no longer attended his rehearsals nor did he call to ask what might be wrong. Eventually, I stopped going to his performances. Either because of age, or because he was focused more on conducting than on the cello, his playing was no longer extraordinary, and I didn't want my memories to tarnish. I couldn't bear the thought of hearing him give a flawed performance, particularly of the Dvořák, his signature piece.

I had little contact with him until he returned to the New York Philharmonic in March 2003, for a series of fourteen performances billed as "Slava and Friends." I had an idea I thought would be irresistible to him—a film of him rehearsing the symphonies of Prokofiev and Shostakovich. These wouldn't be conventional rehearsals but would serve as containers for his comments; they'd allow him to talk. For years at rehearsals, I'd heard him tell stories—amusing and touching—that illustrated important interpretive insights from composers he knew intimately. I didn't want his knowledge to die with him. I wrote a detailed plan for the project, which I could have shown to a TV producer I knew, and went to the Green Room after Slava's first performance of the series. Visibly annoyed, he greeted me with detached coolness. I told him I had an idea about the music of Prokofiev and Shostakovich but before I could begin to explain, he waved his hand dismissively. "I not have time," he said, and now equally annoyed with him, I left. I didn't see him again until early 2005 when I interviewed him for WFMT radio in Chicago. The taping took place backstage at Fisher Hall between the rehearsals for his New York Philharmonic concerts and, for the first time in our many interviews together, he asked that a translator be present. Slava sat directly opposite me; the young Russian woman sat to my left.

"We have tea, please?" Slava asked a staff member, and when two china cups were brought to the table, he placed one in front of her and took the other for himself. She drank from her cup, leaving a scarlet lipstick stain on its rim. In a dramatic gesture, Slava lifted the cup and kissed the lipstick mark as I watched.

But I still cared deeply about him, and went backstage after his rehearsal the following day. No one else was there. "What happened?" he asked with great emotion. "Why haven't I seen you?" I didn't want to say that he had hurt me by questioning my loyalty, or that I needed a more reciprocal, balanced relationship, so I merely shrugged. He shook his head sadly. We chatted for a few minutes—light talk about some of the problems he had encountered during the rehearsals—then embraced as friends, nothing more. A year later, in April 2006, he returned to the Philharmonic. He had just turned seventy-nine, and I had just learned that he'd no longer give cello concerts. I was feeling sad and nostalgic. I gave him a bottle of Champagne and copies of photos I had taken over the years, including one from the day we had met in 1967 and others from his 1970 performance in Moscow. He looked at me. "I almost eighty years old!" he said incredulously. I suspect that we were both thinking of all the years we had known each other. After I attended the last of the rehearsals, all seemed to have been forgiven and forgotten. "My love, my love," he whispered as we held each other backstage.

"How are you?" I asked, looking into his eyes.

"I still alive," he said wearily. That night, in the reception room after the last in the series of four concerts, he wouldn't let me go, pulling me back each time I tried to leave. In a Green Room jammed with well-wishers, I kissed him goodbye, chatted with several friends of mine in the orchestra, then walked out the stage door onto West 65th Street. A car moved up the exit ramp from the parking garage and made a right turn in front of me. There, in the backseat, was Slava. Our eyes met, and we smiled and waved at each other through the glass.

I never saw him again. A year later, in April 2007, he would die of cancer. As he had wished, he was in his homeland when his remarkable life ended.

More than four decades after his death, Stokowski remains controversial. It's the price he's paying for having been a colorful iconoclast in a stronghold of artistic conservatism. In classical music, the lines between serious art, charisma, and superficiality are still blurred. It's now time to reappraise his work—to listen with twenty-first century ears to the music of a man who was far ahead of his time.

I hadn't returned to England for Stokowski's funeral in the fall of 1977. More than the expense, more than taking time off from Curtis, I hadn't wanted to see evidence that he was gone. I needed time to come to terms with the massive personal and musical loss I had just sustained. The following year, while visiting Austria, I took a bit of earth from Beethoven's grave in Vienna and Mahler's in Grinzing. I didn't place it in a carved box of rare wood or precious stone as it deserved, because I didn't intend to keep it. Instead, I put it in a small, round plastic film container that would keep it safe.

A year later, I made the sad pilgrimage to East Finchley Cemetery in London. There, sitting on the ground to be close to him, I dug deep into the mound under his headstone, mixing the earth with that of the composers whose music he had loved and served so well. It was my final gift to him. His own words, engraved on the stone, reflect the spirituality with which he approached his art: "Music is the Voice of the All."

Chapter Twenty-Two

REFLECTING ON THE PAST HAS compelled me to think about the present and the future. Classical music is now facing challenges on many fronts. Because it's no longer widely taught in public schools, its importance in society has diminished. Particularly in the US, the art form has become so marginalized that people often think the term refers to jazz, swing, or the Great American Songbook (as the body of twentieth-century Broadway, Hollywood, pop and jazz standards is known). If this trend continues, aspiring classical musicians will find it increasingly difficult to build careers. Fewer young musicians will be able to invest time and money in studying, practicing, and purchasing fine instruments; performance standards are bound to decline.

There are now fewer "household name" classical musicians than there were even a decade ago. How many people are able to name a single classical conductor, soloist or singer, dead or alive? Even the figure of The Great Conductor as a larger-than-life tyrant, ubiquitous years ago, has become a relic.

It's hard to think of a less-viable business model than a symphony orchestra: one hundred people onstage and a huge staff backstage, all for performances that can't be "resold" unless they're recorded (and, because of our current technology, the recording industry is now almost defunct).

The historical lack of racial and cultural diversity presents another serious issue. Orchestras are finally expanding their repertory to include more works by women, people of color, and living composers. Contemporary music, however, can be difficult to "sell." Classical audiences, constantly aging, are wary of "new music," fearful of being subjected to the dissonances of the 1960s, not realizing that there has been a return to expressiveness and tonality, if not tunefulness. And even though orchestral personnel is more inclusive today than decades ago, that inclusivity must be increased. Only then will audience diversity begin to match what will be onstage.

The orchestra is struggling to redefine itself. Should concerts still last the traditional two hours, with an overture and a concerto before intermission, and a larger work like a symphony or a tone poem ending the program? Many orchestras are finding that shorter concerts, presented earlier in the evening and having an informal ambience, are now more marketable.

Increasingly, I find myself explaining one of the most basic premises of classical music: that performers should serve the composers' wishes. "Classical music is so rigid, not creative like jazz and rock," even sophisticated listeners have remarked. "Why can't musicians interpret the music as they feel it?" I point out that there's plenty of expressive freedom within the notes and directions composers have written, even when the conductor imposes his or her will on the players. It's also difficult for some people, particularly the young, to relate to music that's basically abstract, lacking a storyline or a compelling visual element. And who knows what place classical music will have in future technology? There is reason for both hope and concern.

Like all the performing arts, classical music is organic—constantly evolving—and a metamorphosis can yield something wonderful. Whatever may happen, I hope that new works will always be performed side by side with traditional repertory. It was this repertory—particularly Beethoven and Bach—that provided a great deal of solace and feelings of unity during the COVID-19 pandemic, as many people watched virtual performances by artists who were continents apart.

Coda

WHEN I LISTEN TO MUSIC now, I no longer know what I'm actually hearing—where the vibrations end and the memories begin. The fanfare opening of the Tchaikovsky Fourth instantly transports me to my childhood home, sitting next to Mom on the sofa in front of the Farnsworth. Midway through a concert by a string quartet, I begin to "hear" the scratchy struggles of my young friends and myself decades earlier, and grimace in anticipation of a high note I couldn't yet negotiate. The Sibelius Second Symphony begins to play on the radio. Superimposing itself over this, note for note, is the interpretation by Stokowski I heard at a concert half a century ago.

The sounds I heard years ago may never be equaled. But perhaps someday, in the peace of the "other country," as Stokowski called it, Mom and I, and perhaps Stokowski and Slava, will listen together as their concerts, still playing, vibrate their way through the universe.

Acknowledgments

MANY FRIENDS AND COLLEAGUES HAVE asked if it has taken courage for me to live the life I've led: surviving a troubled family; sneaking in where I didn't belong; starting and maintaining careers in New York City; taking constant risks. I've told them that I never thought much about fear because I was compelled to do these things. I was more concerned about *not* doing them—not having a productive, interesting life. What *did* require courage was writing this book. I had to recall tragedies as well as triumphs, and relive painful losses. Most difficult, I had to rethink my responsibility as keeper of the family secrets. To become a fully mature person—and an honest writer—I had to release them.

I could not have summoned the courage I needed without the support and assistance of the people named in this section. I could easily have written a paragraph—in some cases, a chapter—about each of them, and I hope they will accept my heartfelt gratitude.

At the top of my list are the members of the Philadelphia Orchestra in the 1960s. Their dedication to music created one of the greatest orchestras in history. Those dear people also nurtured, encouraged and protected the teenage girl in their midst—the opposite of the #MeToo situations that so many young women have had to endure.

I am endlessly grateful to my agent, Julia Lord, of Julia Lord Literary Management, who brought her knowledge, experience, and prestige to representing this book. I so appreciate her insight into the complexities of the publishing world, and her belief in this book. Her love and understanding of music were bonuses!

Moira Hodgson provided superb editorial advice, and Betsy Israel's editorial insights got me off to a great start. William Strachan, Nancy Nicholas and Christopher Freitag all contributed additional valuable suggestions.

My heartfelt appreciation is extended to Robert Grossman, former chief librarian of the Philadelphia Orchestra, for fact-checking and for lively discussions about the orchestra library profession; Herbert Light for relating his memories of playing in the Philadelphia Orchestra in the 1960s; Carmela Bromhead Jones and Andrew Hewson for sharing their expertise in British and American publishing; the Kislak Center for Special Collections, Rare Books and Manuscripts, University of Pennsylvania Libraries, for information regarding Stokowski's archives; and Maria Cooper Janis and the late Byron Janis, who helped me in every possible way, from providing introductions to people in the publishing world, to giving much-needed encouragement.

For offering advice, information and inspiration, I am grateful to Darrin Britting, director of publications and content development at the Philadelphia Orchestra; the late Anshel Brusilow; James Burnham; John Carabella; Daniel Dorff, Theodore Presser Company; Mike Draper in Nether Wallop, England; the late Jill Edelson; the late Robert Edelson; Lawrence Foster; Lynne and Thomas Frost; Jerry Grabey, formerly at the Mann Music Center; Daniel Levine; Lynne Edelson Levine; Steve Robinson; and Elizabeth Wilson. Susan Cheever helped me start to expand my master's thesis into this book, and my other professors at The New School—Zia Jaffrey, Robert Polito, Benjamin Taylor, Jackson Taylor and Brenda Wineapple—imparted wisdom-infused knowledge about writing and literature.

I extend sincere thanks to the staffs of the New York Public Library for the Performing Arts and the Banff Centre for Arts and Creativity, where I did substantial work on the book; and to Steve J. Sherman for his unceasing efforts in many areas. For sharing their musical memories with me, I thank the late Martin Bookspan; Carolyn Jelagina Falb; Janet Frank; Allen Halber; Steven

Honigberg; Marcos Klorman; Judith Kornfeld; Lewis Lipnik; Steven Richman; Jayn Rosenfeld; Ramon Scavelli; the late Robert Sherman; David Teie; and Ellen Taaffe Zwilich.

    I am beyond grateful to so many people for their encouragement and advice. Among them are Peter Bogyo; Ann Close; Nina Coffin, Free Library of Philadelphia; Rob Corp, Royal College of Music; Lisa Delan; Angela Duryea; Anthony Fast; Véronique Firkušný; Stanley M. Goldstein, for his lasting avuncular influence; Daniel Guss; Anne Heausler; Edward Johnson; the late Donna Staley Kline; Barbara Lowin; Mary Ann Maniscalco; Janice Mayer; the late Lynne Mazza; Bruno Monsaingeon; Janice Papolos; Joan Perkes; Alfred S. Posamentier; Charles Prince; Christina Putnam; Amy Rhodes; Claire Roberts; the late Stephen Rubin; Harvey Sachs; Diane Saldick; Beverly Schnall; Charlotte Schroeder; Gregory Smith; Kile Smith; Gene Sperandeo, for deepening my understanding of human nature; Barrie Steinberg; Arnold Steinhardt; Kathryn Taylor; and Nancy Wellman. My fellow Friday evening "Teatime" members have patiently listened to my stories for decades. Thank you, Zelma Bodzin (also for introducing me to members of the publishing community); Melody Bunting; Carol Adrian Cohen; Claudia Flowers; Rena Fruchter; Arlene Gould; Leslie Lefkowitz; Marion Marino; Rinah J. Messier; and Marioara Trifan.

    The dedicated, talented team at Regalo Press has been extraordinary. Thank you to Gretchen Young, Adriana Senior, Caitlyn Limbaugh, Aleigha Koss, Alana Mills, Rachel Paul, and Kate Harris.

    I am profoundly grateful to members of the Stokowski family for their openness, honesty and encouragement, and to my dear mother, Mildred Shear, who didn't live to see this book published, but whose influence informs every page.

    I hope I have not omitted anyone. If I have, it certainly was not intentional.

Nancy Shear
New York
November 15, 2024